Nationalism and
Economic Development
in Ghana

McGill Studies in Development
A Series of the Centre for
Developing-Area Studies,
McGill University

The Centre for Developing-Area Studies was established at McGill University in the fall of 1963. It fosters interdisciplinary research on problems of economic, social, and political change in the developing countries. Fellowships are awarded annually to graduate students seeking advanced degrees in this field. The Centre offers a program of seminars in development and maintains a specialized library of relevant materials in the social sciences. In addition, the Centre participates in programs of technical cooperation with universities, governments, and other institutions in the developing world.

PRAEGER SPECIAL STUDIES IN
INTERNATIONAL ECONOMICS AND DEVELOPMENT

Nationalism and Economic Development in Ghana

Roger Genoud

Published in cooperation with the
Centre for Developing-Area Studies,
McGill University

FREDERICK A. PRAEGER, Publishers
New York · Washington · London

The purpose of the Praeger Special Studies is to make specialized re-search monographs in U.S. and international economics and politics available to the academic, business, and government communities. For further information, write to the Special Projects Division, Frederick A. Praeger, Publishers, 111 Fourth Avenue, New York, N.Y. 10003.

FREDERICK A. PRAEGER, PUBLISHERS
111 Fourth Avenue, New York, N.Y. 10003, U.S.A.
5, Cromwell Place, London S.W. 7, England

Published in the United States of America in 1969
by Frederick A. Praeger, Inc., Publishers

Library of Congress Catalog Card Number: 68-55985

Printed in the United States of America

FOREWORD

During the fall of 1966, Dr. Roger C. Genoud was a Research Associate in the Centre for Developing-Area Studies at McGill University. He has since joined the senior economic staff of the United Nations Development Programme.

From the Centre's point of view, it was a most valuable assignment. Apart from his own research, Dr. Genoud participated actively in Centre seminars, and he was unsparing in his efforts to provide sound advice for McGill staff and graduate students doing research on problems of economic development. His fluency in both English and French yielded special dividends in the form of mutual interchange of ideas with other educational groups and institutions throughout the Montreal community.

It will be easy for the reader to discover that Dr. Genoud's study had a gestation period far longer than his stay at McGill. His four years of teaching and research experience in Ghana are the under-pinnings of a very substantial and innovative work. *Nationalism and Economic Development in Ghana* has a sharp economic focus, to be sure; but perhaps its greatest strength flows from a thoroughgoing attempt to understand the close interaction of social and political forces with Ghanaian economic change.

There are good reasons to believe that the author has made a convincing case for viewing the Nkrumah experience—personalities aside—as having laid the basis for modernization and industrialization in Ghana. But this will be for others to judge. Meanwhile, the most significant thing to be said about Dr. Genoud's study is that from the Ghanaian example, it seeks to formulate a new relationship between nationalism and economic development which will prove widely applicable to the process of decolonization in other developing countries.

The approach is genuinely and pervasively inter-disciplinary. In this fundamental respect, there could not be a more appropriate volume to launch a continuing, in-depth, research series sponsored by the Centre for Developing-Area Studies. It is a great pleasure for the Centre to join with Frederick A. Praeger, Inc. in publishing these McGill Studies in Development.

IRVING BRECHER

Director
Centre for Developing-Area Studies

PREFACE

Between 1951 and 1966, an original and controversial process of decolonization took place in Ghana. This book attempts to analyze these fifteen *Nkrumah years*. It is a study of an experience in decolonization; on its ambitions and its performance; on its strategy and its tactics; on its scope and its limits.

In discussing the objectives of Nkrumah's Ghana and the instruments put to use to attain these objectives, I have been led to re-examine the relationship between nationalism and development in former colonies. Thus, at least by implication, this book deals as much with the general problems of development in Africa as with the contemporary history of Ghana.

I have benefited from the many studies which in varying degrees have contributed to our knowledge of Ghana. But most of all, I have been fortunate enough to live in Ghana during one of these rare *moments* when history appears to be in the making. I am deeply indebted to many friends, Ghanaians and expatriates alike, for whom during these years the *Ghanaian way* was a constant topic of serious reflection. The Institute of African Studies of the University of Ghana under Professor Thomas Hodgkin was one such forum but by no means the only one.

I also wish to thank the Centre for Developing-Area Studies at McGill University and Professor Irving Brecher, in particular, for providing me generously with the material and intellectual support which made it possible for me to write this book.

CONTENTS

	Page
FOREWORD	v
PREFACE	vii
LIST OF TABLES	xi
GLOSSARY	xii

Chapter

1	INTRODUCTION	1
	Notes	13

PART I: NKRUMAH'S GHANA: LIMITS AND
SCOPE OF THE DEVELOPMENT STRATEGY

2	THE SOCIO-ECONOMIC STRUCTURE OF GHANA IN THE 1950'S	17
	A More-Advanced Underdeveloped Country	17
	Equilibrium of Embryonic Classes	24
	Conflicting Elites	36
	The "Model Colony" and its "Misfits"	50
	Notes	55

3	FROM A "COMATOSE VISION" TO THE SEVEN-YEAR PLAN	59
	An Official Theory of Decolonization	60
	The Two-Strategy Theory	78
	Elements for an Alternative Interpretation	86
	The Time-Lag	105
	Notes	110

Chapter   Page

PART II: PROBLEMS OF IMPLEMENTA-
TION: THE POLICY OF EQUILIBRIUM

4   ECONOMIC PROBLEMS AND PERFORMANCE   125

Attempts To Recapture Control of the Economy   126
The Failure To Balance Ghana's Trading Partners 132
Foreign Investments and Neocolonialism   135
Marginal Improvements in Performance   140
The "Ghanaian Way"   148
Notes   154

5   POLITICAL PROBLEMS   159

The Failure To Combine Positive and   160
   Tactical Actions
The Convention People's Party   165
Nkrumah and the Policy of Equilibrium   185
From Nationalism to Socialism?   200
"Consciencism": An Ideological Parry   205
   or the Essence of Nkrumaism?
Notes   210

6   CONCLUSION   215

La tragédie du roi Christophe   215
Notes   229

BIBLIOGRAPHY   233

INDEX   241

ABOUT THE AUTHOR   245

LIST OF TABLES

Table		Page
1	Occupational Categories and Employment Status (Percentages) in 1960	28
2	Size, Income, and Labor Employed in Cocoa Farming	30
3	The Share of Productive Investment in Ghana (1951-1969/70)	77
4	Trade with Socialist Countries	133
5	Exports of Cocoa to the U.S.S.R.	134
6	Gross Domestic Product 1955-62 (At Current and Constant Prices)	142
7	Gross Domestic Product 1955-64 (Indexes)	142
8	Evolution of Gross Domestic Expenditure 1955-62	144
9	Capital Formation: 1955, 1962, and 1964	145
10	Employment in the Public and Private Sectors 1961-64	147

GLOSSARY

AKAN   is Ghana's main ethnic group which can be subdivided into the ASHANTI, FANTI, and the less numerous NZIMA to which Kwame Nkrumah belongs.

ANLO YOUTH ASSOCIATION was one of the EWE movements opposing the CPP.

ASHANTI   is the largest AKAN ethnic group, center of the former powerful Ashanti Confederation.

COLONY, THE   referred to the southern part of Ghana including the coastal savannah and a portion of the forest belt.

COMMONERS   *See*, YOUNGMEN

CONVENTION PEOPLE'S PARTY (CPP) was the ruling party during the entire period (1951-66) of this book. It was founded by Kwame Nkrumah, with the assistance of K.S. Gbedmah, Kojo Botsio, and others, in 1949 as a breakaway party of the UGCC. In the 1951, 1954, and 1956 elections, it won a comfortable majority of the seats in parliament. After independence, in March, 1957, the CPP progressively eliminated all organized opposition and eventually (1964) became the only legal party in Ghana.

DYARCHY   referred to the period of internal self-government, 1951-57. *See also*, TACTICAL ACTION.

EVENING NEWS, THE was the daily newspaper of the CPP.

EWE   is a major group located in the southeast of Ghana.

xii

FANTI   is the large AKAN ethnic group located on the Coast. With its century-old academic tradition (Cape Coast), it provided a substantial portion of the civil servants and professionals.

FLAGSTAFF HOUSE referred to the Office of the President.

GA-ADANGME   is the major ethnic group of the Accra area.

GA-ADANGME SHIFIMO KPEE was one of the regional parties in the Accra area which was formed immediately after independence in opposition to the CPP.

GHANA CONGRESS PARTY (GCP) attempted to mobilize the anti-CPP nationalist élite for the 1954 election. Its most prominent leader was K.A. Busia.

GHANAIAN TIMES, THE was a daily newspaper reflecting the government's viewpoint.

"IDEOLOGICAL WING" of the CPP included the editors of *THE SPARK*, a few other activists, and the staff of the KWAME NKRUMAH IDEOLOGICAL INSTITUTE (KNII).

"INTEGRAL WINGS" referred to the various mass organizations, *inter alia*, the TRADE UNION CONGRESS, the YOUNG PIONEERS, the UNITED GHANA FARMERS COUNCIL, the WORKERS' BRIGADE, and the NATIONAL COUNCIL OF GHANA WOMEN, set up by or brought under the control of CPP. A good description of these mass organizations and their relations with the CPP is given in Gilbert Tixier, *Le Ghana* (Paris: Pichon et Durand-Auzias, 1965), chap. iii.

INTELLIGENTSIA was the "term used locally to refer to the small southern group of lawyers and business men who, from an early date, were active among the limited electorates of Cape Coast, Accra, and Sekondi-Takoradi proto-nationalist associations like the Aborigines' Rights Protection Society (1897), the National Congress of British West Africa (1920), the Youth Conference Movement (1930) and a number of municipal party groups. Their immediate concern after World War II was to replace the chiefs as the heirs of British rule, but with the founding of the CPP they were themselves replaced; they continued, however, as implacable opponents of Nkrumah and the CPP, adding a national element to the local and regional opposition parties." (Dennis Austin, *Politics in Ghana: 1946-1960*, London: Oxford University Press, 1964, p. xiii.)

KWAME NKRUMAH IDEOLOGICAL INSTITUTE (KNII) located at Winneba, was outside the university framework with its own campus, lecturers, and a few hundred students. *See also*, "IDEOLOGICAL WING"

MOSLEM ASSOCIATION PARTY (MAP) was formed early in 1954 among the Moslem "zongo" people (immigrants) of the main towns. It amalgamated with the UP along with the other opposition parties in 1957.

NATIONAL COUNCIL OF GHANA WOMEN was one of the mass organizations included within the "INTEGRAL WINGS" of the CPP.

xiv

NATIONAL LIBERATION MOVEMENT (NLM) represented the strongest threat to the ruling CPP in the 1956 election. With K. A. Busia among its leaders, the NLM was regarded as an élitist opposition but, in addition, it could also be loosely described as the regional Ashanti opposition.

NORTHERN PEOPLE'S PARTY (NPP) was the largest regional party in Ghana. It opposed the CPP in both the 1954 and the 1956 elections.

NORTHERN TERRITORIES (NT) referred to the former British Protectorate in the less-developed northern savannah country.

POSITIVE ACTION corresponded, in CPP political terminology, to the nationalist revolutionary tactic based on mass demonstrations, boycotts, etc., and aimed at obtaining "SELF-GOVERNMENT NOW." This campaign, i.e., of civil disobedience, was launched by the CPP early in 1950. Its spirit was never officially abandoned. However, the CPP switched to TACTICAL ACTION when it entered the 1951 election to win an overwhelming victory.

PRISON GRADUATES referred to the CPP members who had been jailed for their nationalist stands before independence.

SELF-GOVERNMENT NOW *See*, POSITIVE ACTION

SPARK, THE was the weekly ideological paper of the CPP.

STANDARD VII BOYS *See*, YOUNGMEN

TACTICAL ACTION corresponded, in CPP political terminology, to the acceptance of the "rules of the game" within the framework of the DYARCHY. Following the 1950 period of POSITIVE ACTION, this became the CPP policy when it accepted to enter the 1951 elections and won an overwhelming victory.

TOGOLAND CONGRESS (TC) was one of the EWE regional parties founded in 1949 in opposition to the CPP. It merged with other opposition parties to form the UP in 1957.

TRADE UNION CONGRESS (TUC) was one of the mass organizations forming part of the CPP'S "INTEGRAL WINGS."

UNITED GHANA FARMERS COUNCIL (UGFC) was another of the mass organizations included within the "INTEGRAL WINGS" of the CPP.

UNITED GOLD COAST CONVENTION (UGCC) was the first political party in Ghana (the Gold Coast then). It was founded in 1947 by the nationalist Ghanaian élite (businessmen, lawyers, etc.) who brought Kwame Nkrumah from London to become its Secretary General. The leading figure of the UGCC was the late J. B. Danquah. The party was dissolved after its disastrous defeat in the 1951 election.

UNITED PARTY (UP) was formed on November 3, 1957, following the passing of the Avoidance of Discrimination Act, which forbade the existence of parties on a regional, tribal or religious basis. It was composed of all the opposition parties (NLM, NPP, MAP, etc.).

VERANDAH BOYS was the name given to the YOUNGMEN who were active militants of the CPP.

WORKERS' BRIGADE was one of the mass organizations included within the "INTEGRAL WINGS" of the CPP.

YOUNGMEN is " a local expression used to describe the COMMONERS, those who held no stool or office of importance. This expression was also used more narrowly to refer to the educated commoners—storekeepers, petty traders, clerks, primary school teachers—who were likely to be among the younger generation." (Dennis Austin, *Politics in Ghana 1946-1960*, London: Oxford University Press, 1964, p. xii.). In a narrower sense, the YOUNGMEN were also sometimes referred to as the "STANDARD VII BOYS" (i.e., those who had only a partial education, up to the seventh form).

YOUNG PIONEERS was one of the mass organizations forming part of the "INTEGRAL WINGS" of the CPP.

Nationalism and
Economic Development
in Ghana

CHAPTER 1 INTRODUCTION

The last months of 1965 and the first of 1966 saw several military coups put an abrupt end to some widely different political experiments in independent West and Equatorial Africa; from Dahomey's multiparty system to the rule of Maurice Yaméogo in Upper Volta; and above all the Northern-dominated federal system in Nigeria which usually won praise in the West as one of the rare attempts to set up a formal Western-modeled parliamentary regime; and Ghana, where Kwame Nkrumah and his party tried first in the name of independence, then in the name of socialism, to pave the way to an original African approach to development.

The series of military coups—which affected former colonies of France, England, and Belgium alike—may be considered as bringing to a formal end the first postindependence period in West and Equatorial Africa. This first period was characterized by certain illusions and the relative optimism which most Africans and many outsiders shared regarding the possibilities of a fast and original course of development in the newly independent countries of Africa. Africa was thought to be more or less outside the mainstream of the Cold War, its leadership and its nationalism seemed acceptable to both East and West and also seemed to incorporate necessary and adequate instruments of development both in French- and English-speaking countries.[1] Except for France's attitude toward Sékou Touré's Guinea, the governments of the former *métropoles* tended to consider with official benevolence the efforts of the newly independent countries on the road to economic and social progress. They also appeared to accept without too much frustration the new situation and its implications, especially the radical change of attitudes between *métropole* and former colonies, and the increase in

1

technical and financial assistance to these countries. Even
the actual or implied one-party systems prevailing in most
former colonies did not seem to disturb Western governments
and were accepted more or less as inevitable, viz., the
necessary price to be paid for nationalism, which seemed
needed for "reconstruction" in independent Africa. To be
sure, such an idyllic picture of their relationship after
independence represents only part of the reality. It
represents the official attitude and does not include, for
instance, the attitude and policies of private expatriate
firms in Africa. Equally important, nationalist governments
in Africa were acceptable also to the Union of Soviet
Socialist Republics (U.S.S.R.), China, and the European
People's Democracies, as well as the majority of the
Western left. Africa was to become the "promised land of
Peaceful Coexistence," and it was generally agreed that
nationalists and nationalism had and should have a political
monopoly in independent Africa. This was also the heyday
of Afro-Asian solidarity and neutralism.

The fall of several governments that represent different
and even divergent tendencies is occurring at a time when
it is gradually being realized that the process of economic
and social development in Africa may be even more difficult
than originally expected. The illusions of the early 1960's
are being dispelled and a thorough review of the conditions
of economic and social development as well as of the role
of nationalism in contemporary Africa seems necessary.
The years 1960-65 supply enough historical material to put
such concepts to the test and to discuss with some
relevance nationalism as a tool for economic and social
development in tropical Africa.

THE CASE FOR A STUDY OF GHANA

There are three main reasons in favor of giving a privileged place to a case study of Ghana.[2]

First, there is *duration*. The Nkrumah-Convention People's Party (CPP) Government lasted longer than any other government in Africa south of the Sahara (Liberia and Ethiopia are excluded for obvious reasons): fifteen years altogether from 1951 (internal self-government) or nine years from 1957 (self-government or independence). This affords students of African affairs the richest field of research. Unlike most other experiences in tropical Africa, that of Nkrumah and the CPP[3] in Ghana lasted long enough for positive studies to be undertaken (e.g., comparisons between official policies and actual implementation, comparisons of actual policies and their results).

Second is the importance of Ghana's *ideological development:* The Nkrumah-CPP policies of decolonization were set out clearly, if somewhat late, in various official documents (e.g., the CPP Program for Work and Happiness later translated into more technical terms in the Seven-Year Development Plan). If one also refers to the various theoretical books written by the former President of Ghana, it is possible to piece together a "Ghanaian theory of decolonization." The tendency to formulate current issues in ideological terms singles out the Nkrumah-CPP experience compared to that of other independent African countries, especially the English-speaking ones, and makes a discussion of Kwame Nkrumah's policies of decolonization at once more easily theoretical and general in scope (at least by implication).

Third, due to causes that can be traced back to the 1890's, Ghana stood out as a relatively *more-advanced country* in tropical Africa, both as compared to the other Commonwealth countries, and to the former French colonies.

This makes a study of the Nkrumah-CPP policies particularly interesting inasmuch as it deals with problems with which the other countries of the region, sooner or later, will have to come to grips. While most other countries still had (or have) to build up modern infrastructures (physical and educational), Ghana's problems were increasingly problems of making use of such modern infrastructures. In other words, Ghana had to map out a program to move from the first stage of economic development to a second stage, involving more difficult issues, more delicate choices. This point has been made very clear by Samir Amin in his *Trois expériences africaines de développement: le Mali, la Guinée et le Ghana.*[4] In a brief chapter on Ghana, Amin compares the difficulties confronting a more-advanced Ghana with the relatively easier situation of a less-advanced Ivory Coast and makes it quite clear that after some time the Ivory Coast will be confronted with the same type of difficulties which Ghana has been experiencing for the past few years.

In sum, a case study of Ghana should help not only to clarify the Nkrumah-CPP period, but, indirectly, also to permit the discussion of problems and potential solutions which, beyond the borders of Ghana, will become increasingly meaningful in other countries in tropical Africa as these countries reach the same level of economic and social development Ghana attained in the late 1950's. Similarly, Kwame Nkrumah's almost desperate plea for a united Africa, whatever the merits of Ghana's approach to this problem, may appear related not only to the former President's personal background and inclinations, but also, and much more significantly, to the experience of Ghana, i.e., a country on the threshold of real industrialization.[5]

The experience of Kwame Nkrumah's Ghana was basically that of nationalism in modern Africa and had little to do with socialism, despite the claims of a clamorous and highly ideological press. The analysis of the strategy and tactics of Nkrumah's Government as well as those of the ruling Convention People's Party should give ample support to such views. In this respect, an analysis of the policies of decolonization of the Nkrumah-CPP Government ought to throw some much-needed light on the realities of postindependence nationalism as well as on the controversial but still rather obscure role of socialism in contemporary African politics and policies of development.

LIMITS OF THIS STUDY

This study embraces, from a very general point of view, the entire fifteen years of the Nkrumah-CPP Government (1951-66). It covers three rather well-defined subperiods: internal self-government, or, in the words of Immanuel Wallerstein,[6] "the period of the Dyarchy," (1951-57); the first four years of independence (1957-60); and the Republic years until the fall of the Nkrumah-CPP Government (1960-66).

The first period began with the overwhelming electoral victory of the Convention People's Party (1951) and conversely the defeat of the earlier intelligentsia-dominated nationalist movement (J.B. Danquah's United Gold Coast Convention [UGCC]).[7] It followed a period of popular unrest (riots of 1948 and the general strike and Positive Action of 1950).[8] Until 1954, the CPP was so strongly established in power that the only danger for the party seemed likely to come from its own success. Everybody joined the CPP[9] and everybody wanted to share the benefits associated with CPP power. The second election (1954) was dubbed the "Independents' election." In some constituencies there were several dissident CPP candidates competing with the official CPP candidate. In its subsequent effort to streamline the party organization, the

CPP leadership was led to take strong disciplinary measures (*inter alia*, the exclusion of some well-known founding members), and, for motives at least open to debate, guarded itself on the "left" (demoting a few Trade Union leaders and alleged Communist backbenchers).

Such internal difficulties, coinciding with the Government's attempt to impose a fixed price to be paid to farmers for their cocoa, caused the hopes of the non-CPP opposition to be revived: The National Liberation Movement (NLM) was formed. It was based in Ashanti, but also regrouped most of the traditionally anti-CPP opposition at the end of 1954. The period came to a close with the NLM and the rest of the opposition narrowly defeated by the CPP (third election, in 1956) and the Gold Coast eventually acceding to independence as Ghana (March 6, 1957).

The second period (1957-60) covered the first years following independence. Ghana was the only independent country in West Africa and, for that matter, in the continent south of the Sahara with the exception of Guinea (and, of course, as already mentioned, Liberia and Ethiopia, part of an entirely different historical context). The first part of this second period, much like the period of the Dyarchy, was still characterized by the "cocoa boom" or its continuing effects. With the help of accumulated foreign reserves (in Great Britain), the Ghana Government was able to launch a huge investment program without having to impose restrictions on private consumption. The struggle for power with the opposition was still bitter; the United Party (UP), in which all former opposition parties and movements merged, including the NLM and the Northern People's Party (NPP), offered the ruling CPP a tough challenge. For the first time the Ga people of Accra joined the opposition (*Ga Shifimo Kpee*). However, with the new possibilities afforded by a freer and fuller use of the state machinery and its Parliament majority, the CPP was able to consolidate its power, and by 1958-60, the opposition, formally at least, was on the wane. The 1960 Plebiscite and the election of Nkrumah to the Presidential office brought the second period to a close with Ghana virtually a one-party (the CPP) state.

The third period (1960-66) opened with all former French colonies of French West Africa (AOF) and French Equatorial Africa (AEF), Nigeria, and the former Belgian Congo being granted independence. Ghana's leadership in tropical Africa was no longer the automatic corollary of her being independent among French and English colonies. Inside Ghana, the political situation was characterized by a near complete CPP monopoly, even before the CPP was officially made the only legal party by a referendum (1964). Economically, these were increasingly difficult years; cocoa prices dwindled lower and lower, and 1965 eventually recorded the absolute postwar minimum. In 1961, the government presented its first austerity budget to be followed by many others, even more stringent. The immediate consequence of the budget was the Sekondi-Takoradi quasi-insurrectional strike among harbor and railway workers (September, 1961). This came as a shock to the Nkrumah-CPP Government: the people par excellence, the industrial workers, turning against the "party of the people!" The response of the CPP Government was repression first, and more centralization and radicalization as soon as possible afterwards—at least formally (of which more will be said later). It was also this period that saw the rise and fall of Tawia Adamafio (1960-62), formally an ultraradical spokesman within the CPP. The last years were also characterized by an ideological inflation, the development of the activities of the Kwame Nkrumah Ideological Institute at Winneba, and other various attempts to turn Nkrumaism into a full-fledged national ideology.

By and large, the first period corresponded to the first

Development Plan (1951-56), and the second period to the launching of the Second Development Plan (1959-64) after a two-year period of "consolidation" (1957-59). The first plan (completed) and the second (interrupted in 1962) belonged to the "shopping-list" technique type of plans and may be better described as programs of government expenditures. The third period corresponded to the first years of implementation of the Seven-Year Development Plan, which was also the first *real* plan for Ghana.

The convenience of dividing Ghana's contemporary history and the Nkrumah-CPP Government period into three subperiods, (1951-57), (1957-60), and (1960-66), should not however, obscure the fact that there was more continuity during these fifteen years than would appear from the above summary. In fact, the Nkrumah-CPP Government constitutes one single experience in decolonization. In the course of these fifteen years many things happened in the world, in Africa, and in Ghana; Nkrumah and the CPP leadership tried to cope with a world of change and a continent in transition. No doubt, this affected their outlook, their plans and policies, but not to the point where it would be necessary to deal separately with separate historical and political periods.[10]

PRECEDENTS AND METHODOLOGY

The subject of this book is neither the political history of Ghana (already competently studied by Dennis Austin)[11] nor the economic situation of the country during this period (presented in great detail in *A Study of Contemporary Ghana*).[12] It is a study of an experience of decolonization, an analysis of the strategy of decolonization of the Nkrumah-CPP Government, and its implementation.

This experience has already been the subject of careful and well-known analyses: among others, at an earlier stage of the history of the Nkrumah-CPP Government, in the works of David Apter and Immanuel Wallerstein.[13] More recently, another American monograph was devoted to the same experience. Robert Fitch and Mary Oppenheimer's point of view in the "End of an Illusion" is not the usual neo-Weberian approach; it is a rather rigid Marxist-Fanonist analysis of contemporary Ghana.[14] Inasmuch as it also discusses these fifteen years "that shook Ghana" from the point of view of decolonization, we shall have to pay more attention to Fitch and Oppenheimer's essay than to other studies on contemporary Ghana. However, neither these books nor others devoted to Ghana and the many articles published before and after the Coup of February, 1966, have exhausted the discussion. These fifteen years were too important for Ghana and Africa to be reduced to a problem of "political institutional transfer" (Apter) or to a "petty bourgeois mystification" (Fitch and Oppenheimer). Many more essays, books, and articles will no doubt be devoted to the study of the Nkrumah years. This will partly determine whether Nkrumaism itself or some kind of neo-Nkrumaism still has, or will have, a meaning and a future in Africa as a theory and practice of decolonization. To such a question we do not have an answer, but we hope to contribute to the clarification of the real nature and achievement of the Nkrumah-CPP strategy of decolonization.

The purpose of this book is thus to analyze a policy of decolonization, i.e., to examine a series of policy decisions in such varied fields as the national economy, public health, education, administration, diplomacy, defense, arts, and culture, and also a more diffuse and subtle element which could be described as a change of mind, a new attitude towards the country's problems—in short, "a new political line." The new political line is expressed by concrete policy decisions (and its validity also partly depends on the success of such measures), but policy decisions themselves derive their meaning and significance from their degree of relevance to the new political line. In other words, a dollar is not always worth a dollar. More explicitly, policies such as the diversification of agriculture, though always advisable and positive in Africa now, do not constitute per se sufficient evidence of the government's determination to decolonize. Similarly, indicators such as the gross national product (GNP) per capita or the evolution of foreign trade would not reveal much as far as a country's policy of decolonization is concerned. And it would be the same with information concerning changes introduced in the educational system, a new cultural policy, or the evolution of the country's diplomatic relations.

Only a global approach would adequately serve our purpose, and it would have to be based on quantifiable and controllable observations. This would constitute the only truly satisfactory approach: First, determine the actual problems, needs, and possibilities of the country; then, analyze the government's general policy of decolonization in terms of a strategy for the solution of the country's problems; and last, one should turn to the examination of as complete as possible a series of indicators to verify both whether the official political line is actually translated into concrete policy decisions and whether such policy decisions truly represent solutions to the economic, social, cultural, and political problems of the country.

Despite the apparent simplicity and logic of such an approach, the least one can say is that it is seldom applied, mainly, it would seem, because political and economic problems are usually studied separately. In political studies, "economic examples" are more often than not used only as illustrations, and it is only too well-known

how easy it is to find such "examples." In economic
studies, far too often no real difference is made between
growth and development.[15] It is apparently assumed that
when total production increases—this being equated to an
improvement of the economic situation of the country—other
improvements in other fields will more or less automatically
follow. Such a tendency to "economism" is due not only to
the professional specialization of the various authors but
also to the low level of production in Africa and the many
obstacles preventing economic development. Inasmuch as
improvements in other fields are severely limited by economic
stagnation, one naturally tends to give an absolute priority
to economic problems. Moreover—and especially in the case
of observers coming from, or trained in, advanced industrial
countries—what seems to matter most is quantitative
progress, i.e., what seems in the long run best capable of
ridding the country of the nightmare of malnutrition, hunger,
rags, and slums. However, an analysis centered on the
evolution of global quantities does not permit one to grasp
and evaluate the process of decolonization.

This, unfortunately, is not such an all-encompassing
study, but we shall try to retain some of the virtue of a
global approach by keeping the concept of decolonization
as open as possible, by not reducing it merely to an
economic problem, and certainly not to a problem of
production alone. After the fall of Nkrumah, several
economists strongly expressed the view that Ghana was
bankrupt or that, under Nkrumah, "in relation to the size
of the effort the results were poor, for while investment
was claiming more and more resources the growth of the
economy was slowing down."[16] But however objective or
virtuous such views may appear, they account for only one
aspect of the reality; politically, they mean near to
nothing.

Decolonization is not just growth. To decolonize

does not mean to improve upon the former colonial administration in the running of the economy. To decolonize, at the very least, is to remove obstacles preventing the autonomous development of the country. And the obstacles are not only economic ones. It presupposes that the leaders take a clear view of the real situation of the country's needs and possibilities as an independent country, and then map out a full program or strategy to effect such changes and reorientations as are deemed necessary. The first stage of a policy of decolonization is to prepare the bases for the development of a *new* country. The infrastructural investments should not be compared to actual production at the present time but to the new national economy-to-be. In a way, the bankruptcy of the old colonial economy is a prerequisite for the successful implementation of a strategy of decolonization. Of course, this does not mean that financial bankruptcy is to be hoped for, but implies that all the resources that can be derived from the existing economic system must be redirected towards the creation of a new national economy. As such structural changes are rather slow-yielding, there is a considerable risk that a bankruptcy of the old system will precede the successful realization of the new one. This represents the internal peril inherent in any earnest policy of decolonization. The economy of any former colony is fragile; any policy of decolonization is perilous. No wonder so few such policies have been successful as yet.

Although there will be some unavoidable overlapping between the contents of each chapter, we shall first present the socio-economic situation of Ghana in the early 1950's in the form of a few preliminary remarks (Chapter 2), then present and discuss the strategy of the Nkrumah-CPP Government (Chapter 3), and in Part II, we shall examine the economic and political problems posed by its implementation.

NOTES

1. The Congo (Kinshasa) would obviously not fit the above description, but altogether the former Belgian colony represents a special case in the 1960-65 period.

2. In a recent article, Immanuel Wallerstein concluded his examination of the latest studies devoted to Ghana by remarking that "Ghana is still a model for scholars, if not for politicians." Cf., "Ghana as a Model," *Africa Report* (May, 1967), pp. 43-46.

3. The Convention People's Party (CPP) was founded by Kwame Nkrumah in 1949, and banned after the Coup of February 24, 1966.

4. Samir Amin, *Trois expériences africaines de développement: le Mali, la Guinée et le Ghana* (Université de Paris, "Institut d'étude du développement économique et social [IEDES]: Tiers-Monde"; Paris: Presses universitaires de France, 1965).

5. Cf., the sober and serious discussion of the limitations imposed on Ghana's industrialization during the Seven-Year Development Plan period (1963/64—1969/70) by the size of the internal market in the first chapter of the "Plan." *See also, infra,* Chapter 3.

6. Immanuel Wallerstein, *The Road to Independence, Ghana and the Ivory Coast* (Paris-La Haye: Mouton, 1964).

7. The United Gold Coast Convention (UGCC) was founded in 1947. Kwame Nkrumah was its Secretary-General until he founded the CPP two years later. It was dissolved in 1952, after being defeated in the 1951 election.

8. In Ghanaian political terminology, "Positive Action" corresponds to nationalist revolutionary tactics, based on mass demonstrations, boycotts, etc., aimed at obtaining "Self-Government Now." "Tactical Action" corresponds to the acceptance of the "rules of the game" within the general framework of the "Dyarchy" (internal self-government, 1951-57). The CPP switched to "Tactical Action" after its overwhelming electoral victory in 1951—in fact, a little earlier when it accepted to enter the election.

9. "Within eighteen months of taking office, membership was up to 700,000." Dennis Austin, *Politics in Ghana: 1946-1960* (London: Oxford University Press, 1964), p. 171.

10. For a discussion of the continuity of the CPP's strategy, see *infra*, Chapter 3.

11. Austin, *Politics in Ghana*.

12. Walter B. Birmingham, I. Neustadt, and E.N. Omaboe, eds., *A Study of Contemporary Ghana*, Vol. I: *The Economy of Ghana* (London: Allen and Unwin, 1966). Most chapters have been written by Tony Killick and the late Robert Szereszewski.

13. David Apter, *Ghana in Transition* (Rev. ed.; New York: Atheneum, 1963) and Wallerstein, *The Road to Independence*.

14. Robert Fitch and Mary Oppenheimer, "Ghana: End of an Illusion," *Monthly Review*, Vol. 18, No. 3 (Special Issue, July-August, 1966).

15. For a full discussion of this problem, see, Isaac Guelfat, *Doctrines économiques et pays en voie de développement* ("IEDES: Tiers-Monde"; Paris: Presses universitaires de France, 1961), chap. ii, pp. 19 — .

16. T. Killick, "Making Ghana Grow Again," *West Africa* (London), 2568 (August 20, 1966), p. 937.

PART **I**

NKRUMAH'S GHANA: LIMITS AND
SCOPE OF THE DEVELOPMENT STRATEGY

CHAPTER **2** THE SOCIO-ECONOMIC
STRUCTURE OF GHANA
IN THE 1950'S

A MORE-ADVANCED UNDERDEVELOPED COUNTRY

Before the British granted their "model colony"
internal self-government, the Gold Coast had been the
scene of some rather violent political agitation, starting
with the 1948 riots. These more or less spontaneous riots
had themselves been prompted by a fairly rapid inflation,
the pinch of which was particularly felt by the urban wage-
earner. Meanwhile, in the countryside, cocoa farmers had
also been waging an economic war by opposing compulsory
cutting of diseased cocoa trees ("swollen shoot"). Up to
a point, these were the immediate causes of the strengthening and acceleration of the nationalist movement in the
Gold Coast. But with the cocoa boom of the following
years, such economic difficulties were soon forgotten; and,
by West African standards, in the early years of the Dyarchy
and independence, the country was a prosperous one.

Such an exceptional prosperity points to a peculiarity
in the situation of Ghana. The Gold Coast of the early
1950's was, and was not, an underdeveloped country.[1] The
country was confronted with problems already different from
those of most other (underdeveloped) countries in tropical
Africa. But, by and large, the means at the disposal of the
government to solve these problems were still those of an
underdeveloped country.

A summary examination of the sectoral distribution of
the active population provides a good illustration of this.[2]

The primary sector is dominant but relatively less than
elsewhere in Africa. Just over 63 per cent of the active

17

population is engaged in the primary sector (61 per cent in agriculture) as compared to 10 to 30 per cent in advanced industrial countries or between 70 to more than 90 per cent in other African countries. About 35 per cent of the Ghanaian peasants are cocoa farmers or employed in cocoa farming.

The industrial secondary sector is not as developed. In 1960, 13 per cent of the active population were engaged in the secondary sector, of whom 230,000 (out of 340,000) were in the "manufacturing industries." However, such a large figure is somewhat misleading, for, in fact, more than half the persons employed in the "manufacturing industries" were artisans rather than industrial workers—the average number of persons employed per "manufacturing firm" being 2.7! In 1962, there were only 14 firms employing more than 500 persons, and most larger industrial establishments had been set up after 1950.[3] Altogether these 14 firms employed 10,500 workers or about 4 per cent of the labor force of the secondary sector. The type of activity of these large firms reveals the pattern of industrial development in Ghana: 6 sawmills, 3 firms manufacturing beverages and tobacco, 2 firms producing transport equipment, 1 furniture factory, 1 printing works, and 1 chemical plant. Among firms employing more than 100 persons, the distribution is about the same: 54 firms out of 92 are sawmills, firms producing beverages and tobacco, and transport equipment. Textiles and metallurgy are both much less important: three for each category among the firms employing more than 100 workers.[4]

The tertiary sector is typically very large and not modern. Twenty-three per cent of the active population were engaged, in 1960, in this sector (18 per cent of the male active population and 31 per cent of the female active population). The share, as well as the type of activity of women in this sector, show that the tertiary sector in Ghana is not modern and perhaps partly parasitic: 275,000 "petty traders'' (who more often than not do not even possess a selling stand)[5] out of a total labor force of 526,000 (male and female) for the whole sector, i.e., more than half.

Robert Szereszewski also mentions regional imbalances, particularly between the North and the South of the savannah and the forest and coastal strip. The more developed South (viz., Western and Eastern regions, Ashanti and Accra regions, or the whole of the forest zone) had in 1960 the following characteristics: territory, 34 per cent; population, 61 per cent; urban population, 81 per cent; production (value added), 75 per cent; capital stock, 82 per cent.[6]

Last, but not least, Ghana's dependence on foreign trade is rather high as revealed by her foreign trade ratio: 46 per cent in 1955 and remarkably constant at 43 to 44 per cent in the following years before dipping to 39 per cent in 1962.[7] But it must be stressed, such trade dependence was more a dependence on the world market in general than a dependence on the former colonial *métropole;* the sterling zone supplied 60 per cent of the total value of Ghanaian imports in 1951 (42 per cent in 1960) and absorbed 45 per cent of Ghana's exports (36 per cent in 1960). Such proportions are far smaller than those of trade between France and her former colonies in Africa.[8]

The above summary of some essential economic characteristics of Ghana reveals the typical picture of an underdeveloped country; but, at the same time, as in the particular case of the primary sector (smaller), the country's economy is already more complex than that of most other tropical countries in Africa. In fact, if one looks a little more closely at the economy of Ghana in the 1950's, one is impressed by many such "differences" and "complexities." The subsistence economy is much less important than elsewhere: Subsistence consumption ("own produce consumed") amounts to only one fifth of the national

consumption expenditure, or about 40 per cent of the total
consumption of local food, or about 17 per cent of the
private consumption estimate in the national accounts.[9]
If one also remembers that "petty traders" were as
numerous in the rural areas as in the cities and towns, one
cannot but agree with Szereszewski: The subsistence
element "takes account of the subsistence activities
carried out primarily by the rural population but it does not
represent an identifiable sector, in the sense of households
detached from the market or from the money economy and
supplying their own needs. Such a sector does not occur in
Ghana"[10] (with a few strictly localized exceptions,
particularly in the northwestern part of the country). That
this is a situation different from the classic model of
economic structures in underdeveloped African countries
and from the types of economic structures in Ghana's
neighboring countries is clearly stated by Szereszewski:

> Agriculture, forestry and cocoa supply the economy
> (in 1960) with 29.2 per cent of all output and create
> 36.5 per cent of the gross value added. Mining,
> manufacturing, electricity and construction together
> contribute 23.0 per cent of output and 17.7 per cent
> of gross value added. Dissected in this way, the
> economy of Ghana presents a rather sophisticated
> picture, certainly different from the stereotype of an
> underdeveloped economy in which the bulk of output
> originates in agriculture. A real symptom of under-
> development is, however, the low value of sales to
> producers indicating that only a very small proportion
> of the output of the economy is delivered to other
> sectors of production. More than half of those sales
> are by the fuel sector, public utilities and services
> and not commodities—since the fuel sector is actually
> the distribution system, no processing of fuel having
> been done in Ghana in 1960. The sectors producing
> commodities have a very low degree of linkage in the
> economy.[11]

Ghana's relatively more complex, more-developed socio-economic structure is to be explained primarily by the historical origin and the main form of the colonial development of the country.

First, just as her neighbors in tropical West Africa, Ghana, or rather the then Gold Coast, was not a European settlers' colony, partly because of the difficult climate of the whole of the intertropical forest belt. (As one knows, the Gold Coast had the awesome reputation of being "the Whiteman's grave.") Even though the Gold Coast was not the only "grave" on the Gulf of Guinea, there were proportionally fewer Europeans there than in most other countries, either French or British colonies. The main reason for this may be that the Gold Coast was fully occupied rather late. After repeated incidents with the Ashanti population, the colonial conquest seemed almost halfhearted; it was aimed at checking the progress of French and German penetration into the interior through the Ivory Coast and Togoland. Another well-known reason is that English settlers were more attracted by British territories in other parts of Africa (Rhodesia, South Africa, Kenya, etc.) and had the possibility of choosing.

Second, and this is far more important, cocoa planting in the then Gold Coast, from the very beginning, was undertaken by Ghanaian farmers, and not by European settlers employing local labor. Although the marketing of cocoa for quite some time was a European monopoly, the fundamental fact that production was, from its origin at the end of the last century, exclusively in the hands of Ghanaian farmers resulted in a relative prosperity of the rural areas of southern and central Ghana, in the constitution of a semimodern rural middle class, and in the progressive withering away of the subsistence economy. This is also the reason why today Ghana is not characterized, as so many underdeveloped countries are, by the economic, social and psychological dualism which corresponds to the continued existence, side by side, of a more or less closed traditional sector and a modern foreign colonial sector.

It must be further stressed that such a development of a colonial economy by local farmers, at such an early stage, also reduced colonial contradictions and spread, more widely than elsewhere, the benefits of colonial growth while developing the monetized sector of the economy. This relative rural prosperity also eventually reached the urban, mostly commercial, sector, and in its turn strengthened and accelerated the development of a modern intelligentsia whose origins can be traced to the establishment of European forts on the Coast (Fanti country and, up to a point, the Ga region of Accra-Christianborg). "Rich" and "less rich" cocoa farmers and businessmen could pay for the studies of some of their children in British and other overseas universities. Their family ties as well as the mode of financing their studies tended to give the Gold Coast professional workers and intellectuals the charac-teristics of a nationalist and bourgeois-minded intelligentsia. Several observers have insisted on the élitist attitudes and limitations of the early intelligentsia-dominated nationalist movement in the Gold Coast. This is an important element which has to be stressed at this point, for it is particular to Ghana, at least to such a degree, and because it is essential to the understanding of the country's political development.

Lastly, as is well known, Ghana was fortunate enough (and this again was a difference in relation to other tropical countries) to be able to draw on fairly large sterling reserves at the time of her accession to independence: about £200 million. Such huge reserves had been piled up before 1957, thanks to positive trade balances, or in the last analysis, thanks to cocoa.[12]

In sum, at the moment of Ghana's accession to internal self-government (1951) and then to full self-government (1957), i.e., when Kwame Nkrumah and his party, the CPP, took over the Government of Ghana, the country's situation and problems were as follows.

Despite relatively higher average standards of living and relatively more-advanced economic development (only 60 per cent peasants), Ghana remained essentially an underdeveloped, pre-industrial country, exporting primary commodities only (cocoa, timber, gold, diamond, manganese) and having to import the bulk of her consumption of manufactures. Moreover, because of her relative prosperity and rising standards of living, Ghana also imported part of her foodstuffs.[13] A larger output of cocoa and higher prices caused total and personal incomes to rise; this permitted private consumption to become more diversified and sophisticated, but structurally the economy remained essentially the same. Thus, under the circumstances, Ghana's relative prosperity could be seen as the source of dangerous illusions. From a different point of view, Dudley Seers and C. Ross were the first to reach a similar conclusion: In the 1950's, Ghana's economy was extremely fragile.[14]

The country was more prosperous, but this was a colonial type of prosperity. Ghana's Government (through export taxes) and Ghana's cocoa farmers could both derive substantial benefits from the country's colonial development. These were positive elements which singled out Ghana among other African tropical countries at the time, but they could not prevent Ghana's economic structures from being and remaining colonial, i.e., Ghana was to be, and remain, a pre-industrial and underdeveloped country.

EQUILIBRIUM OF EMBRYONIC CLASSES

Confronted with such a situation, both typical (underdevelopment, imbalances, dependence) and specific (a relatively more-advanced and more prosperous economy), the Ghanaian leaders, Nkrumah and the CPP, had to make a series of choices, strategic and tactical ones.

Strategic options concern the policy of development. Tactical problems concern the methods, the implementation of the strategy of development. They depend on the consciousness of the leaders, on their awareness of the real situation of their country, their determination to solve the problems, and, last, but not least, their ability to mobilize the "people" on a program of development, i.e., their ability to impose constraints on the people's consumption, attitudes, preferences, etc., while consolidating, or at least maintaining, their power. Thus, strategy and tactics also depend on the socio-economic structures of the country, either directly or as they are reflected in political and other movements, institutions, and organizations—and the limitations such structures, institutions and movements, set upon the nationalist party's freedom of choice.

An attempt to distribute the active population of Ghana[15] according to a three-class system—bourgeoisie, middle class, proletariat—or even into a more refined form, including subdivisions within the three groups, only supplies very broad indicators. It shows, however, that there was practically no bourgeoisie in Ghana. To be sure, although large rural estates do not exist in Ghana, there are, as we shall see later on, some "large" farmers and cocoa brokers who constitute elements of a rural middle bourgeoisie.[16] There are also a few Ghanaian firms in the industrial sector, in the building industry, and the services, whose owners may be described as the embryonic elements of an urban bourgeoisie, but it is difficult to estimate the number of these firms with any precision; available data concerning firms which employed ten or more workers in 1960 does not usually indicate the nationality of their owners. But we know that most mines and quarries (15,000 workers in the private sector) are expatriate firms.[17] The larger establishments of the manufacturing industry (25,000 workers) are also foreign-owned, and the same situation prevails in the building industry (20,000), commerce (25,000), and the services (18,000). In other words, an examination of private firms employing ten or more persons in 1960 essentially reveals the importance of the expatriate sector. The ultimate beneficiaries do not even reside in the country; they are the directors and shareowners of the large trading and mining firms: the British Unilever and Ashanti Goldfields, the Swiss Union Trading Company, the *Cie française de l'afrique occidentale*, etc.

However, in association or in competition with large expatriate firms, there are a few hundred "small" and "less small" Ghanaian entrepreneurs who constitute what could be considered an embryonic bourgeoisie, and whose activity is most significant in the building industry and the tertiary sector.

The "middle classes"[18] include, as one might expect, the overwhelming majority of Ghana's active population (1.7 million persons out of a total active population numbering 2.6 million), i.e., 59 per cent of the male active population and 76 per cent of the female active population. It is mostly a rural population, mainly of farmers (1.0 million out of 1.7, i.e., 60 per cent of the "middle classes"). To these must be added 315,000 persons engaged in retail trade (evenly divided among rural and urban zones), 200,000 artisans, 42,000 fishermen, 17,000 persons in the services, 15,000 in transports, 10,500 professionals, 9,000 engaged in forestry work, and 7,000 gold and diamond diggers

("African diggers"). Thus, in a rough approximation based on the 1960 Population Census, 300,000 people constitute the urban middle classes and 1.4 million their rural equivalent.

Their incomes vary greatly and may even be very low for those categories of peasants living in isolated areas and farming essentially for their subsistence, especially in the northwest. The monetized component of such incomes may be limited to a few pounds per annum (e.g., surplus sold at the local market). Nonetheless, over the years, these rural middle classes have supplied the government with a good deal of its resources. From 1959/60 to 1963/64, export taxes on cocoa have averaged 23 per cent of the total value of cocoa exports and, during the same years, they have represented alone 20 per cent of the government's income, despite steadily and rapidly falling cocoa prices during this period.

These middle classes thus represent a fundamental characteristic of Ghanaian society: Sixty-five per cent of the active population are self-employed ("middle classes"), 80 per cent of which live in rural areas. Their income, especially its monetized component, even if not high in most instances, globally has nonetheless been sufficient for the Ghanaian Government to draw from it a substantial part of its considerable resources. Distributed all over the country, engaged in varied economic pursuits, belonging to several different ethnic groups, to be sure, this population of farmers, artisans, and shopkeepers and traders does not share a common group or class consciousness. However, they are well aware of their substantial contribution to the government's resources. In many ways, they think they are Ghana. And they are not altogether wrong.

The last group, the proletariat, according to the figures and definitions of the 1960 Population Census, would have numbered some 350,000 active persons, a third of them employed in the public sector and two thirds in the private sector. A little more than a quarter (108,000) were agricultural laborers, 25,000 miners, 35,000 employed in the transport and communication industry, and 140,000 were recorded as "industrial workers" though most of them, as already mentioned, were in fact employed by artisans rather than by industrial concerns. Another 30,000 worked in the services. Thus, despite the fact that, on the employers' side, a few larger expatriate mining and export trade firms as well as a growing public sector must be added to the local private employers, the Ghanaian proletariat is not a large group. There is, obviously, nothing surprising about this fact: The Ghanaian proletariat is marginal because the process of industrialization is in its very early stage. In the 1950's, Sekondi-Takoradi, and to a lesser extent Accra, were the only places with strong concentrations of urban proletariat. There were also some fairly dense concentrations in the mining districts of Western Ghana and Ashanti; some of these miners were not nationals of Ghana and would come to work in the mines only for relatively short periods. The turnover of employment in the mines bears this out: Many miners are almost to be considered as seasonal workers. Furthermore, unlike what can be seen in some other African countries, because there were no European settlers and no indigenous large rural estates, there wasn't, and there still isn't, in Ghana, a large rural proletariat, *stricto sensu*. Takoradi is not Casablanca and the *abusa* [19] worker in the cocoa-farming areas is not a North African *khammes* [20] or a plantation worker.

The Ghanaian proletariat exists—and the lively first period of the Trade Union movement is a good illustration of this—but, in the 1950's as well as in the 1960's, it remains a marginal group. Except in Sekondi-Takoradi, and this was well demonstrated in September, 1961, during the strike, the Ghanaian proletariat is not an autonomous force.

The summary distribution of the active population
according to the main occupational categories and
employment status reveals another aspect of the socio-
economic situation of Ghana in the 1950's and 1960's. The
state through its public sector now employs the bulk of the
professionally qualified working population.[21] The modern
sector is gradually coming under the control of the state
while the huge traditional activities are still essentially
carried out by self-employed workers.

TABLE 1

OCCUPATIONAL CATEGORIES AND EMPLOYMENT STATUS
(PERCENTAGES) IN 1960

Employment Status / Occupations	Employees in the Public sectors	Employees in the Priv. sectors	Family workers	Employers and Self-employed	TOTAL
Professional workers	66	13	marginal	20	100
Admin. workers	50	27	marginal	<20	100
Clerical workers	<50	44	marginal	5	100
Sales workers	marg.	4	4	<90	100
Farmers, agricultural workers	marg.	7	20	>70	100
Fishermen	marg.	14	10	>75	100
Craftsmen	<20	20	marginal	60	100
Loggers and forestry workers	marg.	50	marginal	50	100
Miners	marg.[a]	75[a]	marginal	<25[b]	100
Workers in transport and communications	25	42	marginal	>30	100
Services	32	40	4	<25	100
TOTAL	7.5	12	13.5	67	100

Notes: a   Before the nationalization of five mines.
             b   The so-called African diggers.
Source: Ghana, Census Office, *1960 Population Census of Ghana,*
           Advanced Report of Volumes III and IV (Accra:
           Government Printer, 1962).

Cocoa Farmers

Before we go any further, we must comment briefly on the question of cocoa farmers, whom we have all included in the "middle classes," as suggested by the 1960 Population Census, but who, obviously, present a great variety of situations. Indeed, everybody knows that cocoa plays an essential role in the relative prosperity of Ghana, as the main source of foreign receipts and as the backbone of rural affluence and monetized economy, but this is about all that is known. It has almost become a rite for students of Ghana, whether economists or political scientists, to formally acknowledge that whatever is known, is to be found in the writings of Polly Hill. Unfortunately, as Miss Hill herself already pointed out in the introduction to her much-quoted book, *The Gold Coast Cocoa Farmer*,[22] it is not really possible to add up the figures obtained in the survey on which the book itself is based. It is not possible either to make estimates covering the whole cocoa area. It would be nice, we are told, to know how many cocoa farmers there are in Ghana, how many laborers they employ, the size distribution of farms, among many other questions. Indeed, it would. But this is not possible on the basis of the scant information available at the moment. According to Miss Hill, the very "concept of the 'cocoa farmer' could be rather elusive."[23] This is most regrettable, not so much from an economic point of view, but in relation to the real social structure of the country. Thus, bearing in mind all the restrictions suggested by Miss Hill, we feel that it may prove nonetheless useful to summarize those among her findings which may be relevant to our purpose here.

Table 2 uses materials presented by Miss Hill on the basis of a survey conducted in 1954-55, covering 10 villages, and totaling 483 cocoa farmers. These villages

TABLE 2
SIZE, INCOME, AND LABOR EMPLOYED IN COCOA FARMING

Loads	Net Income[a] or 50 shil. per load	Size of Farmers	Number of Farmers	%	Share of Production (Percentage)	Examples of Labor Employed by Individual Farmers
< 20	< 50	very small	130	27	7	
20 – 40	50 – 100	small	136	28	16	
40 – 80	100 – 200	middle	100	20	19	2 *abusa*[b] (farmer's own sons); 3 annual[c]; 4 annual; etc.
80 – 100	200 – 500	large	83	17	33	6 *abusa*; 3 *abusa*; etc.
> 200	> 500	very large	34	7	24	10 *abusa*; 15 *abusa*; 11 annual; 9 *abusa*; 10 *abusa*; 6 *abusa*; 9 *abusa*; 15 *abusa*; 9 *abusa*; 5 *abusa*; 8 *abusa*; 9 *abusa*; 4 *abusa*; 7 annual; 3 annual; 7 annual; etc.,

Notes: a Seventy per cent gross income.
  b Refers to the *abusa* workers. *See*, Chapter 2, n. 19.
  c Refers to annual laborers.

Source: This table is based on the findings reported by Polly Hill,
  The Gold Coast Farmer – A Preliminary Survey (London: Oxford University Press, 1956).
  The survey made, in 1954-55, covered 10 villages and 483 farmers.

cover most of the typical cocoa regions of Ghana: "British Togoland" (2 villages, 70 farmers), the Eastern Region, around Koforidua, in the "Colony," i.e., the first cocoa-growing center of Ghana and that which was most severely hit by the "swollen shoot," (2 villages, 102 farmers), the Ashanti heartland, around Kumasi (3 villages, 167 farmers), and Western Ashanti (Brong), a relative late-comer in cocoa farming (3 villages, 144 farmers).

If the results of this survey represented accurately the situation in Ghana in the mid-1950's, it would appear that more than half the cocoa farmers were "small" and "very small" farmers with a production not exceeding 40 loads per annum, whose net income did not exceed £100 per annum. "Middle" farmers (between 40 and 80 loads or £100 to £200 annual net income) accounted for another 20 per cent, or, with "small" and "very small" farmers, formed altogether about three quarters of the cocoa farmers. "Very large" farmers (more than 200 loads or more than £500 annual net income from cocoa) did not represent more than 7 per cent of the farmers, or along with the other "large" farmers (80 to 200 loads, or £200 to £500 annual net income from cocoa) not more than a quarter of all the cocoa farmers in Ghana. As expected, the shares in the total cocoa production of these various groups are almost the exact reverse: "Small" and "very small" farmers (more than 50 per cent of farmers) share less than 25 per cent of the production. Taken with the "middle" farmers (altogether about 75 per cent of the farmers), they only produce a little more than 40 per cent of the cocoa. The "large" and "very large" farmers (25 per cent of farmers) produce together a little less than 60 per cent of the cocoa.

But obviously, 10 villages and less than 500 farmers out of 200,000, according to the rough guess of Polly Hill (and almost twice as many according to the 1960 census of population), cannot be expected to represent accurately the

situation of the cocoa industry as a whole. Besides, the
averages just mentioned hide considerable variations from
one village to the next, from one region to the other. One
of the extremes is represented by Hwidiem in Western
Ashanti, where there are practically no "small" farmers
and where 80 per cent of the total production is shared
among 14 farmers (out of 30) with each one having an
individual production of more than 200 and more than 500
loads ("large" and "very large" farmers). The other
extreme is illustrated by the village of Asafo in the Eastern
Region (the oldest region, where hundreds of thousands of
trees were destroyed by the swollen shoot disease, and
where, therefore, production fell sharply). In Asafo, 47 out
of 57 farmers interviewed, i.e., 80 per cent of the farmers,
were "small" or "very small" (less than 40 loads or less
than £100 annual net income from cocoa). Together they
account for less than 50 per cent of the production and
there are no farmers marketing more than 200 loads or
making more than £500 annual net income from cocoa. For
obvious reasons, as farmers tend to move their farms to
other regions, i.e., other than those hit by the swollen
shoot disease, there are more and more farmers similar to
those found in Western Ashanti or in the upper part of the
former British Togoland, i.e., farmers of a substantially
larger "size." The increasing quantities of cocoa produced
in Ghana in later years is evidence of such a movement,
affecting both the geographical distribution of cocoa
production and the average "size of the farmers." In other
words, if we were to derive any useful, however approximate, information from the above figures, we should
consider that, altogether in Ghana now, the "size of the
farmers" is larger than it would appear from our average
figures—perhaps substantially larger.

Assuming that the figures are not entirely irrelevant,
it seems that, at the very least, half of the cocoa farmers

of Ghana are "small" and "middle" farmers, deriving not more than £200 per annum from their cocoa farms. Many of these farmers have another job, and not infrequently a full-time job; their farms are cultivated either by *abusa* laborers or by themselves and their families. The other cocoa farmers, "large" and "very large" farmers, also seem to represent a substantial part of the cocoa-farming population, perhaps a third of the population, perhaps more. It may be useful to point out that the information given by Polly Hill on the labor employed by cocoa farmers (information even more scant than that given on the "size of the farmers") indicates that "very large" farmers employ between 4 and 18 *abusa* laborers (taking a third of the crop) and also annual laborers (paid in cash) on several new farms (in one instance, 7 new farms). "Large" farmers employed between 3 and 6 *abusa* laborers. There were also indications of some "middle" farmers employing some annual laborers on new farms and some *abusa* laborers on their fruit farms, but the only example given was a "middle" farmer employing his two sons as *abusa* laborers! No indications were given concerning investments in new farms or employment of *abusa* or paid laborers by "small" and "very small" farmers; this does not necessarily indicate that such farmers never employ labor or do not buy or prepare new farms. The system of production and the extended family are such as to make possible all sorts of combinations of contract, daily or annually paid, *abusa*, *nkotokuano*,[24] or family labor at the various levels of production. Rich farmers may prefer to build large houses, send many children to school, or give substantially to such traditional functions as funerals, rather than buy cars or other modern durables to fill their houses with, but, as Miss Hill notes,[25] it is quite clear that the typical cocoa farmer is not a "small" or even a "middle" farmer going about his business alone or with the additional help of his

family. There are many such one-man or one-family ventures
in cocoa farming in Ghana, but there are also many fairly
large farming businesses relying on the employment of 5,
10, 15, and even more *abusa* and paid laborers.

There is no doubt that, in Ghana, a substantial rural
middle bourgeoisie exists and is quite capable and willing
to develop its businesses (to wit: the investment in new
farms through the employment of paid annual laborers). At
the same time, it should be equally stressed that cocoa
farmers across the country represent many different things,
many different "sizes." Furthermore, cocoa farming may
be a full-time job or a part-time job; it may be a rent, when
the farm is permanently taken care of by an *abusa* laborer
who, as a rule, even markets the cocoa himself.
The cocoa farmer may then be a clerk, a trader, a
school teacher in a neighboring town or in Kumasi or Accra.
It may be a relatively big business, with farms scattered
in different areas sometimes far from one another, with the
farmer supervising the work of his *abusa* men and other
laborers. In other words, the rural "middle classes" (self-
employed), mentioned earlier, include a substantial
semimodern rural middle bourgeoisie, which employs labor,
paid or on a contract basis, whose level of affluence may
not be very different from that of the "middle peasants" of
many parts of Western Europe before World War II. They
produce for their own consumption and for the market. They
are modern enough to use pesticides and spraying machines,
but they are not cut off from the rest of the rural community.

Such a socio-economic structure (embryonic bourgeoisie,
huge "middle classes," marginal proletariat), even though
it is more complex than that of most other tropical countries
in Africa where the subsistence sector is far more important
than in Ghana, suggests that it might have been perilous
for any ruling nationalist party to base itself on *one* social
group (e.g., the urban proletariat), or even on a narrow

alliance (e.g., the urban proletariat and the embryonic bourgeoisie). Thus, Frantz Fanon's rather popular theses on the landless and poor peasants do not seem to apply to a situation such as that of Ghana in the early 1950's. As we shall see later, this may partly account—much more at least than Nkrumah's personal political philosophy—for what appears to David Apter and Dennis Austin as a puzzling ambiguity in the CPP, which is seen as a nationalist party *and* the "Party of the People," i.e., a class party, and what Fitch and Oppenheimer dismiss as a "petty bourgeois" treason of Ghana's truly exploited and toiling masses by the CPP leadership.

Furthermore, one should also note the relative fluidity of the social structure in the later years of the colonial regime, even more so after 1951. Despite some institutional obstacles—such as the fact that almost throughout the Nkrumah-CPP era, secondary schools were not fee-free[26] — this fluidity was quite noticeable. Wallerstein, following the examples set by George Balandier and Thomas Hodgkin, has paid some attention to this phenomenon and shown the importance attached to education as well as active involvement in the many political, cultural, sportive, and religious associations by the younger generation, particularly among the so-called commoners.[27] Obviously, most of the interest manifested toward voluntary associations was to shift at the end of the 1940's to the more attractive, all-embracing nationalist party. It happened in Ghana as elsewhere in Africa. In a series of very short biographical notes which Austin obtained from a majority of the CPP MPs,[28] this relative fluidity of the social structure is rather well illustrated. At the same time, the constant shifting of occupation of these future MPs also indicates the limitations of social mobility in the then Gold Coast. Young men escape from the pattern of traditional society and *successively,* rather than successfully, try their hands at various jobs and careers. But the number of attempts points as much to the difficulty of successfully moving *into* a new group, a new type of activity, as it does to the relative ease with which, by then, one could move *out of* one group, out of one type of activity.

We shall have more to say about this, but it is clear that, however limited, social mobility in Ghana must be counted as a negative factor as far as class or group consciousness is concerned. If one, rightly or wrongly, thinks one can find an individual solution to one's problems, one is little inclined to feel much concerned by the general problems, needs, and interests of one's social group of origin. This is rather obvious, even though family ties remain strong in Ghana. It is the family which hopes to solve its problems by financing its most gifted son's university studies in Great Britain. On his return, the "been-to" will become a lawyer or a high-ranking civil servant, and this will help the whole family. It may be a family affair, as distinct from a strictly individual one as would often happen in European or American circumstances, but it is not the struggle of a social group.

CONFLICTING ELITES

This sketchy summary of the socio-economic structures of Ghana based on the 1960 Population Census supplies only a very rough picture of Ghanaian society. However, it serves one useful purpose, that of establishing orders of magnitude: how many petty traders, how many farm laborers, miners, professionals, cocoa farmers, etc.? It does not say much about the embryonic bourgeoisie, the huge "middle classes," and the marginal proletariat, but at least it says that these groups are embryonic, huge, and marginal. In the case of some analyses, a clear awareness of such orders of magnitude for the various socio-economic groups might have prevented their authors from making statements about Ghana and the CPP which are obviously not based on the socio-economic realities of Ghana as it was and is, but rather as the country was supposed or hoped to be.[29]

At this point, one more remark must be made. Most analyses of political developments in contemporary Ghana, by English or American political scientists or historians, have discussed the problems not in terms of socio-economic groups or social classes but in terms of conflicting élites (usually the chiefs, the intelligentsia, and the "youngmen").[30] And there is more than one possible justification for such an approach. In the short period at least, the problem may not be so much a problem of what the various groups are and what they want as it is a problem of expression. How do these various groups express themoclvcs? What channels do they use? Who speaks on their behalf? These are difficult questions and here one may wonder whether the Anglo-Saxon, neo-Weberian analysis really supplies the answers. Do these conflicting élite groups actually correspond to clearly definable clienteles among the socio-economic groups/classes which we have just examined? One may entertain more than reasonable doubts. It would rather seem that each élite group tries, or tried at the time, in the early 1950's, when it was still possible to contend openly for the devolution of British power, to speak on behalf of the whole community, but, obviously, each group gives this community a different definition: The chiefs are the "natural rulers from time immemorial," the intelligentsia are the living examples of "modern Ghana," and the CPP "youngmen" are the political expression of "the people."

However, it is interesting to try to relate the various élites to the socio-economic groups/classes composing the Ghanaian society of the 1950's. To this effect, we must now briefly examine in turn each of these élite groups.

The Chiefs—Bypassed and Frustrated

It would be presumptuous to pretend that the problem
of the chiefs in their relations with the nationalist
movement in Ghana is a simple one or even that the
question has been made entirely clear by the many studies
devoted to this subject by sociologists, historians, or
political scientists, from Rattray to the most recent ones.
Although the subject has long been a popular one for both
expatriate and Ghanaian scholars, there are many question
marks left, even on such essential aspects as the role of
chiefs vis-à-vis landownership.

However, practically all students of contemporary
Ghana, who by the way draw their information mainly from
the same sources,[31] agree on a few fundamental facts and
conclusions.

The power of the chiefs—the only pre-existing power—
is not, in general, based on the ownership of tribal land.[32]

The chiefs, in the countryside especially, are
powerful, "even awesome" (Austin) but they are not
autocratic because their (traditional) power is both limited
and controlled. Limits are set by the tradition (there are
many things which a chief is expected to do and not to do,
lists of which are solemnly recalled when a new chief is
enstooled), and control is exercised by the *elders* and, up
to a point and under certain circumstances, also by the
"commoners" (or "youngmen"), either directly or through
their mouthpiece, for instance, the *Nkwankwaahene* in
Ashanti. Although such adjectives as "constitutional" (and
conversely "despotic"), sometimes used[33] in connection
with chieftaincy may be misleading, it is nonetheless true
that, if the selection of chiefs remained restricted to some
families (royal families), they had to be elected to the

stool and, more important still, could be, and often enough
were, destooled (through clearly set traditional procedures).

The stool, not the chief himself, is sacred.

Unfortunately, there is no concensus (except when it
comes to recognizing our lack of a clear knowledge of the
facts) on the economic and social relationship between the
various components of traditional society, viz., the chiefs,
the elders, and the youngmen (commoners).

On the contrary, there is a general agreement that
traditional chieftaincy was deeply affected but not broken
by British colonization.

The chiefs represent a local and a traditional authority,
not a national one. With the exception of the *Asantehene*
in Ashanti, their power did not extend beyond a fairly small
community or territory. Inasmuch as nationalism is to be
understood as a dialectical response to the modern colonial
impact, the ability of the chiefs, as local and traditional
authorities, was bound to be limited and, in the last
analysis, only incidental unless the chiefs first renounced
themselves as chiefs and took up new roles and functions
not previously attached to the stools' prerogatives and
duties. In point of fact, far too much attention has been
focused on the chiefs—and this may be partly a hangover
of the traditional ethnological approach to African studies;
the chiefs played near to no part in the modern nationalist
movement in Ghana. We shall, however, devote some
attention to the problem of the erosion of chiefly power in
the Gold Coast during the colonial period because what
happened to the chiefs reflects, more generally, what
happened to traditional society and traditional values, and
this is far more important. The youngmen's frustration is
the potentially positive, modern counterpart to the chief's
loss of prestige and power, and it results from the same
historical process. From this point of view, it is interesting
to pay some attention to this process.

The contact with Europeans (at first, entrenched in
their forts on the Coast and not too keen on getting
involved in the affairs of the Interior), was limited to the
Fanti and Ga areas and in the beginning almost exclusively
commercial. It then became more intense, all-embracing,
covering the whole area of Ghana,[34] introducing elements
of disintegration in the traditional tribal system, and
directly and indirectly began to erode the monopoly of
traditional chiefs as the political and spiritual authorities
in the Gold Coast.

In the course of a first phase, ending roughly with
World War I, the authority of the chiefs was directly
challenged and circumscribed by British colonial administration. Chiefs were held in suspicion by the British and
the imposition of new central and regional authorities (the
Governor, the District Commissioners) as well as the
passing of new and different laws contributed to reduce the
power of the chiefs, and to free those youngmen who felt
the need to escape the grip of tradition and traditional
authority. It may be pointed out here that, as early as the
middle of the nineteenth century, a few representatives of
the African (mostly Fanti) intelligentsia were offered seats
in the Legislative Council of the Colony (Southern Ghana);
this happened to no chief.

In the course of the second phase, beginning after World
War I, the attitude of the colonial authorities shifted. For
the implementation of the Gold Coast brand of indirect rule
they had to turn to the chiefs. To many observers, this
belated colonial support given to the chiefs was ultimately
to prove more detrimental to their prestige and authority
than whatever direct action the colonial authorities ever
took against the chiefs. The argument is twofold. First, the
British did not understand precisely the function of the
chief in Akan and, in general, in traditional society; they
did not see the delicate balance of power between the

chiefs, and the elders and the commoners; they did not see the importance of the notion of consensus. (Although a decision is expressed or even taken by the chief, it nonetheless reflects a consensus of the unit, whether village, clan, or tribe; the discussions have taken place previously.) The British, oversimplifying the real situation and perhaps too strongly influenced by the specific situation of Northern Nigeria in their "lugardian" conception of indirect rule, equated *native authority* with the chiefs. Thus, while some of his functions (e.g., war) had been eliminated by the *Pax Britannica,* others (e.g., religious ones) were being gradually eroded by the spread of missionary schools and similar institutions. The chiefs found themselves loaded with new roles and functions (judicial, administrative, including tax collection). At a time when many of the commoners found increasingly attractive alternatives to the traditional values of village life, the new roles and functions imposed on the chiefs by the British administration could not really strengthen their power. Rather it added new elements (modern ones) of discontent to the traditional ones.

Second, and just as important, is the fact that the chiefs became the local authorities of the colonial administration; this did not add a new (colonial) element of legitimacy to the traditional (i.e., belonging to royal family, being elected by one's fellow-villagers, clansmen or tribesmen, etc.). On the contrary, this new source of legitimacy could not but clash with the traditional ones. This was well illustrated by the fact that to be officially recognized as such, a chief had to be *gazetted.* The CPP, thus, could easily dismiss the chiefs in the competition for national representation by pointing to their colonial legitimacy: "Chiefs no longer sit on Stools but on Gazettes."[35]

More important, however, than the subjective attitudes of the colonial authorities (whether their opposition first or their support later) is the objective impact of colonization itself. The development of a modern, or at least, a new sector, in the economy initiated a process of erosion of the chief's power. To the traditional values, a set of new, modern values was progressively opposed: material values (new objects, new ways) and also new sources of prestige, especially what the Western culture represented, and what was accepted by many as the only culture, as culture itself, both because of the technological advance of the West and because of the need to acquire new techniques (i.e., a new culture) in order to be able to enter the new, colonial world (jobs in the colonial service or in the large expatriate firms). Similarly, the missions added their own disintegrating contribution through the introduction of Western education (Western culture and techniques) and Christian religions (external to the tribe and the clan, but universalistic despite internal conflicts between the various brands of Protestantism and the Catholic church). Despite the relatively small number of converts and the limited school enrolment of the early colonial period in relation to the total population and the school-age population, the importance of new sources of prestige, new values, and new techniques (including techniques of propitiation) as disintegrating factors of traditional society and chiefly power can hardly be overestimated.

Confronted by this classic situation (classic inasmuch as it was, in varying degrees, reproduced in practically all African colonies), the chiefs as centers of local authority might have reacted in many different ways. They might have, overtly or not, refused to cooperate with the colonial authorities. Thus, they might, as it were, have continued, in a nonviolent way, the historic period of resistance to colonization. (This might have applied with particular relevance to Ashanti where resistance had been stronger and had lasted to the end of the nineteenth century, and where the deported *Asantehene* had already set an outstanding example of personal resistance.) The chiefs, thus, might have represented a traditional rallying-point of, at least, passive resistance to colonial occupation, and to the introduction of new values and new ways. In so doing, they would have represented a clear alternative to the process of colonization; they would have set an example for all to see how to resist and oppose colonization even after colonial authority had been established in the Gold Coast. But, with a few exceptions, they did not.

It must be said, however, that in Ashanti, despite the gradual acceptance of some formal modern ways, the authority and person of the *asantehene* continued to appear essentially as a traditional, exclusively Ashanti authority, and one which was little inclined to cooperate fully with the colonial, and for that matter, after 1951, with the national authorities. But, once again, with a few exceptions, it may be said that the chiefs allowed themselves to become the trusted local agents of indirect rule, i.e., in the last analysis, of colonization, if not of colonialism. This is particularly true of the later period of colonial rule, after 1925, and even more so after 1932 and 1935 (the successive stages of the reorganization of both the Legislative and Executive Councils). They became the local wheels of the colonial administration.

The implementation in the Gold Coast of the so-called system of indirect rule unbalanced the delicate equilibrium of traditional authority in favor of the chiefs. Although this increased the chief's powers, it proved detrimental to them as it was obtained at the expense of their prestige. The story is well-known, and not only in West Africa. It would suffice to recall the unhappy fate of Maghrebian *caids* and *bachagas* (in whose case the scandal was more obvious because tribal structures were weaker and the process of

modernization had been carried on further) to indicate how
perilous a mechanism is the system of indirect rule for
those traditional authorities who allow themselves to be
caught in it. Apter summarizes the whole situation rather
well:

> Insofar as it was the design of the colonial authorities
> to maintain the traditional system intact and use it
> as a basis of political administration, much of the
> effective maintenance of the traditional system
> increasingly came from external sources rather than
> from internal support by the members. .... The net
> effect was that, in terms of subsequent events, the
> maintenance of the structure of traditional authority
> was in fact countenanced by law, and by British
> support to the chiefs, while internal support waned.
> *The use of external—non-traditional—means to support
> traditional legitimacy was dysfunctional to the
> maintenance of traditional authority.*[36]

However, when the 1946 Burns Constitution was
promulgated, it seemed that the authority of Ghanaian chiefs
had never been so well established and solidly entrenched.
The Burns Constitution seemed to formally recognize the
chiefs (along with some representatives of the intelligentsia)
not only as the useful and indispensable auxiliaries of the
system of indirect rule but also as the logical prospective
heirs of colonial devolution. This was an illusion, and five
years later (1951), the Local Government Ordinance brought
the chiefs back to their pre-indirect rule roles, minus local
sovereignty.

As a conclusion to this point, one may say that,
because of socio-economic changes introduced by the
process of colonization (including the process of urbanization, the population of most large towns doubled between
the census of 1931 and that of 1948) and because of their
cooperation with the colonial system as its native local
authorities, after World War II, the chiefs no longer
represented the source of undisputed authority to which

they still tried to cling when pretending to be the country's "natural rulers from time immemorial." Chiefly power and prestige were particularly low among the more or less detribalized urban youth and also the more or less dissatisfied rural youth: the many thousands of young and less young "misfits" whose primary education was sufficient to sever their sentimental and cultural links with traditional society, but hardly adequate to permit them to settle in new, modern urban jobs and careers.

The Intelligentsia—Trained for Nothing

The intelligentsia, as often noted, was partly linked to the royal (chiefly) families, and thus, the dividing line between the chiefs and the intelligentsia often cut across families, and appeared in some cases as a problem of generations. Such was the case of K. A. Busia and that of J. B. Danquah, the two best-known leaders of Ghana's intelligentsia and of the opposition to the CPP, who renounced chiefly stools in order to be free to develop fully their cultural-political careers as leaders of the intelligentsia "party" (the UGCC first, then the Ghana Congress Party [GCP], and eventually, the United Party [UP] before it was disbanded). However, the intelligentsia, as an élite group, stood in opposition to, and was in competition with, the more traditional élite group represented by the chiefs; whatever the origin of its members, the intelligentsia's pretensions to inherit British power derived from another source: its members' acquisition and mastery of modern techniques. If the chiefs could feel that the British had, by force, usurped part of their sovereign powers, the intelligentsia increasingly felt that the British had outlived their historical usefulness in the Gold Coast, and only performed roles and functions which the new élites could perform just as well. To them, Africanization did not imply

a return to the status quo *ante* or to any neotraditionalism,
but simply filling with Africans (Ghanaians) the posts
occupied by the British, in the Civil Service, at the
University, and also in the private sector.

The strength of this intelligentsia, in the broadest
sense, is estimated by the 1960 Population Census
(professional and administrative workers). These two
categories represent altogether about 50,000 people, among
whom one finds 27,000 teachers (410 at the University);
3,500 clergy;[37] 9,000 scientific workers, engineers, and
technicians; and 5,000 middle and higher-ranking cadres of
the Civil Service (down to executive officers). If, in the
Ghanaian acceptance of the term, the intelligentsia was
limited to the 410 University professors and lecturers, the
220 jurists, and the 350 physicians, surgeons, and dentists
(many of them especially at the University were and are
expatriates), a good many of the 49,000 others nonetheless
potentially represented their clientele and could have
spread further the intelligentsia's views and, if necessary,
mots d'ordres. In fact, this was the case until the CPP
was formed. Until then the less educated, the less
successful, the less rich, saw in the leaders of the UGCC
their logical leaders; the reason why the UGCC leadership
brought back and hired Kwame Nkrumah was to capitalize
on this potential following, to organize them into a strong
nationalist movement, and perhaps a popularly based
political party. We know what happened: Nkrumah organized
them, but in his own party, the CPP.

The CPP breakaway is not only a testimonial of
Nkrumah's and his closest associates' organizational
ability, but first and foremost a reflection on the
intelligentsia's reluctance to go down into the streets
and villages. The UGCC was a club and a rather exclusive
one at that. The well-known interview of J. B. Danquah by
Richard Wright[38] has clearly established this point. But

the intelligentsia was not simply the slightly contemptuous narrow group of Cape Coast and Sekondi-Takoradi lawyers, doctors, and businessmen. It also included the more sympathetic group of high-ranking civil servants—Christians[39] dedicated to their jobs and truly nationalists—even though they perhaps hoped and tried to maintain, even after independence, the celebrated and somewhat old-fashioned ways and standards of the British Civil Service. Their bedside books were the Bible and the many volumes of the General Orders. These men, meanwhile promoted to the ranks of principal secretaries and the like, were trained by the British; they served the Nkrumah-CPP Government; and they are still in charge. They formed an interesting group, seldom to be found in Africa, and whose work-style, although they served the Nkrumah-CPP Government more honestly and faithfully than the party press would ever allow, was a sharp contrast to the populist and radical style of the former President or the government or party press. They followed Nkrumah and served him; but by inclination and style, they would have been closer to the more conservative UGCC.

Historically, the lawyers and doctors as well as the high-ranking civil servants represented the direct product of British colonization—those ''African echoes of Europe.''[40] Essentially, they thought that by learning the trade they would get through; they believed they could beat the British on their own grounds. It is true that in the Gold Coast-Ghana, as in the rest of British Africa, the process of assimilation was not carried as far as in the French colonies. However, with due allowance for the differences and nuances, in the last analysis, there is little doubt that the intelligentsia in the Gold Coast-Ghana wanted anything else but a Gold Coast without the British. The chiefs dreamt of times bygone; the intelligentsia dreamt of an independent Gold Coast.

The "Youngmen"—The Destoolers

In the late 1940's, a new group surged forth and named its leader: Kwame Nkrumah. During Nkrumah's detention, it was organized into one of the strongest mass political parties of the continent by K. A. Gbedemah. These were the so-called youngmen, who should not be confused with the general body of the "commoners" of the traditional Ghanaian society who are also sometimes referred to as the youngmen (as distinct from the chiefs and the elders). Balandier, Hodgkin, Wallerstein, Apter, and Austin, among others, have given the clearest description of these "youngmen." They were the semi-educated, the historical dissenters, or rather the "misfits" of the colonial system.

> It was among the elementary school leavers that the nationalist movement gathered force with such astonishing speed. By the end of the Second World War they had begun to cohere as a distinct social group, marked out by the limited system of elementary education through which they struggled to reach a minimum of qualifications—and thereby very different in outlook from the better-educated, older-established, intelligentsia class.
> . . . .
> It was from this broad social group of elementary school-leavers that the leaders of the radical wing of the nationalist movement were drawn in 1949— locally rooted in the village, yet beneficiaries also of an educational system which, for all its short-comings, endowed them with a common language— English—and an awareness of common interests which cut across tribal boundaries. In 1948 they burst suddenly upon the political scene, attributing their grievances to the operation of colonial rule and sweeping aside the UGCC. But, although a new phenomenon in national politics, they were already a familiar element in the Colony and Ashanti chiefdoms, where they were persistent opponents of a native-authority system which offered them no outlet for their energies.[41]

Until the arrival of Nkrumah in the Gold Coast, they followed the UGCC and identified their own grievances and objectives with those of the intelligentsia. They formed the troups and were more or less satisfied with this secondary role in the nationalist movement. When the leadership of the UGCC was openly challenged by Nkrumah, when someone spoke to them in the more radical language of populist nationalism, when they were told of their potential role as the people's avant-garde, they left the UGCC and joined *en bloc* the CPP, a party made-to-measure for them. In the Gold Coast of the late 1940's, they were in absolute terms, a small group; but relatively, they represented a strong force. They were more numerous than the intelligentsia properly speaking and more than the chiefs also. In other words, they were, by far, the largest élite group, although the word is hardly fit to describe this rapidly growing group of low income and few real opportunities. More educated than most chiefs and more frustrated than the intelligentsia, they formed an aggressively dynamic group. While the power of the chiefs was limited geographically (one chief for each community) and the prestige of the intelligentsia leadership was restricted, after the CPP breakaway, to a social group, the "youngmen" found themselves much closer to the mass of the people throughout the country, in urban zones as well as in rural zones, although their characteristic ambition was to move out of the rural areas, out of the menial jobs in the urban areas. This phenomenon is partly to be explained by the spread of primary education in the country, and is another illustration of the relatively more-advanced situation of Ghana.

THE "MODEL COLONY" AND ITS "MISFITS"

Although the situation differs from region to region, for the impact of colonization was far longer and stronger in the Colony (the Fanti- and Ga-populated South of the Gold Coast), the end product of colonization in this country can be described as follows:

1.   The pattern of traditional economy and society was altered but not broken.

2.   The development, by Ghanaian farmers, of cocoa production resulted in the establishment of a fairly large semimodern rural middle class, including elements of a rural middle bourgeoisie.

3.   By its increased demand of many goods no longer, or simply   not,   home-produced,   this   relatively   affluent semimodern rural middle class helped spread a limited colonial, but not inconsiderable, prosperity among farmers producing foodstuffs and in the urban areas.

4.   The opening of mines and the setting-up of a foreign-oriented network of communications and commerce resulted in the formation of a proletariat concentrated in a few strictly   delineated   zones,   whose   capital   city   was Sekondi-Takoradi, the only large harbor of the colonial period.

5.   However   limited   in   their   activities   by   the   large European firms and the smaller Syrian and Lebanese firms, a number of African entrepreneurs managed to develop their commercial and, less frequently, industrial enterprises enough to form the embryo of a local bourgeoisie.

6.   The chiefs, by cooperating with the colonial authorities as the local wheels of the system, apparently strengthened their power (reaching an apogee with the 1946 Burns Constitution), but in reality lost much of their prestige and real power.

7. The development of education resulted in, as early as the middle of the last century, and much more rapidly later on, the constitution of a local intelligentsia whose models were British, and yet, one which initiated the first actions of the nationalist movement.

8. The spread of primary education and the development of new productions (e.g., cocoa) as well as urbanization produced another group of modern Ghanaians—the so-called youngmen, neither members of chiefly families nor as successful or as well-educated as the intelligentsia: a group unable to stay in the villages of their parents and unable to find satisfactory alternative opportunities in the towns. While the chiefs and the intelligentsia might appear as successful adjustments to the colonial system and (along with their relative prosperity from cocoa) thus justify the British illusion of a *model colony*, the "youngmen" stood as the living illustration that there could be no such thing as a "model colony." Colonization introduced contradictions in the colonies which not even the granting of independence per se could solve.

9. The chiefs, whose power and prestige rest in the narrow communities which they formally represent, spoke the language of conservatism, sometimes in the form of resistance—for instance when they opposed the compulsory cutting of diseased cocoa trees. At best, under special circumstances, they could truly speak on behalf of their local communities as opposed to the central seat of authority, but ordinarily they represented only themselves, i.e., a no-longer existing group. The richer chiefs, in cocoa-growing areas, sometimes, individually, represented a rural upper middle class or middle bourgeoisie, and perhaps, in a few cases, the element of what has been termed an *"agro-mercantile"* class (but not as chiefs).

10. The intelligentsia, *stricto sensu*, represented, despite its aspiration to express a truly nationalist movement, a

narrow group of interest, including that of the embryonic
urban bourgeoisie. But, essentially, the intelligentsia
represented itself. As we well know by now, to quote an
Algerian saying, "in the colonies, there are more
bourgeois-minded people than bourgeois," for the simple
reason that what truly makes the bourgeoisie is commerce
and industry; and in the Gold Coast as elsewhere in the
colonial world, industry was in the *métropole* and commerce
essentially in expatriate hands.

11. The "youngmen" also essentially represented
themselves, but they formed a larger group, and they could
seek and obtain, far better than the intelligentsia or the
chiefs, the support of the Ghanaian proletariat and, in the
villages, of the smaller farmers—in short, of this *commoner*
stratum from which they originated.

12. As already noted, Ghana's social structures were
relatively fluid. Therefore, the relations between élite
groups and their relations with social groups/classes
were also.

In such a transitional situation, and as long as a group
such as that which, in Ghanaian political parlance, is
referred to as the "youngmen" does not become conscious
of its own interests as distinct from those of the
intelligentsia (which always leads the nationalist movement
in its early stages), the only group with a clear awareness
of its own possibilities and with some degree of
homogeneity is the nationalist bourgeois intelligentsia. At
this point, it must be clearly stated that the intelligentsia
includes the embryonic bourgeoisie but stretches further to
include in its social composition other elements and
embrace in its aspirations a much wider field of activities
than those of the embryonic bourgeoisie. The intelligentsia
aspires to replace completely the colonial power. It does
not usually wish to change the system completely. On the
contrary, the colonial system represents its model; its

objective is to control it, to fill the posts, and take up the roles and functions of the British civil servants and other officers and professionals. In this sense, it aspires to much less, and much more, than the embryonic local bourgeoisie which is in competition with expatriate firms in the essentially commercial sector. The intelligentsia is recruited partly from the embryonic bourgeoisie and partly outside this narrow group; it is bourgeois-minded in the sense that its education and its models were provided by the colonial *métropole*. Inasmuch as it does not, in general, identify its nationalist struggle with a social struggle, the intelligentsia is not simply the mouthpiece of the local bourgeoisie. If it were, it would be far smaller. Besides, the intelligentsia is a product of the colonial system and in this system the real bourgeoisie, as the real industry, is not in the colony but in the *métropole*.

At the same time, before independence, the embryonic bourgeoisie sees in the intelligentsia and its various political and other movements and organizations its true representative. There is no conflict of interest. The position of the rural upper middle class, particularly the richer cocoa farmers, is not quite the same; and it seems that, in the last analysis, because the richer farmers were in Ashanti while the overwhelming majority of the intelligentsia was Fanti and Ga, the rural upper middle class could never really see in the intelligentsia its true representative; at least, not until 1954-57, with the rise and fall of the NLM which combined, for a short period, most of the opposition to the ruling CPP. The other components of the rural middle classes (until the formation of the CPP) either followed suit or remained passive.

In conclusion, until two years before the Gold Coast was granted internal self-government, i.e., until 1949, the year the "youngmen" coalesced into, at one and the same time, a self-conscious new *élite group* and formed the original militant element of the first real mass political party, i.e., the CPP, the intelligentsia led the nationalist or the proto-nationalist movement while the chiefs hoped at least to maintain their hold. The logical sequence seemed to lead to a compromise between the intelligentsia, who could have taken up the roles and functions of the British, and the chiefs, who could have retained their local roles and functions. Indirect rule had set a pattern of devolution in which the intelligentsia had been trained for one job and the chiefs for the other.

The resounding victory of the CPP in the 1951 election changed everything. It split the intelligentsia (those who followed the CPP and those who remained in opposition, those who served and those who rebelled) and, in a way, it split the chiefs also. However, accustomed as they were to putting up with the directives of Accra under the British, they continued under the Nkrumah-CPP Government.

Whatever Kwame Nkrumah's qualities as a charismatic leader, "charisma" is not too relevant here. What matters is that when—for the election—the *élite groups* were put to the test of getting votes, the *youngmen* were the only ones who could go down into the streets and villages to talk to the people. They would have done more or less the same for the UGCC, if a CPP had not been formed in 1949. The results of the election show that almost everybody voted CPP in 1951. In other words, the CPP managed to represent in the eyes of the overwhelming majority of the voters of 1951 what they officially stood for: "Self-Government Now," i.e., independence. In 1951, the CPP victory was not the victory of any particular social class; it was the victory of the *youngmen* over the intelligentsia, who were out-numbered and outtalked on the nationalist platform, and over the chiefs, who did nothing at all to win the day, because they were not, and had never been, a national force.

In a certain sense, the 1951 election was an accident

which a politically more-skillful and less-contemptuous intelligentsia could have avoided. But after the election the dye was cast and a more radical and more popular nationalist party, the CPP, was put to the test.

What would be the government program of the CPP? How would the party maintain its popular support once in government? What would it do to solve the problems of the country's economy? To what degree were its leaders aware of the real problems of their country? These are the questions we must now try to answer.

NOTES

1. Although some criteria apply, but to a lesser extent than in most other former African colonies (primary economy, sectoral imbalances, trade and economic dependence), others clearly don't: economic dualism, average level of income, malnutrition, hunger, etc.

2. Ghana, Census Office, *1960 Population Census of Ghana*, Advanced Report of Volumes III and IV (Accra: Government Printer, 1962). The figures are, in point of fact, the most reliable and complete source of information on the population of Ghana, despite shortcomings. However, the difference between the population distribution in 1950 and 1960 is not too important, at least not for our purpose here, viz., to supply broad indicators concerning the relative importance of the various sectors of the Ghanaian economy.

3. Out of the 234 firms recorded in 1959 (larger firms), 130 had been set up between 1950 and 1959. Tony Killick, "Manufacturing and Construction," *A Study of Contemporary Ghana*, ed. by W.B. Birmingham, I. Neustadt, and E.N. Omaboe (London: Allen and Unwin, 1966), I, chap. xii, 274-75.

Provisional figures for 1962 show the following picture:
1. Number of establishments   92,095
2. Number of paid employees   61,529
3. Other persons engaged   189,646
4. Total number engaged   -   251,175
5. Average number engaged per establishment   2.7

4. *Ibid.*, p. 278.

5. However, a few of these "petty traders" are indeed rich "mammies" and "supermammies."

6. Robert Szereszewski, "Regional Aspects of the Structure of the Economy," *A Study of Contemporary Ghana*, I, chap. iv, 89.

7. *Ibid.*, "The Performance of the Economy, 1955-62," chap. ii, p. 43. Szereszewski further comments: "Although Ghana ranks below some African economies, such as that of the Congo and Zambia, in her dependence on external transactions, it is nevertheless one of the typically open economies of the world and her foreign trade has a dominating influence on the level and the pattern of her economic activity."

8. Tony Killick, "External Trade," *A Study of Contemporary Ghana*, I, chap. xiv, 338.

9. Szereszewski, "Patterns of Consumption," *A Study of Contemporary Ghana*, I, chap. v, 108.

10. *Ibid.*, chap. ii, p. 47.

11. *Ibid.*, "The Sectoral Structure of the Economy," chap. iii, p. 69.

12. The importance of such reserves in an underdeveloped country also corresponds, of course, to the somewhat sluggish expenditure pattern of the British Government.

13. However, some of these were imported from neighboring African countries—and this, of course, poses different problems.

14. Dudley Seers and C. Ross, *Report on Financial and Physical Problems of Development in the Gold Coast* (Accra: Government Printer, 1952).

15. *1960 Population Census.*

16. In this respect, it should be noted that what is known—and this is not very much—of landownership in Ghana does not lead to any definite conclusions. All that can be said is that landownership did not and does not represent an obstacle to the development of an affluent rural middle bourgeoisie. On landownership and land transactions in Ghana, see, *inter alia*, R.J.H. Poguski, "The Main Principles of Rural Land Tenure," in *Agriculture and Land Use in Ghana*, ed. by J.B. Wills (London:

Oxford University Press, 1962), pp. 179—.

17. Several of these mines, however, were subsequently nationalized.

18. For the purpose of this preliminary appraisal of the socio-economic structure of Ghana, we have simply equated "middle class" with "self-employed" in order to be able to draw some broad quantified information from the 1960 Census, but it goes without saying that this is far too vague a definition, and that we shall have to return to the definition of Ghana's "middle classes" later in this chapter. It will permit us to distinguish from among these "middle classes," a semimodern rural middle bourgeoisie engaged in cocoa farming and the production and marketing of foodstuffs.

19. The *abusa* worker is a sharecropper who usually grows and markets the production of a cocoa farm, and retains one third of the proceeds.

20. The *khammes*, also a contract worker, receives a fifth *(khemis)* of the value of the crop, which he does not market himself. His condition is usually extremely miserable.

21. This, up to a point, had already been characteristic of the colonial period, but it developed much more rapidly after independence, and, with the change in scale and the parallel process of Africanization, took an almost completely different significance.

22. Polly Hill, *The Gold Coast Farmer—A Preliminary Survey* (London: Oxford University Press, 1956), pp. 1-2. See *also*, Miss Hill's numerous articles and her later book on the *Migrant Cocoa Farmers of Southern Ghana*—although the information provided by later studies does not differ much from that given in *The Gold Coast Cocoa Farmer.*

23. *Ibid.*, p. 88.

24. Another, less frequent, type of sharecropper.

25. Hill, *The Gold Coast Farmer*, pp. 98-101.

26. Not to mention that even fee-free secondary schools do not, by the mere fact that they are free, solve the problem of democratic access to secondary and higher education.

27. I. Wallerstein, *The Road to Independence, Ghana and the Ivory Coast* (Paris-La Haye: Mouton, 1964), *passim*.

28. Dennis Austin, *Politics in Ghana: 1946-1960* (London: Oxford University Press, 1964), pp. 196-97.

29. This is rather well, although briefly, stated by Colin Legum in his short essay "Socialism in Ghana: A Political Interpretation," *African Socialism*, ed. by W.H. Friedland and C.G. Rossberg, Jr. (Standford, Calif.: Stanford University Press, 1967, 1964c), pp. 132-34.

30. *See infra*, in this chapter.

31. Cf., Austin, *Politics in Ghana*, pp. 21—.

32. Of course, nuances should be introduced to account for the considerable difference in status among Northern chiefs, Akan chiefs, Ewe chiefs, etc. Most of the attention has usually been paid to the Ashanti (Akan) system of chieftaincy.

33. Cf., Nkrumah stating that the CPP was wrongly accused "of being anti-chieftaincy," but was simply "against despotic chieftaincy and in favor of constitutional chieftaincy," in "Movement for Colonial Freedom," *Phylon*, XVI, 406, quoted by Wallerstein, pp. 152-53.

34. The year, 1901, marks the conquest of the Ashanti and the establishment of a protectorate on the Northern Territories (NT).

35. Quoted by Austin, *Politics in Ghana*, p. 26.

36. David Apter, *Ghana in Transition* (Rev. ed.; New York: Atheneum, 1963), pp. 150-51.

37. Excluding 2,700 "fetish priests" who more logically should be listed with the traditional chiefs.

38. Quoted by Robert Fitch and Mary Oppenheimer, "Ghana: End of an Illusion," *Monthly Review*, Vol. 18, No. 3 (Special Issue, July-August, 1966), pp. 60-61.

39. Belonging to the established churches as opposed to the more numerous members of the proliferous and popular syncretic and prophetic neo-Christian churches.

40. Jean-Paul Sartre in the "Preface" to Frantz Fanon, *Les damnés de la terre* (Paris: Maspéro, 1961).

41. Austin, *Politics in Ghana*, pp. 13-17.

CHAPTER 3

FROM A "COMATOSE VISION" TO THE SEVEN-YEAR PLAN

Although the CPP members elected to the Legislative Assembly in 1951 represented only a narrow majority, the party had, beyond all doubt, won the election: Out of the 38 popularly elected seats, they took a lion's share of 34. The voices of the other members of the Assembly (those who had not been directly elected) were comparatively weaker. The British Administration showed no hesitation in recognizing this fact and called on Kwame Nkrumah to form the government, first as Leader of Government Business, then as Prime Minister. This formally marked the end of Positive Action, to be replaced by Tactical Action, in the general framework of what Wallerstein calls the "Dyarchy." In point of fact, this shift of emphasis from Positive to Tactical Action may be considered to have taken place earlier, with the apparent hesitations of Kwame Nkrumah over the question of the line to adopt vis-à-vis the Coussey Report, viz., to reject it and demand "Self-Government Now" (Positive Action), or to accept it provisionally (Tactical Action).[1] The mere fact that the CPP entered (and won) the election indicates that the leaders of the CPP could see the advantages offered by the "step-by-step" kind of devolution offered by the British Administration via the all-African Coussey Commission.

This early recognition of the tactical usefulness of gradualism may be considered to be as important as its formal and frequent rejection later. It may be considered a *pis-aller* to which Nkrumah was reluctant to resort, but to which he would not fail to resort if no better alternative presented itself. Indeed, Nkrumah was not the only one in the CPP to show considerable reluctance to the approach

of Tactical Action, and at the Tarkwa Conference of the
CPP in 1952, there was still an active and vocal internal
opposition on this issue, which eventually led some
founding members of the party to resign. It may be useful
to point out that more than ten years later, the problem of
African Unity through the Organization of African Unity
(OAU), again showed Nkrumah pressing for African Unity
Now, but at the same time accepting the framework of the
Organization and its inherent "step-by-step" approach.

Whatever the limitations set upon the CPP as the first
nationalist government in Ghana (the Gold Coast until
1957) by the Dyarchy, the CPP *was* the government, and
all the more so, after the confirmation of its early majority
of 1951 by the general elections of 1954 and 1956 (although,
as we shall see later, the overwhelming majority of seats
for the CPP, both in 1954 and in 1956, somewhat conceals
the strength of the opposition). As the popularly elected
government of the country, the CPP was confronted with
the reality of power, and, as far as we are concerned here,
with the problems of development and decolonization.
Therefore, the question which we shall discuss in this
chapter is the strategy of development of the CPP. This
strategy has been developed rather fully in two important
documents: (1) The CPP Program for Work and Happiness,
adopted at the Kumasi Congress of 1962, and (2) The
Seven-Year Development Plan of Ghana for 1963/64—
1969/70. A question immediately comes to mind: Why so
late? It is indeed an important question, which will be
discussed later in this chapter.

AN OFFICIAL THEORY OF DECOLONIZATION

When reading these two essential documents, one is
easily convinced of two things. First, the party and

government were keenly aware of the real situation of Ghana, and they knew just as clearly what remedies to prescribe: Ghana will be a modern, industrial, and socialist country. Secondly, the party and government did not wait for these two documents to be published to define their policies and apply them vigorously—to wit: the performances and achievements of the first ten years, 1951-61. At least this is the conclusion one is expected to derive from the reading of the "Program" and the "Plan."

If the achievements of the first ten years were undisputably impressive, they did not clearly indicate that precise and definite choices had already been made, especially as far as socialism was concerned. The second Five-Year Development Plan (1959-64)[2] was officially meant only to turn Ghana into a "Welfare State." In fact, it is only, at least formally, with the last plan (The Seven-Year Development Plan 1963/64—1969/70) that the long-term option for socialism was clearly stated in a plan.

Before going any further it may be worth insisting on one point: With the publication of the CPP Program and the Government's Seven-Year Plan, for the first time, a conscious effort was made to state clearly the political objectives and to translate these objectives in technical, prospective economic terms. This has been stressed by several observers, including E.N. Omaboe.[3] It has thus been suggested that one of the reasons Ghana's plan had more chances to be successfully implemented is the unusually close cooperation between planners and political leaders in Ghana. This is probably an overstatement, but there is no doubt that, with the adoption of the CPP Program, the planners were supplied for the first time with a comprehensive statement of the party's objectives. And up to a point, the Seven-Year Plan does represent a conscious and systematic effort to translate those objectives into technical terms.

The CPP Program for Work and Happiness

In its 181 paragraphs the Program is concerned mainly with socio-economic problems. However, it also touches briefly upon other problems, cultural and political as well as problems of legislation.

The first paragraphs deal with the general strategy and contain an interesting statement of the fundamental objectives of the CPP. The strategic objectives are industrialization and socialism, but, and it must be stressed here, the option for socialism was not justified by criteria of social justice or ideological preference, but rather as a more or less inescapable historical necessity.

> The Party has always had a consistent theory for enlarging the country's prosperity. ... This theory has been tried out in practice during the difficult circumstances of the last ten years. The progress that has been made is indisputable proof of the practicability and correctness of the Party's line.
>
> This theory has its basis in the principles upon which the Party is pivoted. What are these principles? They are:
>
> (1) Socialism, because of the heritage of imperialism and colonialism, is the system by which Ghana can progress.
>
> (2) Socialism can be achieved only by a rapid change in the socio-economic structure of the country. To effect this, it is absolutely essential to have a strong, stable, firm and highly centralized government. This means that power must be concentrated in the country's leadership.
>
> Imperialism-colonialism left Ghana without the accumulation of capital in private hands which assisted the Western world to make its industrial revolution. Only Government therefore can find the means to promote those basic services and industries which are essential prerequisites to intensive, diversified agriculture, speedy industrialization and increased economic productivity.[4]

A little further in the document, this "consistent theory" of the CPP is also related to "Nkrumaism"—"the well-defined ideology on which are founded the policies of the Party." Nkrumaism itself is defined both as the application of *scientific socialism* to Africa and as the theoretical result of an objective study of the conditions and circumstances of Africa.[5] We shall devote more space to the questions of socialism and Nkrumaism in Chapter 5.

The Program then summarizes the usual criticisms leveled against the colonial economic system.[6] Although fundamentally correct, the formulation is not particularly original: international division of labor, Colonial Pact, low wages (cheap labor), inadequate educational system, inadequate health services, etc. In view of the above, the Party and Government must "grapple quickly with the problem of reorganizing the whole of the life of the nation based on improvements" in all sectors.[7]

Such a thorough reorganization of the whole economy is necessary because

> the basic aim of our economic development is to free our economy from alien control and domination. To achieve this, it is necessary for the State to participate in the wholesale and retail sectors of trade throughout the country. This is the only means of protecting the people from unbridled exploitation by alien monopoly interests. The Party is firmly of the view that the planning of the national economy can only be really effective when the major means of production, distribution and exchange have been brought under the control and ownership of the State.

There will be no development without first real liberation, and liberation is necessary because

> Ghana's trade and industry remains largely under the domination of alien monopoly interests. This is a relic of colonialism which the Party is determined to

> eradicate. .... In pursuit of this objective, the Party and Government lost no time in setting up Statutory Boards and Corporations in the fields of commerce, industry and agriculture in order to control effectively the national effort for progress and development.[8]

The main underlying reason justifying the option for a socialist way of development was not an ideological one but rather a historical necessity:

> Owing to the absence of facilities for capital formation, it was clear from the very beginning that this prodigious task could only be accomplished successfully by the institution of socialism. There is no half way to socialism. The total industrialization of the country, the complete diversification and mechanization of agriculture, and a national economic planning based on the public ownership of the means of production and distribution must be the order of the day.[9]

And, in conclusion of the same paragraph, one finds a sentence which evokes the Volta Scheme but at the same time, something else, another country, another time: "This pre-supposes the complete electrification of Ghana!"

Such a bold program must, of course, have the support of the people of Ghana. This is stated[10] in a way quite typical of the political literature published in Ghana and about which we shall have more to say further on. "This means giving the Farmers' Council, the TUC, the local authorities, *the house of chiefs* [italics mine], the women's organizations, and other similar bodies, an opportunity to make suggestions as to planning, and the targets set and to criticize the draft plans produced."[11]

Socialist planning in Ghana also has enemies. They are imperialism and neocolonialism, and at home the "evils of bribery, corruption and nepotism, ... careerism, opportunism, and bureaucracy." It may be interesting to point out here that the internal enemies of socialist planning in Ghana are described as "evils," and what is more, evils which "are basically alien to the general Ghanaian nature." Such evils may afflict a few (even many) individuals in the community, but they are not characteristic of any particular group or class. Further in the text, we shall see that the TUC leaders and the civil servants are both requested to "change their mentality," to switch to new, socialist methods and approaches, but nowhere in the CPP Program is any group of the community denounced as being as a group, objectively, inimical to socialist planning. It is worth quoting the Program a little more. We have already seen that "evils" are basically alien to the general Ghanaian nature. Now we are told also that they

> can be attributed in part to the hangovers of colonialist practises and to the serious social effects of the imposition of a money economy upon our traditional social customs. At the present time we are in a transition stage, emerging into new ways of life brought into being as a result of the new developments in industry science and technology. [However] at the same time, there are certain of our customs—like that of 'dash' and service to the family and the 'oman'—which are being accommodated to the new ways.[12]

In sum, socialism in Ghana was a historical necessity, because there was no accumulation of capital and because, therefore, only the state was able to industrialize the country. Socialism had no internal enemies except a few "evils," which were "hangovers" of the colonial period and which were to be stamped out by the Party and Government. On the contrary, it had external enemies, imperialism and neocolonialism, which not only manipulated Ghana's economy from the outside but which also were well entrenched in the country itself through their control and domination of important sectors of Ghana's commerce and industry. Hence, the necessity to free the economy from external domination. The way to achieve this economic liberation of Ghana was for the state to effectively control the national effort for progress and development; this was to be possible when the major means of production, distribution, and exchange had been brought under the control and ownership of the state.

The Party Program also, more specifically, devoted some attention to the development of agriculture, industrialization, the types of enterprises, and the problem of productivity.

The progress of agriculture was to result from the following developments: (1) increasing the production of export products, (2) introducing new cash crops which can find a market abroad, (3) using at home for food and in industry the cash crops now produced or which would be produced but for which at present there is no method of processing in Ghana (e.g., cocoa), and (4) producing at home foodstuffs to replace those that are at present imported. [13] The Program, however, was not quite clear as to who was to bring about such changes and developments. In any case, as the Party Program was completely silent on the mode of production and the forms of ownership in agriculture, it may be assumed, as most observers do, that the CPP did not see the traditional and neotraditional modes of agricultural production in Ghana as obstacles to the development of this sector. It seems that the Program envisioned state intervention in this field mostly as a series of additions, rather than any significant alteration of existing patterns, as illustrated by Paragraph 78. "In connection with the establishment of State and Co-operative Farms, the Party will also establish national tractor stations. Our country is fortunate in possessing large tracts of uncultivated land on which will be constructed agricultural towns and villages to provide new settlement centres for our patriotic young men and women."

Industrialization was to result from the creation of three main types of industries. First, "the Party proposes that the Seven-Year Plan contain proposals for establishing those types of heavy industry which are large consumers of power and for which raw materials are available locally." This, obviously, is nothing but a description in general terms of the aluminum smelter project at Tema (Kaiser) which was to use large quantities of cheap Akosombo-produced electricity and which would ultimately be based on Ghanaian bauxite. But heavy industry in Ghana was not to be limited to the Kaiser smelter project: "Immediate study should be made of the possibility of starting a heavy chemical industry (fertilisers, artificial yarns and plastics)." In addition, "the use of our iron ore resources might form the basis of an iron and steel industry."[14]

> A second type of industrial development consists of industries which utilize new cash crops and thus provide very considerable agricultural employment. The sugar industry is a case in point. For every man employed in the factory, ten agricultural workers are needed. ... The saving in foreign currency by Ghana producing her own sugar is very considerable. ... The third type of industrial development comprises light industry such as textiles and the making of shoes, clothing, furniture, diamond polishing, and fittings for building.[15]

As can be seen, there is nothing particularly original about the role and type of industrialization foreseen in the Program—except, perhaps, the emphasis placed on heavy industry in such a relatively small country and one which is not particularly rich in mineral resources.

Far more interesting are the indications concerning the "sectors of the economy," i.e., the views of the government concerning the ownership of the means of production in Ghana and the relations between these and the development of the country's productive forces.

"The government recognizes five sectors, all operating side by side in the nation's economy. These sectors are: the state enterprises; the enterprises owned by foreign private interests; the enterprises jointly owned by the State and foreign private interests; the co-operatives; and the small-scale Ghanaian private enterprise."

According to the Program,

the main aims of state enterprises [are] to ensure an ever growing and steady employment for the people; to increase national income and the revenues of the state; ... to have at the command of the State significant and growing stocks of commodities in order to be able to influence the market, this influence being aimed at the stabilization of the price level and that of the currency; to supply those services, which the private sector does not wish or is not allowed to supply.

At the same time, "the Government accepts the operation in the country of large-scale enterprises by foreign interests"—"the objectives of this policy [being] firstly, to accelerate the growth of Ghana's capital stock, [and], secondly, to conserve Foreign Exchange and maintain the national reserves at a safe level."

Lastly, the government

will support and encourage the formation of co-operative enterprises of producers both in agriculture, trade and industry and will also assist small-scale individual Ghanaian Farmers through such institutions as the Investment Bank [and] in order to encourage and utilize personal initiative and skill, Ghanaians can undertake small-scale enterprises, provided that they are not nominees or sleeping partners of foreign interests.

It is hardly necessary to insist on the importance of these seven paragraphs,[16] for they represent the clearest statement of the government's strategy, at the same time as they deal with the respective roles of state, private foreign, and private local enterprises.

Although the ultimate objectives as stated in the Program were to build a socialist society and to achieve the total liberation of the country's economy from external domination, Ghana's economy was to remain for an unspecified transitional period, but probably a long one,[17] *a mixed economy*. The state sector was to perform roles and functions that could not be performed by the private sector, at the same time as it was to be sufficiently developed to exercise over-all control on prices and, presumably, to facilitate the implementation of the government's economic policies at the level of production and distribution.

The role of the private sector was quite clearly defined also: It is to act as an accelerator (foreign capital) and to cater to the needs that can be satisfied better, or just as well, by small-scale enterprises (national entrepreneurs). The economic and political implications of this policy of encouragement to a foreign private sector in Ghana will be discussed later on (Chapter 4), but we may immediately stress the fact that, while practically everywhere in Africa, foreign capital is considered an important tool for the economic development of the country, not much faith is being placed in the potential of a local private sector.[18]

However, in the case of Ghana, domestic private enterprise is specifically restricted to small-scale ventures and this has given rise to some speculations. In particular, it has been argued that Nkrumah and the CPP, as representatives of Ghana's "petty bourgeoisie," had openly allied themselves with foreign capital ("neo-colonialism") and systematically acted in such a way as to prevent the development of a potential national bourgeoisie.[19]

Less dramatically, one could simply observe that on the basis of past performances and in view of the task ahead, the CPP leadership, which was not directly linked with the limited group of Ghana's businessmen, did not expect much from domestic private enterprise. At the same time, they wanted to make it quite clear to the hundreds of thousands of artisans and shopkeepers, from which they recruited many of their partisans and members, that CPP socialism did not imply a threat to their small businesses. As far as foreign capital was concerned, although it is not specifically mentioned in the Program, it seems quite clear that it was not the "traditional," colonial type of expatriate firm which was welcomed and expected to contribute to the economic development of Ghana. This point was made several times and, in particular, in an important speech delivered in 1964 by President Nkrumah on the occasion of the inauguration of the Tema Soap factory, in which Unilever was in partnership with the Government of Ghana.

Nkrumah's statement contained three main arguments. First, he criticized the colonial type of expatriate firms which only imported raw material from the colonies and manufactured them in the "mother country" or sold them to manufacturers. (This was conspicuously the case of Lever Brothers, now Unilever.) Second, he said he was pleased to see that some firms "had seen the writing [of history] on the wall" and were now prepared to invest in secondary industries. These firms, he said, realized that new opportunities were created by the drive toward industrialization in the newly independent countries. What is implied in this argument is that although some industries (e.g., textile industries) can see the industrialization of former colonies only as a source of competition to their own products, other industries (e.g., machine-tool industries) find, or could find, in a real process of industrialization in Africa, new and very considerable opportunities. Whether they sold their products to, or whether they invested directly in, these new industries, such firms would find new and considerable opportunities in the industrialization of former African colonies.

For this period of rapid industrialization, therefore, a new type of foreign enterprise shares, up to a point, common interests with the nationalist, and, in particular, the most radical nationalist governments in former colonies. Although their ultimate objectives are different, both have vested interests in the rapid industrialization of former colonies. Such cooperation, however, implies that both parties respect the "rules of the game," which are, *inter alia*, set out in the Capital Investment Codes, exchange controls regulations, taxation systems, and other elements of the economic legislation of the newly independent countries. Whether such "rules" are to be faithfully observed and whether such a strategy is to be really effective in accelerating the process of industrialization is rather conjectural, but it seems established that the confidence placed by the Nkrumah-CPP Government in its cooperation with foreign capital was not as naive as some thought. Besides, for the huge programs the government had in mind, it goes almost without saying that, with or without its sterling reserves, it could hardly contemplate financing the whole program out of domestic savings and taxation.

Nkrumah's third argument is familiar: If the Tema Soap factory, seen here as a symbol of Ghana's industrialization, is not larger, it is neither Unilever's fault nor that of the Government of Ghana. It is due only to the limited size of the Ghanaian market. Only the artificial borders inherited from the colonial era prevent such investments and such factories from being larger. The answer, thus, once again, is African Unity. And, on this count also, the "true" interests of foreign investors in Africa and nationalist African governments are the same. Both have vested interests in a real process of industrialization and in African Unity.

This is the "vision" which had inspired the early years of the day-to-day economic decisions and which were to be translated into a more systematic program of development through the Seven-Year Development Plan. But before we mention briefly the Plan, we must complete this comment on the Program by a short remark on the role of the Trade Union to which the Program devotes a dozen paragraphs.

As many observers have already noted, and, in particular, T. Killick,[20] the role of the Trade Union is seen almost entirely in the light of the necessity of increasing productivity: "To strengthen labor's interest in increased productivity and national progress, it is the party's policy that there shall be the strongest form of workers' participation in management." And: "Such participation will not be confined to simple representation on management boards."[21]

In point of fact, some paragraphs sound almost like a warning or an injunction:

In the present stage of our development, Trade Union officials must discard their colonial mentality and methods and remember that they are not struggling against capitalists. When they have to fight against exploiters, the State will be their protector. Today, the work of Trade Union officials must be different. The Trade Union Movement must spearhead their efforts to raise production and productivity and cease to be advocates for out-moded conditions, [for] the Government which is formed by our Party

is a People's Government [and] the interest of
workers is therefore well protected by the State. The
Trade Union Movement must therefore pursue a
different role from that of Trade Unions in a capitalist
society.

. . . . . .

The party will ensure that our Trade Unions do
not limit their activities to the education of the
workers only as regards their rights, but also
regarding their duties and responsibilities. The Party
will take steps to inculcate in our working people
the role of labour and increased productivity. The
Party and Government will continue to pursue those
socialist policies which will be to the ultimate
benefit of the workers and will see to it that Trade
Unions explain these measures to the rank and file
instead of becoming mere agitators for rights already
protected and guaranteed by the State.[22]

For good measure, Paragraph 123 also indicates that
"arrangements will be made for the Trade Union Congress
to take full advantage of the courses at the Kwame
Nkrumah Ideological Training Institute at Winneba and at
our Universities."

It may be that the rather harsh tone of these paragraphs
devoted to the Trade Unions, which led some observers to
criticize the "corporatist" tendencies of the Program,
is to be explained partly by the fact that the CPP met to
adopt this Program less than a year after the quasi-
insurrectional Sekondi-Takoradi strike of September, 1961.
However, it also reflects a deeper concern: For the
Nkrumah-CPP Government, the central objective was to
be achieved neither by merely "Africanization" of the
system, nor by any kind of rearrangement of the inherited
structures or within these structures. On the contrary, as
already mentioned, the objective was "to reorganize the
whole of the life of the nation based on improvements
in all sectors," which meant "the total industrialization

of the country, the complete diversification and mechanization of agriculture."[23]

In other words, the problem was not to improve within
the system, for not much benefit could be derived from
such improvements in an underdeveloped economy; but the
problem was to establish a new, modern society, which
meant, first of all, to create the basis of this new society,
i.e., its economic, political, and technological infrastructure.
This was the main problem, and the whole strategy reflected
this conviction. Thus, socialism—or what is considered to
be socialism, i.e., essentially a predominant role of the
state and the public sector in the building of the economy—
was justified and officially presented as a historical
necessity; the state in Ghana had to perform functions
which in the capitalist industrial countries were performed
by the national bourgeoisie (capital accumulation,
entrepreneurship, etc.). Similarly, foreign private capital
was invited into Ghana as a necessary accelerator of this
process of industrialization.

Somehow, in the Ghanaian strategy, both socialism
(i.e., the development of a large public sector) and foreign
private capital have the same justification, viz., the
rapid industrialization of the country. Not surprisingly,
the Trade Unions were to concentrate on productivity, an
economic objective, and not on social objectives, for the
essential "battle" was on the "economic front." All
sections of the population were mobilized to build a modern
nation, there must be discipline under the direction of the
"country's leadership" in whose hands "power must be
concentrated," and which must form "a strong, stable,
firm and highly centralized government."[24] Whatever the
terminology used in this document, what was being
proposed was a straightforward nationalist program of
development.

The Seven-Year Development Plan

The Seven-Year Development Plan reflects this
strategy.[25] This consistency between the objectives
of the CPP Program for Work and Happiness and those of
the Seven-Year Development Plan is all the more remarkable
when considering that those who drafted and approved the
Program and those who drafted the Plan represented two
different groups, the party leaders and the civil service,
and two groups which were often at odds, even publicly.[26]
The Plan has a similar starting point to that of the
Program: Ghana was to become a socialist state and this
long-term objective would be achieved through the successful accomplishment of a series of development plans in the
general framework of a *mixed economy* in which both
private and public sectors would have specific and clearly
defined tasks to perform. In the course of the twenty years
or so to come, roughly until the end of the 1970's, the
government was to progressively acquire a dominant
position in the economy through its investments in the
productive sector.

There would be no point in summarizing the Plan
now,[27] but it is important to stress that, although it
reflects the same strategy as that defined in the CPP
Program, it nonetheless adds an important emphasis of its
own to the strategy.

The Plan insists that the dominant position of the
state sector in the economy is to be achieved

> without our ever having to resort to such expedients
> as nationalization which, if carried out with full
> compensation, would only change the ownership of
> the means of production without adding to productive
> capacity or employment opportunities, and, if carried
> out without such compensation, would inevitably
> incur such a large measure of hostility as to make
> our development plans very much more difficult to
> achieve.

Instead, the state sector is to "surpass" the private sector by investing more in the course of the transitional period ahead. This, the planners insist, will be achieved if the state concentrates its investments "on the most strategic sectors of industry and agriculture," and if it now gives a priority to productive over infrastructural investments. In addition,

> the projects chosen for State investment must include a large proportion with high rates of return and short pay-off periods, [for] only thus can we ensure that the investable resources in the hands of the State will grow rapidly, thereby enabling the State to extend further its participation in economic activity without having to impose intolerable increases in the burden of taxation falling on the people.[28]

This is the main difference between the political leadership and the planning bureaucracy, and in retrospect, it might seem to contain all the explanation that is required for the Coup which ousted Nkrumah and the CPP, and, in fact, this is the explanation which has been repeatedly given by professional economists since February, 1966. We will show, however, that it is only one element of a more complex reality, and, in truth, it was not the bureaucracy that ousted Nkrumah and the CPP, but the army whose positive contribution was not highly valued by the authors of the Seven-Year Development Plan.[29]

Nevertheless, at the time the Plan was drafted and adopted, it represented a significant switch in favor of productive investments as compared to preceding plans.

TABLE 3
THE SHARE OF PRODUCTIVE INVESTMENT
IN GHANA (1951–1969/70)

(Percentage of total)

	Productive Investments	Investments in the Infrastructure and Social Services
First Five-year plan (1951-56)	11.2	88.8
Second Five-year plan (1959-64) discontinued after two years.	20.3	79.7
Seven-Year Plan (1963/64 – 1969/70) discontinued after two years	37.3	62.7

Note: The Seven-year Development Plan gives slightly different figures (p. 27). Productive investments would have represented 9.9 per cent of total investments between 1951 and 1959, i.e., almost four times less than planned productive investments for the Seven-year Development Plan (37.3 per cent).

Source: Walter B. Birmingham, I. Neustadt, and E.N. Omaboe, eds., A Study of Contemporary Ghana, Vol. I: The Economy of Ghana (London: Allen and Unwin, 1966), p. 455.

As can be seen, the strategy, whether expressed in the Party Program of 1962 or in the Government Plan of 1963, is clear enough: It aims at pooling all the resources available to build up a modern industrial economy. This can be accomplished only through a transitional period of mixed   economy   during   which   the   state   sector   is progressively to reach, through its investments, a dominant role—and this is more or less identified with socialism in both documents. During this transitional period leading to "Socialism," the state is to play the leading role, foreign capital is to contribute the "accelerator," while domestic enterprise is limited to small-scale industrial and commercial ventures. All sections of the population are mobilized for this national undertaking—if necessary, the various groups must "change their mentality," but, in the traditional sector, particularly in agriculture, the state is not to interfere. Landownership, in particular, is to remain as it is. Although the official terminology insists on socialism, the strategy appears to be both nationalistic and modernistic. All-pervading, there is the vision of a modern nation, Ghana. This is *the* vision, the "Nkrumaist vision."

THE TWO-STRATEGY THEORY

We must come now to the much-debated question of the delay: Why is it only in 1962 and 1963 that such fundamental documents concerning the strategy of development of the CPP and the government were adopted? Many answers have been given to this question, but without doubt, it is the book published by Bob Fitch and Mary Oppenheimer, which proposes the most dramatic and challenging answer. "The answer is that there was not one Ghana but two—a pro-Western Ghana from approximately 1957 to 1961, and a prosocialist Ghana from 1961 to February, 1966." According to Fitch and Oppenheimer, pre-1961 Ghana had been guided by a development strategy formulated by W. Arthur Lewis. Post-1961 Ghana, on the contrary, attempted to adopt socialist planning techniques, tried to build up the state industrial sector, and finally brought the British banks under some measure of control. [30]

But why this sudden change? Because, by 1961, the Lewis approach had clearly failed. During the "Lewis era" Ghana experienced rapid deterioration of her balance of payments position, loss of huge amounts of external reserves, and failure to attract anywhere near the amount of foreign capital which Lewis counted on to assure Ghana's industrial future.[31] In 1961, the Second Development Plan was abandoned. Increasing balance of payments deficits, dwindling reserves, and failure to attract foreign investment forced Ghana to search for a new development strategy. This point is strongly emphasized: It is not "flirtation" with socialist planning, not hostility to British entrepreneurs operating in Ghana, but complete reliance on the conventional wisdom reflected in the Lewis approach which had led Ghana into this predicament.[32]

After 1961, the policies of the Nkrumah Government changed: They included large government outlays for consumer- and capital-goods factories, Soviet-inspired planning techniques, stringent import controls, and expanded fiscal and monetary powers. All these policies were part of Ghana's natural reaction against the failures of the neocolonial period.[33] But this also failed! Indeed, comment Fitch and Oppenheimer, it failed because the attempt to break with Ghana's colonial past was not made soon enough, and because when it was made, it was not complete enough.[34]

Apart from its intrinsic interest, this "two-strategy theory" is also interesting inasmuch as it is a study which attempts to analyze the Nkrumah-CPP Government in Marxist terms. To be exact, this analysis is also strongly influenced by Fanon's model as presented in his last book, *Les damnés de la terre*. (Some passages of Fitch and Oppenheimer's book are but illustrations of Fanon's third chapter.) Besides, the conclusions of Fitch and Oppenheimer are diametrically opposed to the general attitude of leftists vis-à-vis Ghana. While leftists, in general, supported Ghana under Nkrumah and considered his overthrow a disaster, Fitch and Oppenheimer bring peace to the camp: It was not socialism in Africa, it was not even effective nationalism; it was at worst, neocolonialism, at best, an illusion.[35]

Considering the fragmentation of contemporary Marxist thinking, including its official forms, into several schools, it may not be useful to discuss the degree of Marxist orthodoxy in Fitch and Oppenheimer's analysis. It seems, however, that their interpretation, although it will not satisfy all Marxists,[36] is not an isolated one. Similar analyses have been made of the Algerian National Liberation Front (FLN) Government and of the Tunisian *parti socialiste destourien*.[37] Indeed, it seems that after a decade or so during which no serious criticism was made—during the Algerian war and for a few years after—the national liberation movement in the colonies and former colonies is being discussed once again by a rigid Marxist analysis as an essentially bourgeois movement with very limited purposes and perspectives.

This appears in Fitch and Oppenheimer's interpretation, particularly when they attempt to trace back to its origin what they consider as the CPP's "revolutionary failure," and when they try to explain why the Nkrumah-CPP government adopted, in the earlier period of independence, the Lewis model, which, in Fitch and Oppenheimer terminology is a "neocolonial" model. The answer to this question is in fact the very substance of their book. It may be summarized briefly (and somewhat schematically) as follows: First, although anticolonial agitation started in the Gold Coast before Nkrumah came back in 1947 to become Secretary-General of the UGCC, the founder and Life-Chairman of the CPP did play a major role in shaping the movement, and his political ideology was not a simple one. Strongly influenced by the themes of the Sixth Pan-African Congress, Nkrumah's political ideology "embraced a series of contradictory positions: anti-Communism and anti-imperialism; national liberation and abstract non-violence; non-alignment and economic development through foreign investment. ...It was the clash between these contradictory principles that produced his erratic course in foreign and domestic policy and led finally to his undoing."[38]

Second, the popular basis of the CPP, the youngmen, the commoners, was "essentially a petty-bourgeois stratum." These storekeepers, petty traders, clerks, junior civil servants, and primary schoolteachers were engaged in conflict on three fronts: with the indirect-rule chiefs; with the colonial system; and finally with the wealthier commoner stratum—consisting of big cocoa brokers, lawyers, upper civil servants, and contractors— which was represented by the UGCC. In other words, this lower middle class did have a number of serious grievances and was numerous enough to put the CPP in government, but it was not the "real oppressed class," this being "the landless agricultural laborers and sharecroppers." Thus, when the CPP came to power, it was not the entire colonial system that these youngmen sought to change; the Gold Coast petty bourgeoisie had no radical chains to break, it was not opposed to a society ruled by an economically privileged, all-powerful bureaucracy. It simply wanted that bureaucracy to be African. Consequently, the answer to the problem posed by the bureaucracy was not democratic control—either now or in the future—but "Africanization." And Fitch and Oppenheimer conclude: In this respect Nkrumah was the perfect representative of the Gold Coast petty bourgeoisie.[39] An ideologically confused leadership coupled with a mass party of the lower middle class could

hardly be expected, even in Africa, to follow a strikingly
revolutionary course. And, in fact, the last part of
Fitch-Oppenheimer's argument is precisely this.

Third, a turning point was reached when the CPP
leadership, after reluctantly ordering that Positive Action
should be started, eventually accepted Arden-Clarke's
terms, viz., to enter the election (1951), and, after winning
it, to form the Gold Coast Government and cooperate with
the colonial authority.[40] Fitch-Oppenheimer score this
decision as catastrophic. The CPP's cooperation with the
colonial authorities, from 1951 to 1957, prevented the
Party and Government from tackling the real problems of
the country. During the early years of its rule, "the CPP
made no effort whatsoever to restructure Ghanaian society;
the leaders did not see the institutions left behind by the
British colonialists as barriers to national economic
development. The CPP, at this time, believed that in order
to achieve rapid economic growth the institutions of
colonialism needed only to be administered by Africans."[41]
In the very last pages of their study, Fitch and Oppenheimer
come again on the same point. The failure of Ghana under
Nkrumah and the CPP must be traced back to this original
compromise with the colonial power.

> Arden-Clarke's announcement that the CPP could
> achieve power under certain narrowly prescribed con-
> ditions split the movement in two. ... Within the CPP,
> those who accepted Arden-Clarke's temptation—and his
> conditions—prevailed. In a sense, therefore, the
> CPP's first mistake was its last—for clearly a
> coalition with colonialism is fatal to any party which
> seeks to base itself on the strength and aspirations
> of the colonized.[42]

In sum, Fitch and Oppenheimer first identify the
"youngmen" of former studies on Ghana as Ghana's petty
bourgeoisie, and then infer from this that these "youngmen"

who are assumed to *be* the CPP, cannot possibly want a total revolution. Therefore, they can accept Arden-Clarke's Dyarchy, i.e., the nonrevolutionary transition to independence par excellence. They also assume that this choice of 1951 implied that the CPP would follow a neocolonialist course, relying principally on foreign investments for the country's development (the so-called Lewis model), and that this led to an impasse ten years later. Then, these same "youngmen," Nkrumah and the CPP, after a visit of the former to the U.S.S.R., decided to choose another course of action, this time a truly revolutionary one, although still somewhat timid. We shall discuss the CPP, including its class nature, in our fifth chapter. However, the postponement of this discussion will not affect our analysis of Fitch and Oppenheimer's interpretation of the Nkrumah-CPP strategy, for, whether the CPP was essentially petty bourgeois or not, it remains to be established that Nkrumah and the CPP made these two fundamental, and fundamentally different, choices, in 1951 and in 1961. It remains to be proven that they followed two different courses of action, that there was first a pro-Western Ghana until 1961, and a prosocialist Ghana between 1961 and February, 1966.

We find in our own observations in Ghana, particularly during the later years of the Nkrumah-CPP regime, no evidence to support this two-strategy theory. First of all because the identification of the Dyarchy with neo-colonialism is possible only if one completely leaves out the power struggle which took place during those years and particularly between 1954 and 1958. The second and more important reason is that, as we have just seen, neither the CPP Program of 1962 nor the Seven-Year Development Plan of 1963 represent a fundamental departure from previous strategical options. Although more systematically presented, if not always implemented, the strategy remained essentially the same after 1961 as before 1961.

When all is said, the two-strategy theory is based on the rather abstract and doctrinaire notion that Nkrumah and the CPP made first an ideological choice in 1950-51 and another one about ten years later, that these choices determined the course of events in Ghana, and that these were choices between capitalism and socialism.

To be sure, the acceptance of the Dyarchy set upon the CPP some limitations for the entire duration of this transitional period, but these were not the only limitations. Within the Gold Coast, the struggle for power between the CPP and its opposition posed more important and more urgent problems, but Fitch and Oppenheimer almost completely overlook this fact; they play down the problem of the opposition and particularly the danger of tribalism and federalism.[43] A careful reading of Austin's study—to which Fitch and Oppenheimer themselves refer frequently— as well as direct observations in Ghana would lead to a reverse conclusion. Not only were the electoral battles extremely severe, and often violent in the physical sense, but strongholds of resistance to the CPP were far from negligible long after the opposition was formally eliminated—in fact, to the very end.

These internal political difficulties (the struggle for power), along with other elements, such as the evolution of the economic situation in Ghana between 1951 and 1961, go a long way to explain why it was only in 1962 and 1963, and not immediately in 1952 and 1953 or even in 1957, that the Party and the Government eventually turned their full attention to the economic problems of the country and systematized their strategy of development in the Program and the Plan. At any rate, it goes a longer way to explain these delays than the suggestion that the CPP first chose the "capitalist road" and then the "socialist road"; for although one can see that the first "road" was not a socialist one, one does not see how the second, after 1961, was supposed to be essentially different.

The two-strategy theory, in the final analysis, seems to be only an attempt at minimizing the failure of socialism in Ghana under Nkrumah by arguing that during most of these fifteen years, the government did not follow a socialist policy, but drew its inspiration from the "Lewis model." Indeed, this is correct: Ghana's strategy of development had little to do with socialism, and not only until 1961, but in fact until the very end. Ghana's experience is plainly within the logic of anticolonial nationalism, despite the fact that its leaders have made profuse use of the socialist terminology, and it must be replaced within this framework to be analyzed correctly.

It goes without saying, however, that Ghana's experience during those years contained elements of socialism, but this was not central to the text. A discussion of Ghana, between 1951 and 1966, in terms of a socialist experience or not, is both misleading and generally irrelevant, for it does not focus on the essential question,— which is *decolonization*. Under the circumstances, socialist, or what is described as socialist options and approaches could only, and did only, represent some of the modalities of this experience in decolonization. In Ghana, the central question was, and remains, that of the country's decolonization and development. And this can be more fruitfully discussed in the more logical framework of postindependence anticolonial nationalism. The many questions which may be raised in this framework are of immediate relevance to Ghana, while those concerning socialism in an essentially pre-industrial former African colony are, to say the least, rather abstract. It would amount to looking at Ghana through an ideological—and, given the state of crisis of socialist theory at the moment, an essentially rhetorical—mirror, instead of looking at these fifteen years directly.

Similarly, it is not necessary to identify the CPP with the Ghanaian petty bourgeoisie to explain the CPP's strategy. Pending a full discussion of the CPP in our fifth chapter, we may, however, recall at this point Hassan Riad's perceptive analysis of the Egyptian *Wafd* and his remark that "it is not necessary, in order to explain the *Wafd*, to invent a middle bourgeoisie for whom there was no real economic basis. We believe that it is a simplistic interpretation of Marxism to see in all political parties at all times the expression of specific economic class interests."[44] *Mutatis mutandis*, this remark seems to apply also to the Ghanaian CPP and to Fitch and Oppenheimer's interpretation. Let us now see how the much-delayed publication of the Program and the Plan could be explained without "inventing" anything.

ELEMENTS FOR AN ALTERNATIVE INTERPRETATION

The Struggle for Power

Although the results of the electoral battles do not reveal the whole political picture of the Gold Coast during the 1951-57 period, they nonetheless supply a first and useful indication of the intensity of the power struggle in the country. It must also be emphasized that such elections were not contested in an independent Ghana, but in the Gold Coast of the Dyarchy. In fact, the last general election before independence, that of 1956, was forced upon the CPP by the British authorities, to probe once more, in the face of a growing opposition in the country (the NLM alliance), the popular support enjoyed by the CPP. It is only with great reluctance, and after trying almost everything to avoid the election, that the CPP eventually started its third electoral campaign. The optimism of the NLM headquarters in Kumasi was matched only by the reluctance and pessimism of the CPP leadership in Accra. In a sense, it is true that, because it had agreed to play its part in the Dyarchy, the CPP was forced to fight for power in the electoral framework set by the colonial authorities, and thus was, one might say, co-responsible for what, in 1956, became a real predicament for the party.

As already mentioned, if looked at in terms of seats won, all three elections between 1951 and 1956 were great victories for the CPP, and seemed to reduce the opposition to not very much of a challenge, and the electoral campaigns to rather formal exercises.

In *1951*, out of 38 popularly elected seats to the Assembly, 34 were won by the CPP: 29 against 4 to the oppositions, in the rural areas (indirect suffrage) and all the 5 municipal seats (direct suffrage). In the municipalities, out of 90,000 registered voters, 47 per cent cast their votes in the proportion of about 90 per cent for the CPP (58,000 versus 5,000 for the opposition). In many ways, the 1951 election was the greatest victory of the party.[45]

In *1954*, the first general election (more or less universal adult suffrage), the CPP won 72 seats out of 104. The seats lost by the CPP went mostly to regional parties (15 to the newly formed Northern People's Party, and (3 to the Togoland Congress) and to independent candidates (11 seats), a good many of them CPP dissidents (i.e., CPP members whose candidacies had not been approved by the CPP headquarters). The 11 seats won by the independent candidates do not represent the full extent of this phenomenon (the 1954 election was dubbed the "Independents' election"), for the independent candidates polled more than 22 per cent of the votes, and presented altogether 154 candidates, out of which 103 were CPP "rebels" (59 in the "Colony" for only 44 seats.)

In *1956*, despite its fears, the CPP maintained its majority with 71 seats out of 104. In terms of seats in the Assembly, as in the 1954 election, the strongest opposition party was the NPP (Northern regionalism) with the same number of seats, 15 both in 1954 and 1956.[46] The NLM, which had revived the hopes of the opposition and so upset the CPP, obtained only 12 seats—a little more than half the seats of Ashanti, its stronghold. In other words, the danger represented by the opposition may have seemed minimal. The stronger opposition party, the NPP (15 seats versus 72 and 71 for the CPP in 1954 and 1956) being strictly regionally based, did not present any candidate outside the Northern Region, and thus could hardly be considered a serious threat to the CPP at the national level.

Unfortunately for the CPP, the image of a divided, regionally based, and small opposition is superficial. When one looks at the results of the elections in terms of the number of votes polled by each party, the majority of the CPP is striking only in 1951, when the popular direct vote was in fact restricted to the country's five municipalities.

In 1954, with 70 per cent of the seats, the CPP had only 55 per cent of the votes; and in 1956, with again about 70 per cent of the seats, the CPP only attracted a slightly higher percentage of the votes (57 per cent). With this narrower margin of 55 versus 45 per cent of the popular vote, it is clear that the lack of discipline in the party, in 1954, (the Independents' election) could have upset the party, and weakened its position in the Dyarchy. In fact, the 1954 election was followed by renewed efforts by the CPP leadership to strengthen the party organization, and a number of dissident members were expelled.

It is, however, with the 1956 election that the CPP was confronted with a real danger. By-elections in Ashanti had shown the growing strength of the NLM opposition, and this had subsequently had a dynamic effect on the other regional parties. Moreover, after five years of CPP rule within the Dyarchy, its prestige was not left untouched as the party of the "common man" and as the party which had won its first battles with the demand for "Self-Government Now." After five years of delay, "Self-Government Now" was beginning to be questioned even as "an attitude of mind,"[47] while, at the same time, some of the leaders of the "party of the common man," former "commoners" themselves, had already started, and not too cautiously or discreetly at that, to enjoy the many economic advantages of sharing power.[48] The overwhelming strength of the CPP in the "Colony," where in several constituencies the candidate of the CPP was unopposed, as well as the possibility of winning at least some of the seats in other regions, made the CPP a most likely winner—if victory simply meant to win the election. But the meaning of this election was clearly to test the CPP as a majority party, as the party with which further arrangements for the devolution of sovereignty could be arrived at. Very simply, if the CPP did not obtain a clear and sufficient majority, viz., much more than the various regional opposition parties together, to say the least, the whole idea of self-government might be jeopardized. And, as far as the CPP was concerned, the whole purpose of Tactical Action, and acceptance of the rules of the game within the Dyarchy, might come to a disastrous end.

This brief account of the three elections before independence does indicate that the ruling party was confronted by a strong opposition. And, furthermore, an opposition challenge that seemed to grow stronger, not weaker, with the years. To wit: The intelligentsia, which seemed all but completely eliminated in 1951 and 1954, appeared to be resuscitated with the creation of the NLM, being able, for the first time, to find a popular, though regional (Ashanti), basis, and an apparently attractive economic platform—the cocoa prices paid to farmers. While in the 1954 election, the economic demands of the Ghana Congress Party (successor of the UGCC) for higher prices to be paid to farmers for their cocoa and, at the same time, for lowering the cost of living, may have seemed, to whoever was actually reached by the GCP propaganda, both contradictory and abstract, it was no longer the same in 1956. Soon after Gbedemah, on behalf of the CPP Government, introduced into the Assembly, in August, 1954, the Cocoa Duty and Development Funds (Amendment) Bill, proposing to fix the price paid to farmers at 72 shillings per load for a period of four years, unrest started among the cocoa farmers, in Ashanti as as elsewhere; this is usually considered as the immediate origin of the National Liberation Movement (NLM).

As the NLM developed, many other issues were added to the original economic one. In the last analysis, the price of cocoa may not even have represented, by 1956, an essential issue in the struggle between the NLM and the CPP. It was a resurgence of Ashanti "nationalism," already foreshadowed by the Ashanti demand for 30 seats (one third) instead of 23 (according to population proportions) in the next Assembly. This demand in November, 1953, it must be stressed, was made unanimously by all Ashanti members in the Legislative Assembly, including the Ashanti CPP members and Krobo Edusei himself. This resurgence of Ashanti "nationalism" also provided a catalyst for the various forms of opposition to the CPP, the intelligentsia and the chiefs, as well as the Northern fears of Accra and the Ewe separatist tendencies, as the NLM agreed not to contest the election in the North or the predominantly Ewe regions of the country.

In sum, it may be that neither regionalism (Ashanti or Northern or Ewe) nor the intelligentsia's intense dislike of the CPP, nor the price of cocoa, nor even the widely believed and fairly exact rumors of corruption among the CPP leadership, nor anything else, could alone have represented a serious threat to the CPP. But, with the NLM catalyst, between 1954 and 1956, the addition of all these elements did amount to a formidable threat for the CPP, and it is not surprising that its leadership should have devoted a good deal of its attention and efforts to coping with this problem of survival as the ruling party in the Gold Coast.

The electoral victory of the CPP, in 1956, satisfied the British authorities that the Convention People's Party had a sufficient majority, and the Gold Coast became independent under the name of Ghana on the sixth of March, 1957. But, precisely the fears that had started to bring together the various anti-CPP forces in Ghana before independence were multiplied by the accession of the country to independence. While the festivities associated with independence had not yet ended and Nkrumah was already turning his attention to African problems, new threats assailed the party: first, what appeared to be a minor armed uprising in the Ewe region; and, second, and far more serious, the foundation of the *Ga Adangme Shifimo Kpee* (The Ga Adangme Standfast Association), a popular, spontaneous movement of the Ga population of Accra prompted by dissatisfaction with housing and employment conditions in the capital. To the CPP, this must have appeared as the last straw; the initiators of the movement were the so-called Tokyo Joes, the same "Verandah Boys" who had always been the staunchest partisans and even militants and activists of the CPP; and this in the constituency of Kwame Nkrumah! But soon other elements,

more familiar faces in the anti-CPP opposition, were to
jump on the band wagon: When the new party was formally
inaugurated in Accra, on July 7, 1957, there could be seen
on the rostrum, Antor, of the Togoland Congress, Danquah,
and other opposition party leaders.

Whatever the other causes of dissatisfaction on which
the opposition parties capitalized, the CPP thought to
formally deprive them of their best platform, and at the
same time, give itself additional, legal weapons to cope
with the opposition. The Assembly passed in December,
1957, the Avoidance of Discrimation Act, which forbade
the continued existence or the creation of parties on a
regional, tribal, or religious basis. Even before the formal
vote on the Act was taken, the various opposition groups
reacted by merging into one single opposition party: the
United Party (UP), comprised of the former NLM, NPP,
Moslem Association Party (MAP), Togoland Congress (TC),
the Anlo Youth Association (also an Ewe movement), and
the *Ga Shifimo Kpee*. The bitter struggle between the CPP
and the UP continued in the same pattern as the pre-
independence electoral battles between the CPP and its
former, numerous regional opposition parties and movements,
on the occasion of by-elections, local government elections,
in the Parliament, and any other occasion as arose. In fact,
if anything, the struggle became more violent than ever,
particularly in Accra where CPP and anti-CPP activists
clashed recurrently and violently. But the CPP now was
no longer controlled by the limits imposed by the Dyarchy,
and could use, to the full, the machinery of Government,
as well as the advantage of its absolute majority in
Parliament.

In August, 1957, in December of the same year, and in
July, 1958, the Deportation Act, the Emergency Powers
Act, and the Preventive Detention Act were passed in
Parliament. These new powers were put to use: Some of the

opposition leaders were jailed, some were deported, and some chose exile. Effective results were not long in coming. In the words of Austin, who was a particularly attentive observer of the political situation of Ghana:

> The sense of defeat bred by the growth and assertion of CPP power began to be seen in 1958 first in a series of election defeats and then in the defection of a number of Northern [opposition] members of parliament. In February came the loss of the Kumasi municipal elections; in June the failure of the Ga vote in the Accra elections, while the growing power of the CPP even in the rural areas of Ashanti could be seen in a number of local-government elections.[49]

The end of this process was to be illustrated by the results of the 1960 Plebiscite which gave 88.5 per cent of the votes to the CPP-backed proposed Republican Constitution, and elected Nkrumah with 89.1 per cent of the votes for the Presidency, against his contender and the symbol of the anti-CPP opposition and the nationalist intelligentsia, J.B. Danquah.

As a conclusion to this summary of the political struggle of the CPP against its opposition, one may say that the combination of the Dyarchy and increasingly strong opposition until independence (1957) diverted a lot of the attention of the CPP leadership toward purely political problems. After independence, and for about a year and a half, the CPP, being more or less unable to find a *modus vivendi* with the opposition, still had to concentrate, and did concentrate, a lot of its efforts on its embittered struggle with the UP. In many ways, when presenting the Seven-Year Development Plan, Nkrumah could have said with even more reasons than Tunisia's Bourguiba, that although the party already had economic planning in mind as early as 1955 (in Tunisia also the period of a Dyarchy of a sort),

> this period was dominated by subversion. ... The situation was seen as 'a step back'; there was violence, bloody clashes. The problem of economic planning was overlooked. The preoccupation of the time was to safeguard the State which was threatened in its very existence. We had to give priority to our fight against anarchy, the persistence of which would have meant the end of the State, that is also the end of our independence, and thus made all economic preoccupation futile. [Under the circumstances] the need for economic planning was not felt as an imperative.[50]

When one compares the long and protracted struggle of the CPP against the opposition parties to the relatively more violent but much shorter *"yussefist* subversion" in Tunisia, one feels that indeed Bourguiba's argument might have fit the Ghanaian situation even better than the Tunisian one, and that between 1954 and 1958, "the need for [more serious] economic planning was not felt as an imperative" in Ghana in the face of the more immediate political problem of the power struggle.

Economic Constraints and Illusions

As a postscript to this discussion of the political situation between 1951 and 1961, as well as an introduction to a short comment on the economic situation of the country during the same decade, it may be interesting to point out that these bitter political battles were largely fought without much reference to the economic problems of the country. Even the platform of the NLM, which sought to embody the grievances of the cocoa farmers, did not really present even an outline of an alternative economic program. This is, perhaps, partly due to the fact that the "socialist" objectives of the CPP, although already stated in the Party's Constitution drawn up in 1949 and adopted in 1951,[51] were only stated in very general and vague terms, and were not clearly and practically translated into a program. And certainly not a program which would have affected (or even frightened) such vested nonsocialist (capitalist or proto-capitalist) interests as they then were in Ghana. In fact, a comparison between the economic content of the CPP electoral manifestos and those of the opposition parties shows no fundamental differences, at least as far as sets of practical objectives presented to the voters were concerned.

In *1951*, both the CPP and the UGCC[52] requested a five-year plan, the implementation of the Volta Scheme, extension of roads, rationalization of the cocoa industry, and the development of education. Both also suggested that a welfare program should be introduced. The UGCC's Plan for the Nation opposed to the socialist claims of the CPP, a ten-point program "to ensure that the optimum diffusion of *private enterprise and ownership of property* shall be developed alongside the maximum attainment of personal liberty, within the framework of the welfare state,"[53] but it requested the creation of a national bank, and a reduction of the importation of light manufactured goods, which should be manufactured locally under a five-year plan—all practical objectives which were not mentioned in the CPP manifesto. So, the CPP stood for socialism and the UGCC for free enterprise, but both claimed almost the same program—regardless, in 1951, the issue was *freedom* and not much else. Austin is certainly right in seeing "very little difference [except in the language used] between the CPP 'Goal' and the UGCC 'Plan'."[54]

In *1954*, the opposition to the CPP, as we have seen, came mostly from inside the party with the CPP "rebels" who stood for election despite the fact that the party headquarters did not endorse their candidacies. The opposition from outside the party was mostly regional

(NPP and Togoland Congress), in both cases, a limited challenge. The only national opposition was that of the GCP (successor of the UGCC, and led by K. Busia), and it was weak (one seat, and about 30,000 votes, only a tenth of the total non-CPP vote). Under the circumstances, the élitist GCP could only criticize the "corruption" of the CPP, its ill-conceived housing program, and ill-phased educational program, while promising higher prices for cocoa to the farmers, and to lower the cost of living. Without mentioning the contradiction of these two electoral promises, what may be considered the economic program of the GCP was not much more than what Austin calls "a moderate view of the CPP's own program of wide social and economic benefits [and was only] likely to attract moderate support."[55]

The CPP, at the time strengthened by a short period of power, could simply and successfully ask the voters to cast their ballots in its favor to enable the party "to complete the job." As Nkrumah was reported to have said to a visitor: "Until independence, there is only one political platform—that is independence—and I happen to be occupying it."[56] As we have seen, in 1954, the trouble of the CPP was no longer, or not yet, with the intelligentsia, but with the beginning of regionalism (Northern and Ewe), and with its own party (the dissidents and rebels).

In 1956, with the rise of the NLM in Ashanti, the CPP had to fight its bitterest and toughest battle. But even then, though the immediate origin of the NLM may be traced to an economic problem—a fixed price for cocoa—its leaders chose not to fight the CPP on its economic program. Apart from that of a higher price to be paid to farmers for their cocoa, such demands as "set up light and heavy industries," or "encourage mechanization of farming"[57] could not appear as much different from those of the CPP. And this cannot entirely be explained away by the fact

that some of the organizers and leaders of the NLM were
former CPP party members.

All in all, what the opposition had to say was that the
CPP was corrupt, that its promises were empty, and that
the opposition could do much better, but basically on the
same lines,[58] except as far as cocoa was concerned.
Obviously, to propose the same program of economic
development, while at the same time suggesting that the
cost of living should be kept down and the price paid to
farmers for their cocoa should be higher, is typical of
opposition parties. In this sense, the identification of the
federalist platform of the NLM with a "katangese"
platform,[59] the NLM leaders allegedly trying to prevent
the central government from redistributing throughout the
country the benefits of cocoa exports (Ashanti being the
center of cocoa production), is not as relevant as may
appear at first. Indeed, the "owning classes" of Ashanti
might, as Fitch and Oppenheimer suggest, have been
"tired of their milch cow role," but this could not
constitute a program of government for Ghana as a whole.
And this is one more reason why the NLM leaders chose
not to fight the CPP mainly on its economic policies. The
victory of the CPP in the 1956 election in many cocoa-
growing constituencies shows that even the cocoa issue
was not all that clear, and certainly not the dominant
factor in the election.

One may now wonder why the economic issue played
such a relatively minor role in the electoral campaigns
and the power struggle in general. In other words, why did
both the CPP, in government, and the other parties, in
opposition, deny prominence to their economic policies by
phrasing them in very similar and vague terms? A specific
answer may be found in the peculiar, and rather atypical
economic conjuncture of the Gold Coast in the 1950's.
Another more general answer is suggested by Dudley

Seers's model of economic development in primary producer countries,[60] as we shall see later on.

Let us look first at the economic conjuncture of the 1950's in Ghana. Cocoa prices, and government income and expenditure, will provide convenient, if broad, indicators. From 1951, government expenses increased rapidly and regularly, but resources increased even more rapidly. From 1950/51 to 1958/59, government expenditures climbed from £17.1 to £61.9 million; but during the same period, government income increased from £20.8 to £66.6 million.[61] Thus, for the whole period, and with only the exception of 1956/57 (a deficit of £5.8 million), government resources increased more and more rapidly than expenditures. During the whole period, Ghana's balance of payment was also positive. This first period was characterized by a continued and fairly rapid development of both private and public consumption.

On the contrary, after 1959/60, the situation was completely altered. The first difficulties experienced on the cocoa market, toward the end of the first period, persisted, and became more acute. It was now quite clear that, for some time to come, resources from exports would not rise significantly. From 1948/49 to 1953/54, the price of cocoa (per long ton) had regularly increased from £190 to £467. In 1955/56, it was down to £221; but, in 1957/58, cocoa was again fetching £352. But this was the end. After this year, prices fell continuously: £285, 225, 177, 170 from 1958/59 to 1961/62. Cocoa was eventually to reach its lowest price during the 1964/65 campaign with a figure much below £100. Cocoa represented more than 60 per cent of the total value of Ghanaian exports (varying between 56 and 75 per cent from 1951 to 1962). The fall of its price on the world market, despite a considerably increased production, eventually brought about a series of deficits to the balance of external payments: £27.6 million in 1961, £1.7 in 1962, £21.5 in 1963, and £6.9 in 1964.

The sheer size of infrastructural investments (in the fields of public health, education, and economic infrastructure properly speaking), already made by then, implied a high level of recurrent ordinary expenditures, including more or less incompressible expenses for imported goods and services. Similarly, the other expenditures of a larger administration (civil service and public corporations) cannot be reduced beyond a point. In fact, from 1959/60 on, government expenses kept growing rapidly (from £76 to £144 million in 1963/64), while resources increased more slowly (from £70 to £122 million for the same years, 1959/60 to 1963/64). Ghana had then entered the period of budget deficits. In the course of the years from 1959/60 to 1963/64, budget deficits increased regularly: £6, 24, 39, 50, and £21 million.

Thus, until 1958/59 or even 1959/60, the Ghanaian Government did not have to make difficult decisions, nor feel it had to. Private consumption, capital formation, and public consumption could all grow without conflicting. It was a period of respite, but also one of illusions. It nonetheless made it possible for the government to launch its first large development projects (roads, schools, public health, the artificial port of Tema, the Volta Dam) in an exceptionally favorable climate. In point of fact, the Volta project was criticized by the opposition in Parliament, not because of its size or conception, but because it was not entirely financed by Ghana and because of the importance of the participation of a foreign private firm (Kaiser). It was thus a period of respite in the sense that the CPP could concentrate on its political struggle against the opposition and at the same time embark, so to speak, on the sly, on its huge program of building a modern infrastructure for the economy.

After 1960 (the year of the Republican Plebiscite), this freedom of movement no longer existed. The party and the government had to choose. They could no longer satisfy themselves and the Ghanaians with general statements on socialism, the African personality, or the paradise-like benefits of industrialization. Above all, they could no longer enjoy the rare possibility of rapidly increasing public consumption and investment, and at the same time, let private consumption grow rapidly. In 1961, the government introduced its first austerity budget, and the reaction is well known: It was the Sekondi-Takoradi quasi-insurrectional strike.

Thus we seem to have a picture which is less, much less, dramatic than that presented by Fitch and Oppenheimer, but at the same time, not entirely different. It is, in point of fact, a pattern of evolution that seems to fit remarkably well Dudley Seers's model. It may be that the policy choices, practically, do not appear so clear-cut to the protagonists themselves. Dudley Seers, who is one of the rare economists who recognize fully the importance of social and political factors in the process of development in former colonial countries,[62] shows in his model a type of evolution in underdeveloped countries in which political decisions vis-à-vis the economic development of the country are at the same time less sweeping and more technical.

Dudley Seers's Model

The starting point of Dudley Seers's model is an "open economy in its pure form."[63]

> A starting point is one elementary fact. A large number of countries exporting primary products show all of the following characteristics: (1) The currency is highly backed, and is held at parity with, and

fully convertible into, the currency of a major international power; (2) There are few quantitative restrictions on imports; (3) Tariffs are relatively low. ... This type of economy can be called 'open' because it responds readily to external influences. The main feature of the performance of this sort of economy, is that the long-period rate of growth is very largely determined by one exogenous variable (exports) and one structural relation (the income-elasticity of demand for imports).[64]

A brief discussion of the functioning of the open economy follows. Taking his examples from the experience of Latin American countries as well as Africa during the postwar period, Dudley Seers shows how the economy of primary producer countries comes under stress. So many studies have been devoted to this phenomenon that it may not be necessary to comment here. Seers's conclusion is that "in practice we have to drop [the] assumption that imports rise parallel to exports." The main reasons for this are, *inter alia*, that "if the inflow of capital is in the form of private direct investment, the profits of overseas companies will probably absorb an increasing proportion of export proceeds, so that the *net* total of foreign exchange receipts available to finance imports... rises more slowly than exports,"[65] and that "there may be a leakage through the banking system; the overseas assets of foreign banks... may grow... or people may invest increasingly in foreign shares. There is one development that may alter this deterministic set of relationships. ... This is import substitution. But," Dudley Seers points out,

here we must allow for the political context of an open economy. If we look at such economies, we notice that many of them are, if not colonies, then very much under the influence of one of the great powers. This power will try to keep the door open for the sale of its products, and will discourage or prevent the establishment of high tariffs or import

quotas. Moreover, a colony, or neo-colony, is typically
in a 'comatose state'; few political leaders realize
the need for an aggressive policy of import substitution, or could mobilise sufficient support to carry it
through in the face of opposition from importers,
landowners, bankers and the dominant foreign power.[66]

In fact, "where the open economy has disappeared,
this has been due to its destruction by two forces. In the
first place, political pressures for development (in the form
of protest against unemployment, demands for higher
wages, etc.) have been too strong. Secondly, exports of its
primary commodity have run into a stagnant or declining
phase."[67] The situation of the world cocoa market at the
end of the 1950's and the Sekondi-Takoradi strike of
September, 1961, seems indeed to illustrate perfectly
Dudley Seers's model in the case of Ghana.

When export proceeds cease to rise, or actually enter
a declining phase, pressures for development stimulated by
the "revolution of rising expectation" tend to grow
stronger rather than weaker: *Volens nolens*, the government
has to make its first choices. But, Dudley Seers shows
that at first, when the economy comes under stress, the
government tries to prolong the "open" stage. Probably,
not so much because of any preference for the open
economy, but because to prolong it allows the postponement of such choices which may antagonize vested
interests. In the case of Ghana, if we accept the suggestion
of Dudley Seers, that is, that Ghana's open economy came
under stress in about 1955, such an escapist attitude
would not be surprising, not only because the country was
not yet independent, but also because this was precisely
the time (1954-58) of the bitterest political battles that the
CPP had to fight against the opposition (NLM and later
UP). According to this model, the various devices that
can be used to prolong the "open" stage are as follows:

> the government can run down reserves, raise the rates
> of taxation of foreign mineral companies, or make
> mild increases in tariffs. A certain amount of import
> substitutes can be achieved without much protection,
> because of the cost of ocean freight; the government
> may encourage this by such measures as setting up
> industrial development institutions. For any of these
> reasons, income can grow for some years more
> quickly than exports without an economy essentially
> ceasing to be open.[68]

Again, this description seems to fit the evolution of Ghana
very well. All these various devices were used and found a
theoretical justification in the 1953 Lewis Report on
Industrialization and the Gold Coast.[69] In the sense that
the Ghana Government may be said to have tried to prolong
the "open" stage of the economy in Ghana, Fitch and
Oppenheimer are not wrong in equating the "Lewis period,"
until 1961, with neocolonialism (if by neocolonialism one
means a policy devised to maintain more or less intact
the structure of the colonial economy, the open economy).
But, as we shall see, this is only part of the picture, and
the "Lewis period" could almost as well be described as
the application of "Tactical Action" to the economic field.

In any case, such devices to prolong the "open"
stage cannot last forever.

> Despite the temporary reliefs which have just been
> described, the period of stress cannot be endured
> indefinitely. Whereas the pressure for economic
> development persistently mounts, the markets for
> primary products show a chronic tendency to sag,
> while countries supplying financial assistance do
> not provide it at a fast enough rate. Moreover, in
> the current political climate of the world, it is
> becoming increasingly difficult to suppress by
> violence political demands for economic development.
> After a while, the forces acting to close the economy
> became cumulative. Governments may concede
> general wage increases to reduce political tensions.
> But such rises in cost may hamper exports[by making

production in marginal farms or mines too expensive][70] and at the same time they are bound to stimulate imports. Official measures to encourage local industries involve an increase in outlays for imported equipment. Furthermore, as the foreign exchange crisis deepens, it is found that loans are harder to float in overseas markets; foreign capital may become more reluctant to enter; and domestic private capital tends to seek safety overseas. ... At a certain point the open economy loses its capacity to cope with the socio-economic demands on it, and a crisis develops, triggered off perhaps by some quite small event [such as a dip in the price of a leading export or a change of government]. The symptom is a fast decline in reserves of foreign exchange.[71]

Again, by and large, the model fits Ghana's experience, and it is precisely at a period of fast-declining reserves of foreign exchange, after the Takoradi strike, that Ghana was presented with a more fundamental choice: to move or not to move to a "closed" economy. Expressed in a slightly different way, the problem of industrialization, which all contending parties in Ghana had advocated since 1951, but in very general terms, had now to be confronted in much clearer and more realistic terms.[72]

"What happens next depends on the balance of forces in the country."[73] But, from then on, the choice was quite clear. At this stage, there were only two possibilities: the government either reduces its expenditures (public consumption) or reduces private consumption, and imposes general controls on foreign trade and the movement of capitals and other transfers, and pushes ahead with its industrialization and other development projects. According to Dudley Seers, it was in 1961 that Ghana was confronted with these problems, and made its move toward the closing of its economy. The question of whether this first period of "closed" economy may actually be described, as in

Dudley Seers's model, as a period of easy import substitution is more open to dispute.

Other aspects of Dudley Seers's description of the early period of the closed economy may not apply so well to the Ghanaian situation, but this at least is quite correct: "The most conspicuous change... is the development of a machinery for planning. A 'plan' may well have existed earlier, but during the 'open' phase of the economy it can be little more than a collection of long-term expenditure plans of government departments, together with some rather vague aspirations for social progress and non-quantitative statements of policy in various fields."[74]

THE TIME-LAG

The interest of Seers's model lies partly in the fact that it takes into consideration the historical experience of a number of underdeveloped countries, either former African colonies or Latin American countries. Our own observations, particularly in Tunisia and in Ghana, seem to indicate that in former African colonies there is, in general, a *time-lag* between the accession of a country to independence and the time when a comprehensive set of economic decisions are taken (in the form of a "real" plan, for example). In Tunisia, the major event that might have accelerated the *prise de conscience* of the actual economic needs of the country was perhaps the decision of the French Government to cut its financial assistance to Tunisia in retaliation for the continued assistance given by Bourguiba's Government to the Algerian National Liberation Front (FLN). For all practical purposes, the decision of the French Government to cut its economic and financial assistance to Tunisia had the same effect as the fall of cocoa prices in Ghana.

In both countries, it may be argued, the first years
were occupied by political problems connected with the
struggle of the party to strengthen its grip on power. This
has already been discussed in the case of Ghana. Then,
again in both countries, when the political situation could
be considered more or less stabilized, a sudden and
serious deterioration of the financial position of the
country occurred (fall in cocoa prices in Ghana, and
interruption of French assistance in Tunisia). In both
cases, this sequence of events seems to have first
postponed, and then accelerated, the *prise de conscience*
of the real situation and needs, of the country's economy,
and eventually brought about a series of concerted moves
to "close" the economy. It may be interesting to point out
that both in Tunisia and Ghana, there is a time-lag of
several years between independence and a serious move to
"close" the economy, and, as we have seen, in Tunisia
the delay in introducing economic planning is precisely
accounted for by President Bourguiba's reference to the
political problems posed by the opposition, the so-called
yussefist subversion. This coincidence, and a comparison
between the two countries, may seem all the more
interesting especially in view of the fact that the official
political doctrines of the two countries were worlds apart.
But the same time-lag is characteristic of the evolution of
both. This naturally raises the question of whether this is
more than a mere coincidence. Obviously, the price of
cocoa might have maintained itself for several more years,
or France might have either cut her assistance to Tunisia
earlier or later, or not cut it at all, or Tunisia might not
have given any logistical support to the Algerian Army of
National Liberation (ALN).

Many things *might* have been different, within the
limits of each country, and therefore might have resulted
in different patterns of evolution. But two things stand.

First, the political struggle for power: It is hard to imagine any country moving from the colonial status to the status of independence, without any political power struggle, in one form or another, whether such a struggle took place between different political formations or within a single party; whether the conflict took violent armed forms or more or less peaceful electoral ones; whether it took the form of a conflict of élites, of leaders, of élite(s) versus masses, of generations, or of regions against the centralizing tendencies of a ruling nationalist party or movement. Second, whatever the actual fluctuations of prices of any given primary commodity on the world market, or the "goodwill" of any assisting former *métropole* or major power, these are factors which escape the control of the former colony.

In other words, one may more or less safely conclude that, by and large, one may expect a typical pattern of evolution of former colonies after independence characterized by a "time-lag" between the moment the former colony becomes independent and the moment the government takes a series of concerted measures which bring the economy under more and more stringent government controls (closed economy). The length of such a time-lag would appear to depend mainly on two variables: the intensity of the political power struggle after (or even just before) independence, on the one hand, and the intensity of the strain on the economy, on the other (including, but with a reverse, delaying effect, the relieving economic and financial assistance that the former *métropole* or another major power may grant the country). The two variables are by nature independent but, if the political power struggle involves economic or development issues, they may be thus related.[75] This was not really the case in either Ghana or Tunisia.

Therefore, the time-lag also measures the evolution of

the ruling party and the government of the former colony
from what Dudley Seers describes as a "typically comatose
state" to a growing awareness of the realities of the
country's economy—the actual implications of a real policy
of development. While the party leadership and government
grow more concerned with economic problems and discover
that independence also means underdevelopment, the
concept of decolonization becomes less vague and tends
more and more to be understood as a prerequisite for
development. The instruments of economic controls, in
order to be applied to the reorientation of the economy,
must be concentrated in the hands of the state. The bureaucracy, and particularly those in charge of the economic
departments within the civil service, also become more
conscious of the problems of economic development.
Meanwhile, their knowledge of the country's economy and
their technical and administrative experience have improved.
As Dudley Seers puts it: "The most conspicuous change
is the development of a machinery for planning." But,
again, this is not fundamentally a technical problem, but a
problem of *prise de conscience*.[76] The very conception of a
national economy, and a better realization of what such a
national economic development entails, clearly indicates
that, at the level of the party leadership and the government
at least, national consciousness is enriched and
strengthened by the addition of an economic dimension.
The economic content of nationalism grows in size and
precision. It tends to become meaningful, and to actually
inform the economic policies of the government.

In Dudley Seers's model, it is implicitly assumed that
the government's behavior is more or less neutral. It is the
"stress" and the popular pressure for more jobs, and better
(or, at least, not worse) wages, that push the country
toward a closed economy. In other words, the process is
given, as Dudley Seers himself is aware,[77] "an appearance

of inevitability." And this, again, implies that the government is more or less neutral, that it is not conscious of the problems before they can be avoided, that, generally speaking, its policies are circumstantial.

This may be true of many countries, and the purpose of such a general model is precisely to be able to fit as well as possible the general pattern of evolution of the majority of countries in similar circumstances (here, the underdeveloped countries). But it does not seem to be so in Ghana. The sheer size and the type of infrastructual investments in Ghana, between 1951 and 1961, imply that the government had in mind, from the very beginning, a general program of modernization and of industrialization. Some indicators are given in the Seven-Year Development Plan. They show that the student population increased between 1951 and 1961 by more than 200 per cent in primary schools, 140 per cent in middle schools, almost 440 per cent in secondary schools, and almost 480 per cent in the universities. Roads of Class I were increased by 46 per cent, roads of Class II by almost 60 per cent. The government more than doubled its production of electricity without even taking into consideration the power to be produced by the Volta Dam, which in 1961 was not yet in service. Investment in the construction at Tema of the largest artificial harbor in Africa amounted to £27 million. Investments in health and other public utilities were just as large, but they did not necessarily represent more than a successful (and costly) program of social welfare.

At the same time, this does not mean that such a broad consciousness of the social and economic needs of the country may not have lacked depth and completeness. Indeed, as we have seen, it coexisted with some illusions concerning the importance of the tasks ahead, and the actual implications of implementing such a program. If we may risk an image, mixing two different types of literature on Ghana, we may say that the "Nkrumaist vision" of a modern Ghana was still somewhat "comatose" in the 1950's. The long period of the Dyarchy and the bitter power struggle diverted the attention of the CPP leaders from the economy at the same time as a relatively favorable economic conjuncture contributed to prolong the "comatose state."

The CPP Program for Work and Happiness and the Seven-Year Development Plan of Ghana were delayed until after 1961, but did not represent a fundamental departure from the policies of the government before this "crucial" year. Instead, they seemed to reflect a clearer awareness of the problems of development. The role of the state as well as that of foreign and local private initiative were clarified, but essentially all were to perform the same functions as before. Clarification, systematization, and acceleration, yes, but not an "agonizing reappraisal." 1961 was not the dividing line between two Ghanas: a procapitalist pre-1961 Ghana and a prosocialist post-1961 Ghana. There was basically only one strategy for economic development in Ghana—rather bold, vague, and empirical in the earlier years, still bold, but more precise and systematic after 1961. In the words of the CPP, the government, and the planners, it was a "socialist" strategy. However, our analyses show that this is a misleading interpretation.

NOTES

1. The Coussey Report contained proposals for internal self-government to be granted to the Gold Coast.

2. The second plan was never strictly implemented and was eventually abandoned after two years.

3. E.N. Omaboe, "The Process of Planning," *A Study of Contemporary Ghana*, ed. by W.B. Birmingham, I. Neustadt, and E.N. Omaboe (London: Allen and Unwin, 1966), I, chap. xviii, 452.

4. *Program of the Convention People's Party for Work and Happiness* (Accra: Government Printer, 1962), pars. 6-8.

5. *Ibid.*, pars. 16-21.

6. *Ibid.*, pars. 28-31.

7. *Ibid.*, par. 32.

8. *Ibid.*, pars. 55, 35, and 36.

9. *Ibid.*, par. 33.

10. *Ibid.*, par. 64.

11. It may be worthwhile comparing Paragraph 64 of the CPP Program of 1962 to the first two paragraphs of the first constitution of the CPP in 1949: "Self-Government Now and the development of [Ghana] on the basis of *socialism*. To fight relentlessly to achieve and maintain independence for the people of [Ghana] *and their chiefs*" (italics mine). *See also, infra*, Part II, Chapter 5.

12. *Program*, pars. 65-67 and 70.

13. *Ibid.*, par. 77.

14. *Ibid.*, pars. 88-89.

15. *Ibid.*, pars. 90-91.

16. *Ibid.*, pars. 103-109.

17. In point of fact, the *Program* does not say that this is to be a transitional period, but the *Seven-Year Development Plan* makes this point clear and suggests that the transitional period of mixed economy is to stretch over several "plans," i.e., probably fifteen to twenty years at least.

18. And this cannot be entirely accounted for by the fact that this was also the view of the colonial authorities.

19. Cf., *infra*, "The Two-Strategy Theory," in Chapter 3, in which the arguments of Fitch and Oppenheimer, who have fully developed this point, are discussed at some length. Cf., also "The Conventions People's Party" in Chapter 5.

20. Tony Killick, "Labor: A General Survey," *A Study of Contemporary Ghana*, I, chap. vi, 142-43.

21. *Program*, pars. 117-18.

22. *Ibid.*, pars. 119-22.

23. *Ibid.*, pars. 32-33.

24. *Ibid.*, par. 7.

25. The Seven-Year Development Plan was prepared by an all-Ghanaian commission (with the exception of Prof. J. Drewnosky, of the University of Ghana) under the chairmanship of J.H. Mensah. Most of the members of the commission were civil servants. A draft text of the Plan was submitted in April, 1963, to a panel of economists of international repute, from both socialist and Western countries, including Profs. Hirchman, W.A. Lewis, Kaldor, Dudley Seers, etc.

26. *See*, the public polemic between the party press and J.H. Mensah in August, 1964. Cf., in particular, *The Ghanaian Times*'s editorial of August 22, and Mensah's cyclostyled and widely circulated reply dated August 26.

27. The Plan had only begun to be implemented when, after the Coup of February 24, 1966, it was abandoned altogether.

28. Ghana, Office of the Planning Commission, *Seven-Year Plan for National Reconstruction and Development*, Financial Years 1963/64 — 1969/70 (Accra: Government Printer, 1964) p. 3.

29. "The alternative policy [to the one proposed in the Plan] would, in the long-run, leave Ghana with an economy dominated by an army of domestic servants, bootblacks, bureaucrats, and petty traders, and *most likely, an overblown military establishment* such as characterizes so many economies in the contemporary world which have been allowed to *develop along the wrong lines*" (italics mine). *Ibid.*, p. 11.

30. Robert Fitch and Mary Oppenheimer, "Ghana: End of an Illusion," *Monthly Review.* Vol. 18, No. 3 (Special Issue, July—August, 1966), p. 82.

31. *Ibid.*, p. 83.

32. *Ibid.*, p. 91.

33. *Ibid.*, p. 94.

34. *Ibid.*, pp. 83-84.

35. Fitch and Oppenheimer insist on the importance of making such a clear distinction between the Lewis period and the period after 1961, because

> by telescoping Ghanaian history into one horrendous 'socialistic-communistic dictatorship,' the NATO intellectuals are able to ignore the neo-colonial background from which Ghana tried to escape; they are not required to defend the embarrassing Lewis period...[and] by treating Ghanaian history as a monolith, it is possible to ignore entirely the reasons why Nkrumah at last tried to take a non-capitalist path. Instead, his increasingly bitter attacks on neo-colonialism can be discussed in psycho-pathological terms: 'paranoia,' 'love-hate relationship,' 'increasing megalomania,' 'transference,' etc. Finally, if all of Ghana's post-independence history was an experiment in socialism, and if that experiment failed, then it can be argued that socialism is really unworkable in Africa. *Ibid.*

36. Particularly in view of their reliance on guerilla warfare. See, *ibid.*, pp. 23-24 and 129-30.

37. Cf., *Groupe d'études et d'action socialiste tunisien, Les caractéristiques de la période actuelle du développement de la Tunisie et les instruments de la Révolution arabe,* (Paris?, 1967?).

38. Fitch and Oppenheimer, p. 19.

39. *Ibid.*, pp. 21-24.

40. Fitch-Oppenheimer go so far as to argue that this decision of the CPP

> had repercussions on independence movements throughout Africa, especially in British West Africa. Arden-Clarke's 'act-of-grace' (Nkrumah was elected when still purging his time in prison for having started Positive Action) in freeing Nkrumah from prison began to take on the same significance for African nationalists that Dien

Bienphu would soon gain for Asian nationalists—
both marked the end of European colonial power
and indicated a specific means for achieving
power.

Ibid., p. 35.

41. *Ibid.*, p. 82.

42. *Ibid.*, p. 127.

43. Fitch and Oppenheimer almost completely dismiss the problem, and for all practical purposes, equate "tribe-baiting" in Ghana to "red-baiting" in the U.S.! Cf., *ibid.*, p. 58.

44. Hassan Riad, *"Les trois âges de la société égyptienne" Partisans* (Paris), No. 7 (1962), p. 38.

45. Most of the above and following data concerning the election in Ghana has been taken from: Dennis Austin, *Politics in Ghana: 1946-1960* (London: Oxford University Press, 1964).

46. The slight discrepancy with figures sometimes given about the 1954 election (e.g., Apter) is due to the fact that 4 elected independent candidates joined the NPP (3) and the CPP (1) after the election. The results of the election are therefore either 16 Independents, 12 NPP, and 71 CPP, or 12 Independents, 15 NPP, and 72 CPP.

47. Thomas Hodgkin, *African Political Parties* (London: Penguin Books, 1961), p. 21.

48. Cf., among others the "scandal" of the Cocoa Purchasing Company—Krobo Edusei's all too famous "atomic bomb of the CPP."

49. Austin, *Politics in Ghana*, pp. 384-85.

50. Habib Bourguiba, Speech, November 18, 1961.

51. Austin, *Politics in Ghana*, p. 162. Cf., Article VIII: "To establish a socialist state in which all men and women shall have equal opportunity and where there shall be no capitalist exploitation."

52. *Ibid.*, p. 130.

53. *Ibid.*, p. 137.

54. *Ibid.*, p. 138.

55. *Ibid.*, p. 226.

56. *Ibid.*, p. 227.

57. The NLM manifesto was significantly entitled: "Why should you vote for cocoa?" and a cocoa tree was chosen as a national emblem by the NLM. *Ibid.*, pp. 330-31.

58. What the opposition might have done after, if and when in power, is obviously an open question. But what matters here is that economic policies, or strategies of development, were not the central issues of the election, or for that matter, of the power struggle.

59. Fitch and Oppenheimer, "Ghana: End of an Illusion," p. 55.

60. Dudley Seers, "The Stages of Economic Development of a Primary Producer in the Middle of the Twentieth Century," *Economic Bulletin of Ghana* (Accra), VII, 4 (1963).

61. These figures, as well as those given in the next two paragraphs, are drawn from: Ghana, Central Bureau of Statistics, *Economic Survey 1964* (Accra: Government Printer, 1965).

62. "Any theory of development must attempt to incorporate such factors (social and political)—a purely economic growth model is of very limited usefulness." Dudley Seers, "The Stages of Economic Development," p. 59.

63. There are five stages in Seers's model:

I(a)   the open economy in its pure form;
I(b)   the open economy under stress;
II(a) the closed economy: the period of easy import substitution;
II(b) the closed economy: the phase of difficult import substitution; and
III(a) export diversification.

Ghana, according to this Seers model had reached Stage I (b) in about 1955, and Stage II (a) around 1961. *Ibid.*, p. 68.

64. *Ibid.*, pp. 57-58.

65. *Ibid.*, p. 58.

66. *Ibid.*, p. 59.

67. *Ibid.*

68. *Ibid.*, p. 60.

69. *Ibid.* Although the scope of import substitution remained quite modest.

70. In fact, the nationalization of five gold mines in Ghana was precisely those mines which could no longer be run profitably by the private companies. T. Killick, in the chapter of *A Study of Contemporary Ghana*, devoted to labor and wages, insists on the importance of wages paid in mines as a basis for all industrial wages. Because such wages could not be raised much higher at such a level of productivity, the resistance of mining interests acted as a powerful deterrent to wage increases in the industrial sector as a whole.

71. Dudley Seers, "The Stages of Economic Development," p. 60.

72. As opposed to the very vague and happy notions about industrialization and the industrial society common until then. Cf., a CPP election manifesto asking Ghanaians to vote for Nkrumah "to make the Gold Coast a paradise so that when the gates of heaven are opened by Peter, we shall sit in heaven and see our children driving their aeroplanes, commanding their own armies," reproduced in *The Evening News*, July 13, 1956, quoted in Austin, *Politics in Ghana*, p. 334.

73. Dudley Seers, p. 61.

74. *Ibid.*, pp. 61-62.

75. If we were to accept Fanon's model, as expressed in *Les damnés de la terre* (Paris: Maspéro, 1961), we would make a restriction for those countries which became independent as a result of a long and violent liberation struggle, particularly for those which won their independence after a full-fledged war of liberation. In such countries, there should be almost no illusion at all, and the period of the war of liberation should have taken care of the power struggle. Unfortunately for the model, the post-independence history of Algeria is far from confirming Fanon's theoretical assumptions. The power struggle started immediately, on the day of independence, with the "Frontiers' army" on one side (Ahmed ben Bella), and the "maquisards" *(willayas* III and V) on the other (ex-GPRA: [*Gouvernement provisoire de la*

république algérienne] and President Benyussef ben Khedda). Furthermore, in the summer of 1962, both sides allowed the struggle in Algeria to develop without any reference to the fundamental political or economic issues of the time, both sides protesting their fidelity to the Tripoli Program (which, besides, almost no one in Algeria had yet had a chance to see).

76. This had also been expressed by E.N. Omaboe who remarked that the plan "is an attempt to break with the old method of the 'shopping-list'," but also insists on the fact that

> firstly, it could be claimed that the Seven-Year Plan is the first *real* plan which sets out the policies and objectives of the CPP Government. The first plan had already been prepared when the CPP came into power in 1951. Although the second plan was introduced in 1959, two years after the attainment of independence, it could be said with some degree of justification that, in 1959, the Government had not been able to break with the past. This came after the institution of a republican form of government in July, 1960, when the Government took some radical decisions which Ghanaianized the top posts of the civil service. By the time the Seven-Year Plan was launched in 1964, political independence had been forcibly asserted in many ways, both domestically and internationally. The plan is therefore the first true reflection of the economic and social objectives of the CPP.

See, *A Study of Contemporary Ghana*, p. 452.

77. Dudley Seers, "The Stages of Economic Development," p. 69.

PART **II**

PROBLEMS OF IMPLEMENTATION:
THE POLICY OF EQUILIBRIUM

One does not have to be for or against Upper Volta or the Central African Republic, but the case of Ghana is different. Under Nkrumah, one was for or against Ghana. And the question is still debated. Somehow, the debate on Ghana was, and is, an extension of the more general debate for or against socialism. Since the fall of Nkrumah, the debate includes, as already mentioned, a subquestion: Was Nkrumah's Ghana a socialist experience? The purpose of the following pages is to suggest that such a debate, including its subquestion, is almost totally irrelevant, and is essentially due to the extrapolation of non-African analyses to contemporary situations in Africa.

To discuss these fifteen years (1951-66) in terms of a "socialist experience" leads to a series of insuperable contradictions or simply leads nowhere. The problem has to be examined in its historical context, which is anticolonial nationalism in Africa. In other words, after 1951 and, even more so, after 1957, the problem was one of giving economic and, more generally, concrete content to nationalism *after* independence. This posed economic and political problems.

However, it is obvious that, up to a point, the Government of Ghana and the CPP are partly responsible for this confusion as they repeatedly described their policies in terms of a transition to socialism.

In the Constitution of the CPP drawn up in 1949 and approved by the Second Annual Conference of the Party at Ho in Southern Togoland in August, 1951, the words "socialism" and "socialist" are mentioned three times in the national, and once, in the international "aims and objects" of the party. In view of what we have already said about the electoral platforms of the CPP in 1951, 1954, and 1956, we may conclude that if the socialist objectives of the party were allowed to lapse between 1951 and 1961, this was due only to (unfavorable) circumstances. The party had to put up with the limitations set upon itself by

121

the Dyarchy and the struggle for power with the opposition, and thus, it could not immediately implement its fundamental objectives which were socialist. As soon as it had a chance (after the elimination of all opposition), it turned back to the old program and tried to put it into practice. This formal analysis is basically the one proposed by the CPP officialdom in the 1960's. A diametrically opposed one is that proposed by Fitch and Oppenheimer: The CPP never was a socialist party, and, if and when it came to resort to some form of socialist planning techniques and policies, this was only under the pressure of economic circumstances, when clearly enough the liberal policies of the "Lewis era" had failed. Neither of these contrasted analyses is satisfactory in the sense that neither takes sufficiently into consideration what Dudley Seers refers to as the "typically comatose state" in which the leaders of the nationalist parties find themselves at the time of independence. Both assume that the party leadership is perfectly clear about its objectives from the very beginning.

We have already, in our previous chapter, given some reasons to believe that this assumption should be abandoned and that it is more realistic to discuss the evolution of the party's doctrines and policies during the first postindependence period in terms of the interplay of opposed variables. Some of these (e.g., the power struggle) tend to delay a real *prise de conscience* of the problems of development, while others (e.g., the stress on the economy) tend to accelerate it. These analyses are not satisfactory inasmuch as they discuss what in the final analysis amounts to a minor point—a definition of the phenomenon by analogy, not the phenomenon itself. They discuss the fifteen years between 1951 and 1966 not in their historical context (nationalism) but as they are reflected in the ideological mirror of universal contemporary political thought (socialism). Thus, it is only incidentally that they happen to be relevant, that they throw a useful light on one aspect or another of this experience.

With this in mind, we find it more logical to postpone a discussion of the "socialist content" of the Nkrumah-CPP Government until after we have considered the economic and political problems posed directly to the Party and Government by the "Ghanaian Way," i.e., by the implementation of an intermediate strategy of development.

CHAPTER **4** ECONOMIC PROBLEMS
AND PERFORMANCE

The economic problem confronting the Nkrumah-CPP
Government after independence can, for the purpose of this
study, be reduced to a few fundamental questions and,
similarly, the success of the "Ghanaian Way" could be
said to depend on the ability of the Nkrumah-CPP
Government to solve these questions. Inasmuch as the
main objectives of the "Ghanaian Way" under Nkrumah
were to attain development and socialism by way of a
mixed economy in which the state was to play an
increasingly important role, but in which both foreign and
domestic private capital and entrepreneurship were also
to develop (the strategy), the practical problems confronting
the government were tactical—problems of implementation.
How did the Nkrumah-CPP Government go about it? How
did they manage to control the reorientation of the economy
which is implied by such a program? How did they manage
to resolve the contradictions and tensions inherent to any
mixed economy—and particularly in a mixed economy where
one of the elements (the public sector) is supposed to
gradually "surpass" the others (the foreign private sector
and the domestic private sector)? Which social and political
forces did they seek to enlist in support of such policies?
And how?

ATTEMPTS TO RECAPTURE CONTROL
OF THE ECONOMY

The first of these questions concerns the control of
the government over the economy, for obviously, without
such control the orientation or reorientation, not to speak
of development and socialist objectives, would elude the
the government. The problem of economic controls may be
looked at in many different ways. Among others, there is
the one suggested by T. Killick who raises the possibility
of exercising economic control on the type of economy such
as that of Ghana, i.e., the economy of a dependent,
underdeveloped country.[1] This type of analysis is
interesting in that it discusses the problem of development
in practical terms: how to get the economy under control
and how to reorient its development in the direction
decided by the government. It is a technical, economic
analysis. But it only goes to show that the possibilities of
controlling the economy of Ghana were extremely limited,
in the sense that the dependence of Ghana was not only
on some countries and certain interests, but also, more
generally, and typically of the economy of underdeveloped
countries, it was a dependence resulting from the very
structures of the economy. It may be described either in
terms of fragility or dependence on overpowering external
factors and decisions. Another limitation of such analyses
is that they concentrate on stability rather than growth—not
to speak of development. This is well illustrated by the
Seers-Ross Report[2] which, at the beginning of a period of
extraordinary expansion, nonetheless stated in its
much-quoted opening sentence: "If we were forced to sum
up the Gold Coast economy in one word, the word we would
choose would be 'Fragile'." The Seers-Ross Report was
mostly, at the time, concerned with the proneness of the

Ghana economy to inflationary forces, but Killick thinks that, in the mid-1960's, he "may adopt their term—fragility —for a rather more general usage, to draw attention to the general tendency of the economy towards instability." [3]

> First and foremost, there are the large fluctuations in the earnings that Ghana derives from her cocoa exports. . . . Partly as a result of the unreliability of cocoa tax revenues, the general government budgetary balance is unpredictable. Other exporting industries are also subject to widely fluctuating earnings, most notably the diamond, manganese and logging industries. As is the case in most economies with a large private sector, the volume of private investment is also a volatile element. . . . Then there is the instability that stems from the very great importance in the domestic flow of goods and services of local foodstuffs, which comprises over 40 per cent of total private consumption. . . . . . The effects of these destabilizing forces show up in a number of ways. For one thing they affect the price level. A study of month-by-month price changes for the last ten years indicates a seasonal variation superimposed on the general upward trend. . . . Instability is reflected also in the rather drastic changes that are liable to occur in the balance of payments from one year to the next, in the substantial changes that occur in the numbers of unemployed from one month to the next and in the erratic pattern of growth of the Gross Domestic Product. [4]

In view of the above, Killick insists on "the great difficulty that must be experienced in exercising control over Ghana's economy, especially since most of the sources of instability are external. . . . With many of the crucial variables so subject to short-term change, long-term economic policy will be both more difficult to formulate and to enforce." [5] And "the policy weapons that are available for the control of the economy appear slight in relation to the magnitude of the job they would have to do." [6]

This may be so, but, after all is said, one is left with the truism that a country is dependent as long as its economy is that of a dependent country. Or that the road to economic development and economic independence is difficult, and that the state does not have much at its disposal to effect the necessary structural changes at the same time as it aims at increasing the rate of growth of the gross national product (GNP). All this is well-known and simply means that one should not expect rapid and striking results. Beyond this elementary truth, there still remains the problem of controlling what can be controlled. And this brings us to another way of looking at the problem, a more political one such as that which may be implied by Fitch and Oppenheimer when they say that it is only at a very late stage that Ghana tried to "bring the British banks under some degree of control." There is no doubt that it is useful to know that in Ghana, like in any underdeveloped country, the inherited instruments of economic control are not many and not very effective, but such instruments do exist, and moreover, there are at least some areas where something may be done, especially with regard to that aspect of the country's economic dependence which is clearly linked with identifiable foreign elements, such as the well-known and overwhelming economic and trade dependence of Ghana on her traditional Western partners.

What did Ghana do about this? How did the government attempt to recapture and create the instruments of control of the economy? And how did they try to establish a new and better balance among the country's economic and trading partners?

Formally, in 1957 and in the course of the following years, the Government of Ghana did recapture control of the economy. A banking system was created, including a Central Bank and the Ghana Commercial Bank, the latter established with the obvious purpose of competing with the well-entrenched foreign institutions operating in Ghana, Barclays Bank and the Bank of West Africa. In 1961, exchange controls as well as import controls were eventually introduced through the much-criticized import license system.[7] One of the large foreign import and retail firms, Leventis, was acquired by the government. It was renamed Ghana National Trading Corporation (GNTC) and could be said to represent an additional instrument for control of the flows and prices of imported goods on the local markets. A Capital Investment Act in 1963[8] completed this set of tools at the disposal of the Government of Ghana to control the external economic relations of the country. At this point, it must be emphasized that Ghana has no claim to originality or particular firmness as far as these instruments of control of the economy are concerned; a number of other African independent countries have taken similar steps. In truth, it could be said rather that Ghana did not seem to be in any great hurry to recapture such instruments of control of her economy, and that the acquisition of Leventis stores (GNTC) or the creation of a Ghana Commercial Bank to compete with foreign stores (Kingsway, Union Trading Company, *Compagnie française de l'afrique occidentale,* etc.) or with foreign banks (Barclays and Bank of West Africa) only represented an indirect type of state intervention and control. Again, the attitude of the government seems an intermediate one, one of "surpassing" the private, mostly foreign, sector rather than one of replacing it through nationalization or any other form of expropriation.

The impact of such measures could be felt in the later years, particularly after 1963; but at the end of the period under review, it was still rather difficult to say whether these were effective enough to assist in the implementation of the plan's objectives. Partly because at least some of the above measures had been taken only at a rather late stage, and also because, for one, the import policy (a vital enough element though) was still not quite clear. Indeed, it lacked clarity to the point that as late as a few weeks before Nkrumah was overthrown, the party's theoretical weekly paper, *The Spark*, could devote a long and devastating article to the policy of the Ministry of Trade.[9] Moreover, at the level of implementation, the general economic policy itself was not all that clear. This could, *inter alia*, be seen in the absence of centralization of economic power. The Planning Commission, the Ministry of Trade, the Ministry of Finance, and, last but not least, the Office of President, all represented separate centers of economic decisions. Such a fragmentation of power could hardly go on without affecting the efficiency and coherence of Ghana's economic policies. In this sense, Julius Sagoe's article in *The Spark*, inasmuch as it reflected the frustrations of the leftist "ideological wing" of the party, perhaps did not even go far enough in its criticism of this peculiar state of affairs.

All in all, the Ghanaian Government could be said to have eventually begun to recapture most of the instruments of control of the economy, at least as far as external relations are concerned; but at the same time, it could also be said that it had not yet succeeded in reintegrating them into a comprehensive, coherent, and effective system. Competition among ministers as well as a rather high rate of change in ministries, involving both ministers and principal secretaries (with a few exceptions, especially in the Office of the President), did not help either.

Indeed, there was at least one variable on which the government had, or could have had, control, and that was its own policies, not only as they are expressed in the Plan (strategy), but also, more prosaically, as they are reflected in the day-to-day implementation.

This was put rather bluntly by E.N. Omaboe, Government Statistician and now the principal economic adviser to the Army and Police Junta in Accra: "It appears from the course of events since 1951 that the authorities have never been able to stick to the order of priority which the development plans have provided." [10] In a few pages, Omaboe expresses the views of the civil service, i.e., of a bureaucracy repeatedly and publicly requested to "change its mentality" by the party, but, which at the same time, always felt somewhat left out of the major economic decisions concerning the country. We shall have more to say about the civil service later on, but at this point, it is worth mentioning these remarks by Omaboe inasmuch as they make up the best-phrased document concerning the grievances of the civil service vis-à-vis the policies of economic development of the Nkrumah-CPP Government before February 24, 1966. Omaboe reproaches the government for its inability to accept constraints and choices, in other words, to want too much at the same time. But there is more:

> The second reason for the Government's inability to keep to development plans lies in the differences of approach towards development projects which have developed between the politicians on the one side and the technicians and civil servants on the other side. In Ghana, the politicians are always ahead of the civil servants and the planners in the general consideration and implementation of economic and social projects. This has meant that almost all important projects have had to be initiated by the politicians who on many occasions have taken their decisions and committed the nation to a certain course of action before the technicians were consulted. The ideal would be either for the politicians to refer these matters to the technicians for study before a commitment is entered into or for the technicians to move with the politicians and be in a position to

provide them with alternatives from which they should
make their choice. This has not been so and the
civil servants have therefore struggled hard to catch
up with the politicians. [11]

As a result of this analysis, which today would
probably be much less cautious and even more unfavorable
to the politicians, Omaboe concludes: "There is therefore
an urgent need for the centralization in one body of all
decisions relating to the implementation of a development
plan." [12] Here is at least one technical conclusion on
which most observers of the Ghanaian scene until 1966
would easily agree. Although in view of the fact that the
"politicians" really meant Nkrumah himself, particularly
in the last years, it may be that all that Omaboe actually
tried to say was that it would be better for the Plan if its
implementation were completely left to the planners, or
that it would be better if Nkrumah were to be advised on
these matters by the planners alone. Whatever the real
intention of this text, what is certain is that the Nkrumah
Government was always capable of planning ahead
ambitiously, but was extremely reluctant to accept any
constraints and to clearly decide priorities. And there was
very little that the planners could do about it, or anybody
else for that matter.

THE FAILURE TO BALANCE
GHANA'S TRADING PARTNERS

However, even if controls had been more coherent and
stringent, this would not have, *ipso facto,* solved the
problem of Ghana's trade and economic dependence on a
few countries, especially the U.K. and the U.S. To achieve
this, the neutralist policy of Ghana should have found its

logical counterpart in foreign trade and economic and financial relations. Taking as a starting point, Ghana's overwhelming dependence on the West, which absorbed almost all her exports and supplied almost all the external source of finance for her development projects, it may be assumed that Ghana should have tried to develop her trade and economic relations with the socialist countries in such a way as to reduce as much, and as rapidly as possible, her dependence on the West. Such a reorientation of Ghana's trade and economic relations was even more important in that Ghana's economy was more fragile than many in Africa—cocoa as her essential source of foreign receipts (about 60 per cent). On this point, and despite late improvements, Ghana was not entirely successful, to say the least. Two examples will suffice as illustrations.

The first example concerns the evolution of Ghana's total trade with the socialist countries[13] as compared to her total foreign trade.

TABLE 4
TRADE WITH SOCIALIST COUNTRIES
(Millions of Pound Sterling)

	1960	1964
Imports from socialist countries, Israel, etc.	6.5	22.
Total Ghana imports	129.6	121.6
Exports to the socialist countries, Israel, etc.	5.8	15.
Total Ghana exports	115.9	114.6

Source: Ghana, Central Bureau of Statistics, *Economic Survey 1964* (Accra: Government Printer, 1965).

The development of Ghana's trade with her new partners is obvious, but comes rather late, and is still insufficient to free the country from its trade dependence on traditional partners. In 1960, total trade (exports and imports) with these countries (£12.3 million) did not quite amount to as much as that year's trade deficit (£13.6 million). Between 1960 and 1964, imports from the new trading partners increased more rapidly than Ghana's exports to them.

The second example points to an even more preoccupying problem, the extreme difficulty of finding an alternative market for Ghana's cocoa. The evolution of the U.S.S.R. imports of Ghanaian cocoa from 1955 to 1964 will provide a clear illustration of this point.

TABLE 5

EXPORTS OF COCOA TO THE U.S.S.R.

(Thousands of Tons)

	1955	1956	1957	1958	1959	1960	1961	1962	1963	1964
Total export	204	233	259	195	252	297	406	423	404	382
Exports to the U.S.S.R.	13	9	36	1	8	34	19	25	43	33

Source: Ghana, Central Bureau of Statistics, *Economic Survey 1964* (Accra: Government Printer, 1965).

As can be seen, imports from the Soviet Union did not increase very rapidly or significantly with the share in total Ghanaian exports of cocoa for the last year below ten per cent. Besides, Soviet imports of Ghanaian cocoa varied enormously from year to year, moving from 1957 to 1960 from 36 to 1, then to 8, and finally to 34,000 tons. Taking into consideration that the world cocoa price each year is more or less determined by the size of world demand and supply, and taking into consideration the difficulty of stocking large quantities of cocoa in the producing countries, the irregularity as well as the small quantities of cocoa sold to the U.S.S.R. illustrate quite clearly that Ghana's trade with the socialist countries, and her other new partners, had not permitted Ghana to reduce significantly her trade dependence on her traditional partners—the Western countries.

To be sure, Ghana is not entirely responsible for this relative failure; some of the responsibility must be placed on the relative lack of flexibility of the Soviet trading methods and organizations. In addition, the small size of Ghana and the limited variety of her export production (problems of payments), on the one hand, as well as the already rather sophisticated level of consumption in Ghana (quality and variety), on the other hand, did constitute serious obstacles to the development of trade between Ghana and the socialist countries. On the contrary, it is quite clear that the U.S.S.R. supplied a valuable assistance in infrastructure and research (especially geology and nuclear energy). To identify Ghana's responsibility for such negative results, one may point out the lack of knowledge and interest in the markets and economic development of the socialist countries, perhaps a certain amount of reluctance on the part of some civil servants, but above all, as already mentioned from a more general point of view, the defective import license system, and the almost completely separated activities of the ministries of Finance, Trade, and the Planning Commission.

FOREIGN INVESTMENTS AND NEOCOLONIALISM

The second question is that of the role of foreign private investments. In a way, it is again a question of economic control, in this case, control of what has sometimes been described as "internal foreign decisions," i.e., decisions taken by firms established in the country but which are based on interests foreign to the country.

The question may be touched very briefly in view of the nature of investments in Ghana during the period under review, as these were mostly supplied by the Ghanaian Government in the early years and mostly directed to infrastructural projects. Theoretically, the problem posed by such investments is that they might eventually introduce serious distortions in the economic development of the country; foreign private capital is not necessarily, and not usually, attracted by the same type of projects as are needed for the country's general development. The argument is classic and it may not be necessary to enter a full discussion at this point, for in the case of Ghana during the postindependence period, one may safely say that new industrial investments certainly did not pose such problems. It is rather their insignificance or their absence that should be noted. In the later years when fairly large flows of private capital could be attracted, mostly in the form of suppliers' credits, again the problem was not one of possible distortions in the economic development of the country, but rather one of repayment of hard loans.[14] We shall return to this point later.

In point of fact, while a lot of noise is being made about the danger—economic and political—represented by foreign private investments in Africa (neocolonialism), what really appears on closer examination is the general insignificance of such investments. Investments during the colonial period, as is well-known, only ensured such limited developments as were necessary for the commercialization of the colonies' primary production. Now new, postindependence investments seem quite inadequate to make a real process of industrialization possible. There seems to be a great confusion on this question as far as

Africa is concerned at the moment, and this may be partly explained by the fact that there are not many concrete examples to analyze. However, the problem deserves attention since no, or almost no, country in Africa seems to be in a position to tackle the problems of its economic development or industrialization without having to rely on foreign capital—both public and private.

Without entering a full discussion, one may say that, theoretically, insofar as foreign investments are being channeled toward those projects and sectors for which the Plan has made priorities, one should not fear serious distortions in the development, nor should one fear a strengthening of the "colonial" structures of the economy as a direct result of such investments. The combined use of a Code of Foreign Capital Investment and the Plan should constitute an adequate instrument for directing foreign investments toward priority projects and sectors, and by and large, bring such investments in line with the general strategy of development. Similarly, repatriation of profits and capital is not a blind mechanism; in any case, a ceiling may be fixed in such a way as to make each investment a profitable operation for the country. To approach the problem in any other way simply means that one does not want foreign private investments, and then it is something entirely different, another choice, which as yet no African country has made, regardless of what was being said at the time in the press of Guinea, Algeria, Ghana, and other "revolutionary" countries in Africa.

In reality, a survey of the distribution of foreign investments in Africa would show that, with the exception of countries rich in oil deposits or in strategic or other precious minerals (such as Zambia's or Mauritania's copper), such investments are neither many nor important. Moreover, they are concentrated in a few, mostly coastal, places (for example, in the Ivory Coast for a few years), but almost completely neglect the landlocked countries of the interior, whatever their political regimes. The economic criterion apparently used tends to reinforce the existing and contrasted relative situations of the coast and the interior to the detriment of the savannah. From this point of view, it is true that if the process of industrialization were essentially to be the result of private foreign investments, it might well tend, in the long-run, to prolong and reinforce the pattern of development already started during the colonial period.

New industries (new and progressive elements in themselves) are located mostly in centers and towns (often port-towns) already developed during the colonial period in the framework of the exploitation and commercialization of the colonies' primary production. Such a pattern of development would imply, in the long-run, a considerable movement of population (with a tendency to proletarization) from the interior to the coastal centers, as has already been the case, though on a limited scale, since the beginning of the postwar period (e.g., Upper Volta migrants to Ghana and the Ivory Coast, both in agriculture and mines). In other words, such a pattern of development would result in distortions, though not necessarily economic (the process of a real industrialization not being necessarily called in question), but geographical, and not within the limits of one single country, but at the level of a whole region (for example, West Africa).

A government may well give its approval to, or turn down, any particular investment and thus, more or less, control the orientation of the country's economic development, but it may not, of course, compel reluctant foreign investors to invest. Such a development would be almost entirely dictated by the criterion of comparative private profitability of individual projects. Such a pattern could perhaps be altered by a huge foreign public assistance (such as, but on a larger scale, that of the French Government in former French colonies), but it could certainly not reverse the pattern completely. Besides, in the case of Ghana, for example, the choice of the Accra-Tema-Akosombo triangle as the main pole of industrialization seems also to indicate that, even when development decisions are taken by national planners, the very same elements of comparative costs and benefits and external economies play a prominent role.

There remains the case of a country like Ghana. Situated on the coast, having, by African standards, a remarkably well-developed infrastructure, and thus presenting, compared to its neighbors, the advantage of important external economies, Ghana by and large was in a relatively favorable situation; nonetheless, it did not attract much foreign investment.

Such an apparent contradiction can only be explained, so it would seem, in terms of the political options for Ghana. If this is the case, what should be inferred from it? It is a rather delicate question, but to answer it one must probably return to the problem of Ghana's economic dependence on the West. Had Ghana been able to balance better her economic relations with the rest of the world, viz., had the socialist countries eventually come to represent a real alternative, absorbing more Ghanaian exports, supplying more loans and other facilities, it may well have been that the attitude of Western capital (both private and public) might have been altered in favor of Ghana. In this sense, one may wonder whether Ghana was not, in the last analysis, the victim of its own inability to free itself from its economic dependence on the West, rather than the victim of its official choice of a "socialist path of development." A pro-Western, nonsocialist Ghana might have attracted more private foreign investments than a neutralist Ghana such as Nkrumah's Ghana, but a neutralist

Ghana which would have managed with the assistance of the socialist countries to free itself from its overwhelming dependence on its traditional Western partners might have attracted even more foreign capital, perhaps with a different composition. In any case, a rather weak neutralist country, unable to balance better its economic partners, represented the worst possible bargaining position.

In sum, the economic danger implied by this intermediate "Ghanaian Way" seemed, before February 24, 1966, to be far more precisely a danger of not being able to attract enough foreign capital (public or private) than the hypothetical danger that foreign investments might introduce distortions in the economic development of the country. Besides, it seems than Ghanaian planners were aware of it, since they had only earmarked a total of £100 million for foreign private investments out of a grand total of more than £1 billion for total investments during the seven-year plan period.[15] On the contrary, the share foreseen for private domestic investments (from capital held by both Ghanaians and expatriates living *in* Ghana) may seem to be rather high, with a total of £400 million for the seven years, particularly if one bears in mind the increasing fiscal pressure in Ghana during those years and also the tendency to resort increasingly to public borrowing. Lastly, it may be thought that the government might well have been able to obtain, despite the difficulties of 1965, from various public sources, a total of about £200 million in loans. As the experience was interrupted after two years, it is hardly possible or useful to discuss this particular question any further.

MARGINAL IMPROVEMENTS IN PERFORMANCE

At this point, the question of performance should be raised. Did Ghana after all succeed in implementing its strategy? Did Nkrumah and the CPP during their fifteen years in power manage to improve the situation of Ghana? We have already, incidentally, seen that, despite their efforts, they could only marginally reduce the economic and trade dependence of Ghana on her traditional partners. The disastrous effect of the fall in cocoa prices on Ghana's financial position shows that they did not manage, or did not have time, to do much about the structures of the economy which remained predominantly monocultural and export-oriented. Moreover, the labor content of Ghana's exports had not yet been meaningfully increased when Nkrumah was overthrown.

From the above, it would seem that the economic policies of the Nkrumah-CPP Government were but a long exercise in futility, and that the whole experience— considering the present financial position of the country and Nkrumah's overthrow—ended in a failure. But here one may be reminded of the extreme difficulty of exercising controls on an economy such as that of Ghana. For a more sober appraisal of Ghana's performance, it may thus be useful, before concluding, to look briefly at such other indicators that are available. The best source is the already mentioned *Study of Contemporary Ghana* which supplies information and data on the middle period, 1955-62. [16] This data, starting four years after, and ending four years before the period under review (1951-66), does not reveal the whole picture, but it indicates the trend. It should be adequate for our purpose here.

It is only too well-known that the rate of growth of the gross domestic product (GDP) is quite inadequate to seriously prove or disprove anything concerning the real development of a former colony, at least in the early years after independence. However, we may mention the evolution of Ghana's GDP here as a first and very broad indicator.

TABLE 6

GROSS DOMESTIC PRODUCT 1955-62

(At Current and Constant Prices)

	1955	1956	1957	1958	1959	1960	1961	1962
At current prices	334	345	363	383	435	*469*	497	535
At constant (1960) prices	355	376	388	382	433	*469*	476	492

Source: Walter B. Birmingham, I. Neustadt, and E.N. Omaboe, eds., *A Study of Contemporary Ghana*, Vol. I: *The Economy of Ghana* (London: Allen & Unwin, 1966), chap. ii.

TABLE 7

GROSS DOMESTIC PRODUCT 1955-64

(Indexes)

1955	1956	1957	1958	1959	1960	1961	1962	1963	1964
100	106	109	108	122	132	134	139		
	5.9	3.2	1.5	13.4	8.3	1.5	3.4	*	
					7.5	3.2	5.3	2.7	4.5**

Sources: *Walter B. Birmingham, I. Neustadt, and E.N. Omaboe, eds., *A Study of Contemporary Ghana*, Vol. I: *The Economy of Ghana* (London: Allen & Unwin, 1966), chap. ii.

**Ghana, Central Bureau of Statistics, *Economic Survey 1964* (Accra: Government Printer, 1965).

The evolution of the GDP reveals first a most erratic course (cf., the rate of growth of 1958 and 1959, or 1959 and 1961). Second, it shows an average compound rate of growth over the eight-year period (1955-62) of 4.8 per cent. As an indicator of real growth (constant prices) it is rather high.[17] The same at current prices would show a much faster rate of growth but it would be a misrepresentation because of the rising prices during this period. However, the rate of growth at constant (1960) prices is also somewhat misleading, since it does not (by definition) take into account the evolution of prices in a period of rapid fall in cocoa prices (a fall which directly affected the global resources of Ghana). It may also be noted that with the approximate rate of growth of the population between 2.5 and 2.6 per cent, the rate of growth per capita is more or less halved when compared to that of the GDP. At £60 per capita in 1955, it reaches £69 in 1962 (£70 in 1960). Relative to other African countries, this is still a good performance: Nigeria, £29; Tanzania, £21; Zambia, £65; Rhodesia, £75; but U.K., £477; and U.S., £993. [18]

Samir Amin [19] considers this period as "Ghana's second great period of development" (between 1954 and 1962/63) and indicates a rate of growth of 5.5 to 6.0 per cent in Ghana between 1955 and 1963, which is a higher figure than that given by Szereszewski (4.8 per cent), but practically the same if Amin's rate is not compound. In any case, by African standards, this is a fairly high rate of growth at the time. According to Amin, the Ivory Coast was the only country in West Africa during those years which had a comparable rate of growth (6 to 7 per cent). And the same author concludes: "These are exceptionally high rates of growth in Africa, if one leaves aside those countries with a large mining production for which rates of growth become completely meaningless. Ghana's rate of growth is all the more impressive in that Ghana's development is older" [when compared to that of the Ivory Coast]. [20]

Lastly, it may be useful to compare Ghana's average rate of growth (4.8 per cent) during these years to that foreseen by Ghanaian planners for the period of the Seven-Year Development Plan: 5.5 per cent.

During the same years, the table of gross domestic

expenditure shows a nonparallel evolution of three main components, public consumption and gross capital formation increasing much faster than private consumption:

TABLE 8

EVOLUTION OF

GROSS DOMESTIC EXPENDITURE 1955-62

(Main Components)

	1955	(indexes)	1962
Private consumption	100		120
Public consumption	100		162
Gross capital formation	100		153

Source: Walter B. Birmingham, I. Neustadt, and E.N. Omaboe, eds., *A Study of Contemporary Ghana*, Vol. I: *The Economy of Ghana* (London: Allen & Unwin, 1966), chap. ii.

What we know of the later years, after 1962, suggests that the diverging evolution of private consumption, on the one hand, and public consumption and capital formation, on the other hand, was maintained and even accentuated, with all the risks of socio-economic tensions which such a trend implied. Such a policy of diverting resources from private consumption toward public consumption and capital formation may be considered dangerous and unpopular. Indeed, it was—as is any policy of austerity that cannot be identified easily and immediately as a historical necessity (e.g., war effort and war restrictions). At the same time and at another level, it would appear to confirm the claim of the Nkrumah-CPP Government that they were actually committed to a serious policy of development.

However, the breakdown of capital formation into its main components does not entirely confirm this impression:

TABLE 9

CAPITAL FORMATION: 1955, 1962, and 1964

(Percentages)

	1955*	1962*	1964**
Building	51.9	55.2	46.6
Other constructions	23.1	21.9	26.7
Transport equipment	11.5	10.4	11.2
Machines and equipment	13.5	12.5	15.5
Total	100.0	100.0	100.0

Sources: *Walter B. Birmingham, I. Neustadt, and E.N. Omaboe, eds., *A Study of Contemporary Ghana*, Vol. I: *The Economy of Ghana* (London: Allen & Unwin, 1966), chap. ii.

**Ghana, Central Bureau of Statistics, *Economic Survey 1964* (Accra: Government Printer, 1965).

As a first conclusion based on the examination of the above indicators, the rate of growth was still rather high, but showed a tendency to decrease. (From 1961 to 1964, whether one takes Szereszewski's figures or those supplied by the Economic Survey 1964, the rate of growth was almost always inferior to the average rate between 1955 and 1962). Toward the end of the period, private consumption per capita tended to decline as a result of a series of austerity budgets and of an increase in the current prices of commodities, both imported and domestic. Conversely, the rapid increase of public consumption seemed to confirm the growing role of the state in the economy. With an average of 13.8 per cent of the GDP during 1955-62, gross capital formation tended to rise rapidly, moving from 100 in 1955 to 153 in 1962 (indexes). However, it must be emphasized that the composition of capital formation in Ghana was much less favorable than its global rate of growth, with three quarters of all capital formation going to building and construction.

It may also be said that Ghana's general economic situation (as distinct from her strictly financial position which was notoriously bad at the end of the period) was still rather favorable, but that after 1962, the country entered a period of increasing austerity under the double pressure of ambitious development projects and a severe deterioration of Ghana's main export prices. Our own observations during 1962-66 confirmed this. Ghana, after a period of high private and public consumption, entered after 1961/62 a period of restriction of private consumption in order to permit public consumption and capital formation to keep on growing rapidly. This, without doubt, resulted in socio-economic tensions both unknown before and fraught with political risks.

A few more questions remain unanswered. They concern the degree of industrialization, the share of the public sector in industrialization, and the socialist content of this experience. To try to answer the first two, we must now look at another series of indicators. The third one, socialism, will be discussed more fully in the next chapter (political problems).

A comparison between two tables of the GDP for the three-year period, 1955-57, and the three-year period, 1959-61, shows that the global share of cocoa, agricultural production and distribution, and forestry including sawmills, i.e., the bulk of the traditional or colonial economic activities, represented respectively 51.2 and 52.0 per cent of the GDP.[21]

In relation to these figures, the progress of manufacturing industries during the same period appears almost insignificant: 1.2 per cent of the GDP in 1955-57 and 2.0 per cent in 1959-61. Other private industries, mainly building and transports remained practically unchanged: 16.4 and 16.5 per cent. Public enterprises, which include some manufacturing industries, increased from 1.5 to 2.0 per cent of the total GDP.[22]

Although these figures do not reveal the whole
picture, they are a sufficient indication of the trend. At
the end of the Nkrumah-CPP Government, Ghana had built
a remarkable infrastructure (roads, schools, power plant,
harbor facilities, etc.), but the industrial process was still
in its infancy. At the same time, this process was pushed
hard: Out of the 234 larger firms recorded in 1959, 130 had
been established since 1950.[23] And this drive toward
industrialization was definitely the result of the
government's initiative; this is clearly indicated by the
following table which illustrates the growing share of the
public sector in the largest establishments:

TABLE 10
EMPLOYMENT IN THE PRIVATE
AND PUBLIC SECTORS
(Thousands of Persons)

	1961	1962	1963	1964
Total	350	356	368	376
Private	138	131	123	114
Public	211	225	245	261

Source: Ghana, Central Bureau of Statistics, Economic Survey
1964 (Accra: Government Printer, 1965).

In other words, when they were ousted by the Coup of
February, 1966, Nkrumah and the CPP had not yet gone
much beyond the first stages of their program of
industrialization, and the economy of Ghana remained
typical of that of any underdeveloped country with a very
low degree of intersectoral integration: The total input
from all sectors to all sectors represented, in 1960, only
£40.6 million out of a GDP estimated at £484.8 million, or

8 per cent.[24] By the end of 1965, these figures had probably increased, but not very much.

Nkrumah and the CPP were hit when their program had not yet borne the fruits which would have justified its cost, and when its cost was at the highest level.

THE "GHANAIAN WAY"

In sum, empirically first, and then more systematically and more rationally, Ghana's approach during the Nkrumah-CPP period was an intermediate approach. It was a partial compromise. To use again Dudley Seers's terminology, Ghana did not choose to maintain the "open economy" at all costs[25] or to plunge immediately in an attempt to completely reverse the colonial trend, by "closing" its economy. As already indicated, the Nkrumah-CPP line (however wavering it may have appeared at times) was not to be found at the extremes: neither a liberal (neocolonial laissez faire) nor an immediate and complete breakaway from the methods, ideas, and objectives of the colonial and postcolonial (Dyarchy) period.

Even a superficial examination of Ghana's general policies, particularly her African and foreign policies, shows that Nkrumah and the CPP were not prepared, even in the early years of the Dyarchy and independence, to be satisfied with an essentially formal type of independence. This general attitude was also reflected in the press and the many official statements of the party and the government. More convincingly and concretely, Nkrumah's refusal of a passive and neocolonial course is illustrated by the strategic infrastructural investments and their sheer size. We have already mentioned some of them, including the Volta Dam at Akosombo, symbolically inaugurated (not unlike a sort of Ghanaian battle of Fleurus) a few weeks before Nkrumah's ouster. This, as well as Tema, the development of communications and, above all, that of education[26] no doubt constitute many evidences of the government's determination to lay the firm foundations of a real process of industrialization in Ghana, i.e., in the last analysis, the prerequisites for a radical reorientation of the country's economic structures. It may be useful to point out here that most, if not all, criticisms formulated against Ghana's economic policies during the Nkrumah-CPP period by Ghanaian as well as foreign economists do not question the strategy, the intentions, or even the achievements of the period. Rather, what is usually reproached, regarding the government's economic policies, is that too much was invested in infrastructural projects; the country's infrastructure was partly underutilized.[27] It is hardly necessary to emphasize that such a criticism is fairly unique in contemporary Africa.

In other words, the general impression that Ghana was more advanced, more developed than her West African neighbors is not only explained by the incomplete and rather superficial argument of "cocoa prosperity," but also by the large infrastructural investments and the development of education. In this sense, it would be better defined as a reflection of the obvious determination of the Ghana Government to go ahead, to *far da se*. This was also apparent in a rapid and eventually complete "Africanization" of the civil service, including its higher ranks, and, at the most common, individual level, in the lack of inhibitions (racially or otherwise).

If, thus, it may be said that Ghana did not succumb to the temptation of neocolonialism (if this was a temptation at all to the ambitious, radical-minded leadership of the CPP), at the same time, they did not pursue, either in the beginning or later, a clear-cut policy of self-supporting development. Moves to close the economy only came gradually, and, whether before or after Nkrumah's visit to the Soviet Union in 1961, the fundamental concept of a "mixed economy," including an expatriate sector, was never questioned. Despite a growing insistence on "scientific socialism," as opposed to the various forms of "African socialism" popular on the continent, [28] the Soviet model, insofar as it was seen to represent a model of economic development, remained, to the end, extremely remote—not only as far as its class content is concerned (socialism), but also inasmuch as the historical experience of the U.S.S.R. can be described as an extreme case of self-centered, self-supporting pattern of development (the "Iron Curtain" model). It may be readily admitted that, whatever the political preferences of the CPP leadership (and these were not all that clear and simple), an "Iron Curtain" model of development could not be seriously considered in Ghana at the time of independence, or even later. For such a model to have any chance of being effective, there are at least two prerequisites which were both lacking in Ghana: a minimum dimension (a large country and population) and a strong and disciplined party. Behind its protective "Curtain," the country becomes a closed arena where the party and the government tackle their development problems free of external interferences. Foreign show windows (such as more attractive and desirable consumer goods and standards of living) are eliminated, and, by removing elements of comparison, a policy of austerity may be believed as more acceptable. If the party is popular and well organized, it may succeed in convincing the masses of the correctness of its policies. If not, the responsibility shifts to the government and some amount of popular consent may be obtained by government propaganda and coercion. Although the CPP and Ghana did not have much in common with the Bolsheviks and the Soviet Union, one may wonder whether the "Iron Curtain" model might not, at the present level of technological development in Africa, present an additional difficulty that the U.S.S.R. and China experienced only marginally—that of a cultural and technological stagnation (cultural and technological being, of course, understood in their modern sense: modern technology and science). In any case, this is an academic question, for, once again, the possibility of taking such a course was never seriously considered in Ghana.

However, it may well be that the problem of the dimension (the dimension of the country as far as it constitutes a basis for, and sets limits upon, the development of the economy) is one of the sources on which Ghana's pan-Africanism fed under Nkrumah. For a real development to take place, Ghana and most other African countries are seen as being too small. This, better than the misgivings about, and opposition to, Nkrumah's pan-Africanist proposals by most other African heads of state, perhaps explains the near obsessional character of Nkrumah's advocacy of "African Unity Now." The explanation of such an insistence on the urgency of African unity would appear to be linked to a particular conception of development, to Nkrumah's almost desperate conviction that it is impossible in Africa "to build socialism in one country"—hence, the need for African unity.

More generally, before the first Addis Ababa Conference of the OAU, the pan-Africanist policies of Ghana had already been clearly expressed (on the actual day of independence) by Nkrumah: "The independence of Ghana is meaningless unless it is linked up with the total liberation of Africa." The objective was considered a fundemental one; it was to be attained at all costs. Even at the cost of political compromise: Unite Africa from above, with everybody, including heads of state whose policies and positions were repeatedly denounced in Ghana

(Felix Houphouet-Boigny, Ahmadou Ahidjo, Joseph Kasavubu, etc.). Even at the expense of one's self-pride: Go to Canossa-Wagadugu to shake hands with Maurice Yaméogo and other leaders of the Entente. Even at the expense of one's dignity: Expel more or less provisionally the political refugees of the Sawaba and the UPC (Union de Population du Cameroun) parties, among others, at the time of the Accra Conference of the OAU.

Such an approach to African unity, and such decisions, may be considered to be at the origin of the relative deterioration, after 1963, of Ghana's relations with the other "revolutionary" African countries (Algeria, Mali, Guinea, U.A.R., Tanzania), Ghana was prepared to sacrifice everything for African unity. What was seen as an important problem by the other "revolutionary" countries, was seen as far more in the eyes of Nkrumah; it was *the* fundamental problem: "Africa Must Unite." And, indeed, inasmuch as one believes that there can be no real development within the limits of the microstates of Africa, it is obvious that the essential battles are not to be fought within each state, but on the continental level, for the unity of Africa.

The fact that Ghana did not simply try, as the Ivory Coast did with the other countries of the Entente, to set up some kind of regional grouping of countries, perhaps only indicates that Ghana's pan-Africanism had more than one source. It cannot be accounted for by objective economic needs alone *(inter alia,* larger markets and a broader basis for economic development). Thus, Nkrumah's pan-Africanism may not appear as a simple translation in tactical terms of Ghana's objective economic needs and development ambitions ("Africa's Prussia"), but as something far more important: an attempt to solve in advance and on the basis of Ghana's more-advanced experience the same problems with which, sooner or later, all African countries will be confronted.

This is not surprising in view of what is known of Nkrumah's own biography, his prolonged stays in the United States and in Great Britain, his many and continued contacts with American, West Indian, and English pan-Africanists, as well as his lasting companionships with W.E.B. DuBois and especially with George Padmore. Leaving aside all other considerations (feasibility, approach, etc.), it is fair to say that Nkrumah's pan-Africanism was neither pure utopia nor identifiable with some African equivalent of Bismark's Prussian pan-Germanism. For the same reason, it cannot be simply and polemically assimilated with the insidious "proposal to pair the crocodile (Ghana) and the chickens" (the other African countries).[29]

It may also be worth recalling that, apart from the well-known thesis on African unity, the problem of the dimension was also discussed, at least in the later years, in terms of an "optimum zone of development," apparently from the influence of the French Marxist economist, Charles Bettelheim, who spent some time in Guinea and whose ideas probably found their way through to Ghana via the little group of French-speaking Africans, who moved from Conakry to Accra around 1962, and who seemed to have enjoyed some degree of influence on the ideological thinking of the former President of Ghana.[30]

Thus, in order to implement their strategy of development (industrialization, "socialism," etc.), and pending further progress in their efforts to enlist more support for African unity, the CPP and the Government of Ghana chose to accept a *modus vivendi* with the world around them, and tried to take advantage of its contradictions (Cold War, Peaceful Co-existence, etc.) as well as of whatever the end of British rule had left them with—about two hundred million pounds sterling and the state machinery. In view of the starting point, and in particular the still strong foreign interests in Ghana and the fact that most of Ghana's exports went to the U.K., the U.S., and Western Europe, this meant that the *modus vivendi* was also a partial compromise with the forces which so far had played a major orientational role in the economy of Ghana. In economic terms, as we have seen, this meant a transitional phase of mixed economy, and we have just seen what concrete problems it posed and what results it brought about. We must now turn our attention to the political problems posed by the "Ghanaian Way" and try to determine the political meaning and significance of this experience.

NOTES

1. Cf., Tony Killick, "The Possibilities of Economic Control," *A Study of Contemporary Ghana*, ed. by Walter B. Birmingham, I. Neustadt, and E. N. Omaboe (London: Allen and Unwin, 1966), I, chap. xvii, 411—.

2. Dudley Seers and C. Ross, *Report on Financial and Physical Problems of Development in the Gold Coast* (Accra: Government Printer, 1952).

3. Killick, "The Possibilities of Economic Control," *A Study of Contemporary Ghana*, p. 412.

4. *Ibid.*

5. *Ibid.*, p. 413.

6. *Ibid.*, p. 437.

7. "Much-criticized" because it often appeared incoherent, or because its coherence more often than not seemed more clearly related to bribery than to any other consideration.

8. The date, 1963, should not, however, give the impression that the government waited six years before turning its attention to the many problems related to the control of foreign private investments in Ghana. In point of fact, the adoption of the Capital Investment Act in April, 1963, implied that the following Acts were repealed: (1) The Pioneer Industries and Companies

Act, 1959; (2) the same Act, Amendment of 1960, and (3) the Amendment of 1962. The provisions of the Act are rather generous, but the type of industries that are declared "pioneer," and thus, may enjoy government's encouragements and other benefits, is not specified. Instead, a set of criteria is established for important projects. *See,* United Nations, Economic Commission for Africa, *Investment Laws and Regulations in Africa* (E/CN.14/ INR/28/REV.2), 1965.

9. Early in 1966, a long article was published in *The Spark* by Julius Sagoe, the pseudonym of a senior lecturer at the Kwame Nkrumah Ideological Institute in Winneba, a regular contributor, and one of the most perceptive of *The Spark.* The article was a violent attack on Kwesi Armah's (then Minister of Trade) import license policies.

10. *A Study of Contemporary Ghana,* p. 459.

11. *Ibid.,* pp. 460-61.

12. *Ibid.,* p. 461.

13. Plus Israel, the U.A.R., Mali, and Guinea, i.e., all the bilateral agreement trading partners of Ghana, and also most of her new trading partners.

14. As suppliers' credits are by definition tied with a type of goods or services which are being supplied by the creditors, the choices of the debtor, the government receiving suppliers' credits, are restricted and thus some degree of distortion may have to be considered.

15. In fact, much less since out of the £100 million, £55 million represented the Valco aluminum factory at Tema, for which a final agreement had already been reached.

16. Most of the following information can be found in Robert Szereszewski, "The Performance of the Economy, 1955-62," *A Study of Contemporary Ghana,* I, chap. ii. Much of the original material and data was collected by Miss Walters and presented in the Walters Report (unpublished).

17. As exports remained more or less stable from 1954 on, this is partly an illusion. After the mid-1950's, the "boom" was a government-fostered boom.

18. Cf., *A Study of Contemporary Ghana,* p. 42.

19. Samir   Amin,   *Trois   expériences   africaines   de
développement: le Mali, la Guinée et le Ghana* (Université de
Paris, "IEDES: Tiers-Monde"; Paris: Presses universitaires
de France, 1965). Samir Amin's comparative study is all the
more interesting in the case of Ghana as it includes a comparison
with the Ivory Coast, whose remarkable development in recent
years is seen by Samir Amin as very similar to Ghana's first
period of development.

20. *Ibid.*, p. 190.

21. *A Study of Contemporary Ghana,* p. 60.

22. *Ibid.*

23. *Ibid.*, p. 274.

24. *Ibid.*, p. 64.

25. Although too much perhaps has been inferred from the
frequently mentioned Gbedemah's "anchor of safety." To be
sure, when the question of Ghana's currency parity with, and
convertibility into, the sterling was debated in parliament for
the first time, Gbedemah, then Minister of Finance, did say that
the pound sterling was the "anchor of safety" for Ghana's
economy. This also reflects a poor conception of what it entails
to ensure national economic safety in a former colony, not to
speak of economic development. But the debate took place in the
Legislative Assembly on February 5, 1957, i.e., just before
Ghana's accession to independence (March 6, 1957).
    Later developments suggest that Gbedemah's statement
reflected the limitations set upon the CPP by the Dyarchy as
well   as   illusions   about   the   possibilities   and   methods   of
development in Ghana rather than a deliberate choice of a *liberal*
or *neocolonial* course. In point of fact, by definition, the Dyarchy
represents a neocolonial framework, which, no doubt, can be
altered by a very strong nationalist ruling party and government.
Up to a point, despite the continued power struggle of the CPP
with its opposition, it was altered.

26. Enrolment in primary and middle schools jumped from
200,000 to 800,000 from 1951 to 1961. At the end of the period,
Ghana could boast of having achieved almost universal school
attendance in the first form of primary education. It is also had
by then three universities which no longer were dependent on the

University of London (the previous so-called special relations). One of these, Kwame Nkrumah University of Science and Technology (KNUST), in Kumasi, specialized in the training of engineers, architects, and other scientific-technical training.

27. Cf., *inter alia*, Amin, *Trois expériences africaines de développement*, and *A Study of Contemporary Ghana*, chap. xviii (by Omaboe).

28. For a rather full introductory discussion of the various types of African socialism including Ghana's "scientific socialism," see, Jitendra Mohan, "Varieties of African Socialism" *Socialist Register* (London: Merlin Press, 1966), pp. 220-66.

29. As mentioned by a French-speaking West African diplomat to Philippe Decraene. Cf., *"Les régimes militaires de l'ouest africain,"* Part III: "Ghana: *Des officiers qui ont la faveur du peuple, Le Monde* (Paris), July 2, 1966.

30. In particular, the Senegalese-born Habib Niang, a rather enigmatic figure.

CHAPTER 5 POLITICAL PROBLEMS

Politically, the main difficulty confronting a nationalist party after independence, as one knows only too well, is the unavoidable postponement of the economic benefits associated with the attainment of independence in the pre-independence nationalist propaganda. And, up to a point, the more earnest the government's development program, the more complete the postponement of these economic benefits. In addition, when the strategy of development is an intermediate one including an important private sector, as in Ghana and in most African countries for that matter, the economic frustrations of the period immediately following independence are compounded by the mere continued existence of this private sector, particularly its expatriate component. In order to derive a maximum benefit from the continued development of a private, mostly foreign, sector in the economy, it is necessary to let it function and develop in its natural capitalistic framework. This, *inter alia*, includes the repatriation of profits (while stringent exchange controls prevent nationals from taking money out of the country), the conspicuous existence of standards of living for expatriate and, up to a point, national employees of foreign firms which are far above those of the mass of the population, and, by and large, the thousand and one visible signs of a world and a way of life more attractive than the one of the majority of the indigenous population. At the same time as such anomalies—with regard to the official line—are tolerated or even encouraged, the Government requests from the people an austere, self-sacrificing behavior: frozen wages, "human investment," mobilization of the people's "revolutionary energies," etc.

The intermediate way introduces an apparent contradiction in the strategy and a frustrating dichotomy in a community where it seems that there are now two systems of weights and measures. If such a situation is to be tolerable for any length of time, it would seem that there should be no doubt whatsoever concerning the true intentions of the party and the government. A certain degree of austerity, or at least of restraint, among the leaders of the party and the government could perhaps contribute to make such dichotomic tensions more tolerable. If Tactical Action is to be maintained and even widened in scope after the end of the period of the Dyarchy, the ultimate usefulness of such a course must be given maximum credibility.

THE FAILURE TO COMBINE
POSITIVE AND TACTICAL ACTIONS

The best way of achieving this would seem to be a combination of Tactical Action and Positive Action, or, in non-Ghanaian political terminology, an active involvement of the party in the "struggle for development." This poses the problem of the dual function of the party, as a militant mass party and as the party that forms the government. It seems that most nationalist parties felt the importance of this problem, and this perhaps partly accounts for the formulation, in many cases, of development objectives in terms of "battles" to be fought and won.[1]

In Ghana, such a preoccupation appears in the formal emphasis placed on Positive Action. The anniversary of the launching of Positive Action in 1950 was commemorated formally, usually at mass rallies held in Accra and other towns in Ghana. Nkrumah used to attend such meetings in person, at least until 1963. There were "re-dedication" speeches delivered by "Prison Graduates." But both Positive Action and "re-dedication" were rather formal displays of party militancy. In the last years, even such rallies were poorly attended, and this cannot be entirely explained away by the fear of further bomb attempts against Nkrumah, as did indeed happen in January, 1963, at the Accra Stadium. Very simply, in the later years of the Nkrumah-CPP Government, the party had lost a great deal of its earlier militancy and did not seem to be able to "mobilize the masses." There are many possible explanations of this phenomenon which was so obvious at the occasion of any "mass rally" in the 1960's. The simplest and probably the best is that the party was not able to mobilize the masses for rallies fundamentally because it had ceased trying to mobilize them.

When the party was fighting to retain power, during the electoral campaigns of 1954 and 1956 and for some time after, either on the occasion of by-elections or municipal and local elections or, more generally, in the process of liquidation of the opposition, it showed great organizational skills and a definite capability for mass mobilization. In this respect, the 1960 Plebiscite may be considered the last such performance of the CPP. Afterwards, and while the government turned most of its attention to the economic problems facing the country, the CPP, as a mass party, did not follow suit. It did not manage, or did not choose to turn its organization and attentions to the economic problems of the country. Electoral battles were not followed by "economic battles." The only obvious involvement of the party in the "economic battle" was the CPP Program for Work and Happiness, but even this, when all is said, may appear as a by-product of government activity.

The question of the dual function of the CPP was further obscured by repeated statements by Nkrumah and party officials, in the late 1950's, that "Ghana was the CPP and the CPP Ghana."[2] In many ways, it was correct; it was correct in the same sense that the Communist Party (CP) of the Soviet Union could be said to be the U.S.S.R. In the sense that the CPP was wholly committed to the task of creating and developing a modern country, Ghana, the party could be said to be Ghana.[3] The danger inherent in such an approach is that in identifying the party and the state (for in identifying the party and the country, one obviously also identifies the party and the state) one further increases the confusion already implicit in the dual function of the party. Such a confusion is detrimental either to the party or to the state. Either the state absorbs the party or it is the other way round. In Ghana, the state absorbed the CPP. Fanon, who spent some time in Accra after his appointment as Ambassador of the GPRA[4] to Ghana in March, 1960, and who may have been prompted by his disappointment with the political situation in independent countries in West Africa to write his last book, discusses in the third chapter of *Les damnés de la terre*[5] the roles and relations of the party and the state after independence. His analysis may appear rather simplistic, but it contains one fundamental truth: The state tends to absorb the party.

After independence,

> the party disintegrates. There only remains a formal party, a name, an emblem, a motto. ... After independence, the party no longer helps the people to formulate their demands, to increase their awareness of what their real needs are, to consolidate

their power. Now, the party's role is to transmit to
the people the leaders' decisions. ... Local party
cadres are appointed to administrative jobs, the
party identifies itself with the state administrative
machinery, the militants drop out and take the empty
title of citizens.

The party [may even] duplicate the administration
and the police and [help them to] control the masses,
not to ensure their active participation in the affairs
of the nation, but to constantly remind them that the
government expects obedience and discipline.

The party rots. This dismal picture of party disintegration
is followed by a brief description of what "a true party"
should do and be. It should "not become a tool in the
hands of the government. On the contrary, it [should be]
an instrument in the hands of the people." To achieve this
"the party [should] not have administrative powers. ...
The less confusion [between party and state], the less
duplication of powers, the more effective the party in its
guiding role."[6]

Such a description applies rather well to the history
of the CPP after independence, particularly after 1960,
when it could be assumed that the opposition had been
definitely quelled and done away with. This may be, as
Frantz Fanon suggests, a general pattern in the
postindependence period in "those countries in which the
revolutionary commotion has not been sufficient." It
nonetheless remains to be further explained in the particular
case of Ghana.

One may agree that in order to implement their strategy
of development, the Nkrumah-CPP Government could not
afford the luxury of being too particular and thus had to
make the best use of whatever was at their disposal. This
would imply that they had to take whatever assistance
could be obtained from both Western and socialist
countries, that they had to attract as much foreign capital

as they could, private and public. Moreover, they had to rely on a body of civil servants trained by the British in the framework of the colonial civil service, and who are still in charge today. To be sure, they were competent; but inasmuch as they were politically neutral, they could not apply political criteria in which they did not believe, or, more simply, which were totally alien to them.

In sum, the Nkrumah-CPP Government could neither do without foreign capital nor could it replace its competent nonpolitical civil servants by a fresh team of "socialist" technicians and administrators who simply were not available. These, however, were limitations set upon the freedom of movement of the government, not the party. It should not have prevented the CPP from playing its political role—agitation and mass mobilization. One could, on the contrary, imagine a division of labor between the state and the party. The state would, with the help of its civil service, have laid the infrastructural basis of a modern economy. The party would have laid the political foundations of such a modernization, by involving and mobilizing the people, locally and nationally, in the "battle for development." It seems that this might have been all the easier in that Kwame Nkrumah was, at one and the same time, President of the Republic (state) and Life-Chairman as well as Secretary-General of the CPP (party). Moreover, several ministers were also members of the Central Committee.

Such a division of labor, such a combination of "Tactical" and "Positive" actions, such a party-government complementary action were not put into practice in Ghana. At any rate, if it was attempted at all, it was not successful. Why? This is one of the central political questions of Ghana's contemporary political history. In order to answer this question, one must first be clear about the CPP itself. Whose support should the CPP have sought? Whom should they have mobilized? Who voted CPP? Who were its members? What was this party, the CPP, which claimed more than two million members (out of a total population of less than seven million inhabitants), and which, on the morning of February 24, 1966, had none left (except the former ministers, MPs, and high-ranking party cadres, all of whom were locked up at Ussher Fort, and who did not try anything to stop or avert the police-army Coup)?

THE CONVENTION PEOPLE'S PARTY

Most observers have seen in the CPP two major elements: a nationalist mass party and a people's party, or better, a people's party and a party of the common people. This has been particularly well phrased by Dennis Austin:

> There was, ... a significant ambiguity in the title of the [then] new party. On the one hand, it meant the 'whole people'—as indeed a nationalist movement was bound to claim in its struggle against the colonial power. On the other, it stood for the 'ordinary people'—the commoners—as opposed to the chiefs and the intelligentsia.

However, Austin also insists on the fact that, even by 1960,

> it was not easy to see the CPP as the vanguard of a clearly defined social class, since the general appeal of independence enabled the leaders to master a broad front of support ... [but] nevertheless the demand made by the party for self-government was bound up with a struggle for power which had many of the characteristics of a class struggle—provided the words were widened in scope to connote a level determined as much by education, and by social standing within a traditional system, as by economic criteria.[7]

David Apter's description of the CPP is well-known and points to the same ambiguity:

> The CPP is fraternal and open, intimate, and tolerant. It is particularistic in its loyalties and universalistic in its recruitment. It rewards its friends and removes its enemies. It has diffuse purposes with as many different groups of people finding in it social, economic, or political succor as is necessary to provide a mass following; yet it is specific in its political objectives ... a society of the elect to which many are elected. ...[8]

Wallerstein, who also quotes the above description, more or less expresses the same opinion. But Apter, Austin, or Wallerstein's attempts to explain this ambiguity of the CPP are less convincing, partly because they do not really try to clarify the notion of "common people," partly also perhaps because their attention seems to go mostly to the role of the leader, Nkrumah, and his "charisma." For Apter, in the general framework of his concept of "neo-traditionalism," the leader's charisma is necessary to legitimize and make possible the transfer of modern institutions from the colonial regime to the national independent regime, i.e., what Apter calls "political institutional transfer." Wallerstein's thesis is slightly different: Nkrumah's charisma is necessary "to provide material and status security to an expanding new middle class." For Fitch and Oppenheimer, as we already know, there is not an ambiguity, but a mystification. The CPP expresses only the needs and aspirations of the Ghanaian petty bourgeoisie. But, obviously, these cannot be asserted openly. The petty bourgeoisie must therefore disguise its power monopoly, through the CPP, under a nationalist phraseology. In a strict Fanonist analysis, Fitch and Oppenheimer thus also explain the role of the leader: Nkrumah keeps the people waiting, uses his enormous prestige to ask the people to be patient, to postpone the realization of their own political, social, and economic needs and aspirations.

But whether neo-Weberian (Apter, Wallerstein) or Marxist-Fanonist (Fitch and Oppenheimer) all such analyses assume that the CPP—at least most of its militants and leadership—represented a lower middle class, as distinct from both traditional and modern élites (the *chiefs* and *intelligentsia)*, on the one hand, and, explicitly, at least in the case of Fitch and Oppenheimer, the *masses*, the *people*, on the other hand. Their analyses, however diverging in their conclusions, are all based on the assumption that the history of Ghana in the late 1940's and early 1950's is that of the emergence of a new class —the "Standard VII boys," the partially educated. It is important to stress that, as we have already mentioned, most observers define the "new class" in terms of a certain degree of education. These Standard VII boys "were close to the ordinary public and not divorced from the social and institutional structure of Gold Coast life as the intelligentsia might be."[9] They "had completed elementary education [and] were on the whole loath to take jobs involving menial degrading labor."[10] These *youngmen* "who had hitherto been marginal men were now [after the riots of 1948 and the general social and political unrest of the following years] tantamount to effective public opinion. They were organized, and they were many. They had a goal—self-government. They had a devil—British imperialism. They found a God—Kwame Nkrumah."[11]

Thus, "the CPP was to win its first election victory in 1951 over the earlier generation of political leaders, not merely because it outbid the UGCC in terms of 'Self-Government Now' rather than 'later,' but because it enlisted in its ranks the general body of commoners —literate and illiterate alike."[12]

The whole political situation is usually summarized as follows: The sweeping CPP victory in the 1951 election crystallizes both the emergence of a "new class" and the passage from proto-nationalist movements, such as the UGCC, to a fully fledged nationalist party, the CPP. And in addition, this victory is seen as the logical conclusion of a phenomenon which had begun a few years earlier. Tracing the origin of the CPP back to the 1948 riots (though the CPP was founded more than a year later and although these riots were essentially spontaneous), Austin concludes that

> the February (1948) riots were also responsible for the schism which took place between, on the one hand, the reformist intelligentsia and, on the other, the radical 'young men' who listened willingly to Nkrumah as he began to create his own following, nominally within, in practice opposed to, the Convention (UGCC). Thus, the early Jacobins gave place to the *sans-culottes*—in Ghana, the 'Verandah boys'[13] and the revolution began to take a familiar course.[14]

All this is very interesting but, as can be seen, if there was a "significant ambiguity" in the CPP (nationalist party or party of a particular social class), this ambiguity is far from being entirely dispelled, and the indiscriminate use, to describe this "new class," of such terms as "Standard VII boys," "partially educated," "commoners," "common people," "youngmen," "middle class," or "new middle class" tends to further obscure the question of the class nature of the CPP. It also points to the extreme difficulty, in any contemporary African situation, of applying political concepts which were developed in the historical context of the European experience. Indeed, as we have noted in our second chapter, it is quite clear that the *youngmen*, the partially educated misfits of the Gold Coast, who flocked to the CPP but who did not represent the whole party either, originated from the rural and urban "middle classes" of farmers, artisans, shopkeepers, but their relationship with these "middle classes," much like that of the intelligentsia with the embryonic bourgeoisie, was not a simple one. They were, again like the intelligentsia, a direct product of the colonial system. What they wanted was to move *out of* their group, out of the "middle classes." They had no class interest to defend, for, precisely they had nothing, or what they had, they did not want any longer.

As mentioned in Chapter 2, the *youngmen* who were the *sans-culottes* and propagandists of the CPP, as distinct from this *Third Estate* of the traditional society also referred to as the *youngmen* or the *commoners*, can be labeled "lower middle class," "new emergent middle class," or "petty bourgeoisie," only for want of a better definition, to distinguish them from the proletariat, the bourgeoisie or the chiefs and the intelligentsia. But, by doing so, one misses the main point—the essence of colonization and colonial society. A colony is an economy and a society in transition. In such a society, the main contradiction, and particularly if modern education is introduced on a fairly large scale, is that it cannot accomodate in the modern sector all those in the colony whose links with the traditional society have been gradually eroded or severed as a result of the colonial impact (through education or through other forms). This accounts for the frustration of a number of youngmen and their nationalist militancy, as it had accounted earlier on for the development of all kinds of youth associations. To understand fully the role of the youngmen, they must be replaced in their historical perspective, and this perspective is not that of a petty bourgeoisie, but rather that of the relative fluidity of the social structures of a colony, including its limitations.

Thus, as a product of colonization, the youngmen joined the nationalist movement, and indeed, turned it into a fully fledged nationalist party. They were the CPP original militants, but after the 1951 electoral victory, with the party's doors wide open, they only represented one element of a much wider context.

However, despite the fact that the definition of the "youngmen" as a "petty bourgeois stratum" appears superficial, but because the argument is not limited to the CPP's recruitment, it may be useful to discuss the matter a little further.

According to Fitch and Oppenheimer, "the period of open political struggle between the CPP and the Right Opposition was 1954-58. It began with the agro-mercantile strata—goaded into political activity by the CPP's heavy export taxes on cocoa—challenging the CPP for state control." [15] Thus, the whole political struggle in Ghana is reduced to a struggle between two élite groups—the would-be or embryonic bourgeoisie, represented by the *intelligentsia* and its political parties, and the petty bourgeoisie, represented by the *CPP*. "Neither of the forces which might have polarized and deepened the political struggle [the Ghanaian working class—agricultural as well as urban proletarians—and the British owning class] was an open participant." [16] The CPP's fifteen years of power, in such an analysis, only brought about a "partial political revolution," not a "total revolution," for the Gold Coast petty bourgeoisie "had no radical chains to break." [17]

The arguments offered to support this analysis and conclusions, as already mentioned, concern the recruitment of the CPP, its political methods, the relation of the party with the working-class organizations, and the liquidation of what could be described as the left-wing of the CPP (Trade Union leaders and Communists). But the strongest argument, borrowed from Austin's studies of elections in

Ghana, concerns the large proportion of nonvoters in all Ghanaian elections. According to this analysis, when the leaders of the CPP clashed with the leaders of the UGCC for the control of the nationalist movement in Ghana, they did not turn to the working class, but to the youngmen, a large number of whom were already organized in various youth movements. These youngmen vastly outnumbered the intelligentsia and thus had no difficulty in sweeping aside the UGCC in the 1951 election. But this, according to Fitch and Oppenheimer, was a struggle for power which only affected the country superficially. The masses of the people did not even bother to register as electors and even less to cast their votes. [18] If they did not vote, it is because they were not interested; and if they were not interested in the struggle, it is because they were not concerned by the issues at stake. In other words, the masses of the people—rural and urban proletariat—were left out.

This may seem very convincing, but, as a little probing will show, it does not correspond to the reality of Ghanaian elections in the 1950's, which, as we have seen in Chapter 3, were fought bitterly and did not affect Ghana but superficially. The fact that a majority of Ghanaians did not take part in any of the various elections held between 1951 and 1960 does not necessarily imply that they were precisely the urban and rural proletarians of Ghana and did not feel concerned.

The socio-economic structure of Ghana, in the 1950's, [19] does not indicate that there was such a huge rural or urban proletariat in the country. The naive picture of a Ghanaian people of small cocoa farmers toiling on their own plots of forest land is not correct. But, at the same time, large landowners are not many in Ghana and even these rarely employ more than fifteen to twenty workers, most of whom are not proletarians in the strict sense. As we have seen, apart from the type of labor employed for the original operation of clearing forest land for the establishment of new cocoa farms, the typical worker is not a paid laborer but a sharecropper, either the classical *abusa* worker or the *nkotokuano*. And the situation of the *abusa* man (who may himself be the owner of a farm elsewhere or who may become a farmer later on and who in any case is very seldom a native of the region where he works) is far too complex to be simply identified with that of a rural proletarian (say of the Italian *braccianti* type). The importance of migrant labor also makes it very difficult to assimilate all the population employed in mining activities to a mining proletariat. In short, it is quite clear that in the Ghanaian population, the urban and rural proletariat was, and still is, a small minority.

Indeed, if it were not for the relatively advanced socio-economic situation of Ghana as compared to that of her neighbors, all this would be so obvious that it would not be necessary to discuss this question seriously. It is not easy to say exactly who did not vote in the elections, and even less, to ascertain why they did not vote, but surely, it is impossible to assimilate this absenteeism to a lack of interest on the part of the rural and urban proletariat of Ghana.

Furthermore, there seem to be arguments even to the contrary. Austin in his analysis of the 1956 election (mostly NLM versus CPP), shows that the mining constituencies in Ashanti gave their solid support to the CPP. [20]

In conclusion to this point, the suggestion that the masses of Ghanaians who did not vote in the various elections were nonvoting electors appears as a superficial European analogy. What really happened is not a case of absenteeism. What really happened is that in 1951 and even more so in 1954 (the first general election), a voter was almost automatically a CPP voter in the sense that the CPP was at the time the only active mass party in a country where such elections never took place before; the task of contending parties was not simply one of attracting voters to their sides, but one of "creating" them. Austin, gives several detailed descriptions of how militant CPP members went about the huge task of visiting as many villages as possible to convince their inhabitants to register on voters' lists. The same author shows that the British authorities would not have succeeded in registering voters without the cooperation of the CPP. To many citizens in many constituencies, the mere act of registering their names on voters' lists meant giving their support to the CPP, to "Freedom," to "Self-Government Now," in short, to the nationalist movement. And thus, the success of the CPP was precisely that it was able to send militants to the villages and get citizens to register as voters.

In this respect, the crux of the matter is that some observers, when dealing with African situations, seem to share a rather naive conception of what a "mass party" is all about. In the first place, they seem to imply that for a party to be a mass party, a majority of the population has to be involved in the party's activities; but, of course, this, even in non-African conditions, is simply not the case. Even a mass party is always the party of an active minority of citizens. There simply is no such thing as a party in whose activities a majority of the population takes part. Whether a party is a mass party (as opposed to an élite party) depends on its appeal and its recruitment which must both be broad and more or less unrestricted. It further depends on its general objectives which must be broadly democratic and centered on the promotion of the working classes in a general sense. Last, and this is its most distinctive characteristic, its methods must include the ability of the party to organize and mobilize the "people" for mass demonstrations, boycotts, strikes, and other similar mass actions. There is no doubt that, in the 1950's, the CPP was such a party. Its main objective was for several years strictly and simply nationalistic (independence), i.e., the same objective, although formulated in more radical terms, as that of its successive élitist contenders (UGCC, GCP, NLM, UP). And, in a country where the proletariat was a minority, the CPP's appeal was of necessity directed toward the people, the common people in a broad sense. From this point of view, there was thus no serious ambiguity. The large number of nonvoters simply corresponds to the difficulty of involving the country village people in national politics (as distinct from local or regional activities) and particularly through new forms and media. Unlike European situations, in Africa, a national election, particularly in the countryside, is far more difficult to organize for a mass party than mass demonstrations, boycotts or strikes. In any case, it is not a traditional activity and it has to be organized.

In the second place, the very choice of the term *mass party*, to be opposed to *élite party* and presumably to indicate that the party has mass support, popular following, and is democratic in character, organization and policies, is open to debate. The concept of a mass party is more aptly, and more usually, outside the Anglo-Saxon world, used in opposition to a party of cadres, an avant-garde type of party. The modern social-democratic parties are mass parties while, up to a point and typically, the Communist parties are parties of cadres, at least of militants. Party membership or following is irrelevant within this definition of mass party and avant-garde party. As we shall see later on, the CPP was a mass party according to both definitions, but for the sake of clarity, it would be better to discuss Nkrumah's party in terms of a "mass party" when we discuss the *organization* of the party, and in terms of a "popular party" when we deal with the party's *appeal* and the party's *ability to mobilize the people.*

The party, as Apter saw quite clearly, was always open; its membership is supposed to have reached over two million people; thus it was clearly not an avant-garde party of cadres, but a mass party. At the same time, obviously, it could not be an élite party. The CPP, therefore, whatever definition is given, was, by all standards, a mass party. To conclude, on this point, one may say that the CPP's appeal was directed to the *people* in general and not to any particular group. The CPP did not attempt to pose as a class party.[21]

Other arguments which have been used to identify the CPP with a "new élite group" or the petty bourgeoisie concern mainly the party's methods and tactics. To now summarize and discuss them briefly permits us to throw a little more light on the CPP and on the definition of a popular nationalist party in the conditions of contemporary Africa.

Among others,[22] Fitch and Oppenheimer argue that the CPP's political methods were not democratic, that the CPP did not try to mobilize the masses against the NLM or the UP. First, the CPP tried to negotiate with the NLM (to avoid a third general election), and "when negotiation failed, it resorted to administrative repression." By and large, the CPP's response to the relative success of the NLM "was not to 'parachute' organizers into the rural areas to organize the landless agricultural workers, who would have been natural allies in any fight against the capitalist farmers and rentier chiefs."[23] Instead, the CPP played the micro-regionalism[24] and used coercion, bribery, and electoral promises. But, again, this is more of a statement of opinion than a proven argument: Even if one does not dismiss Fitch and Oppenheimer's argument by simply pointing out that the *only* example they give of CPP undemocratic methods is borrowed from Austin and wrongly attributed to the CPP. Austin mentioned it as an illustration of NPP's (viz., Northern People's Party) methods, and more generally of the less sophisticated Northern politics.[25] Even if one takes the argument seriously, one does not find much to support it. In fact, in an analysis of a by-election in Kumasi (Ashanti) following Kurankyi Taylor's death, Austin shows that as late as 1959, i.e., toward the end of the period of open political struggle for power, the CPP had maintained its appeal to the nonprivileged common people.

> A pattern of voting was traced out from the 1956 election to the Kumasi-South by-election in April 1959; and the conclusion was reached that, whereas the NLM-UP was largely confined to Ashanti and Muslim voters in the city, the CPP was able to attract support not only from the Southern immigrants but from a substantial number of Ashanti voters as well. Thus the predominantly Ashanti wards were found to be divided between the Opposition and the CPP roughly in the proportion 60 per cent for the NLM-UP, 40 per cent for the CPP; the Southern immigrants wards voted overwhelmingly (80 per cent plus) for the CPP. ... The pro-CPP Ashanti vote was probably concentrated among the poorer compounds of the city. ... The wealthy Ashanti lawyers and businessman ... voted heavily against the CPP. ... In sum, therefore, it was possible to make a reasonably accurate correlation between tribal origin and party affiliation and to draw the tentative conclusion that while the wealthier Ashanti families were likely to vote for the NLM, the poorer compounds were likely to be divided between the two parties.[26]

Now, if the CPP had managed to maintain its appeal as the people's party, as late as 1959, even in the very heart of Ashanti NLM-UP opposition, it is hard to imagine that the party by then only, or mostly, used undemocratic methods of coercion, bribery, and tribalism. It is true to say that the CPP *also* used electoral weapons other than plain democratic and popular agitation. It did use Brong regionalism against the larger Ashanti regionalism, and not only Brong micro-regionalism. The CPP did enter local chieftaincy quarrels for apparently no special reason other than a possible electoral victory. The CPP also took advantage of the Cocoa Purchasing Company (founded in 1952 and controlled by the CPP) to win farmers' votes with the promise of credits or the threat of not granting them. As Apter said: "The party rewards its friends and removes its enemies." But these were the political weapons of the time used by all contending parties during a period of a bitter power struggle and during which fists, sticks, and other crude weapons were widely used.

But these were not the typical or the only weapons and arguments used by the CPP. Rather what was characteristic of the CPP's methods is that they blended democratic popular mass agitation, a mixture of promises and coercion, and in some cases, micro-regionalism against the NLM-UP and NPP macro-regionalism. The CPP was more democratic inasmuch as it added democratic arguments to others used by its opponents. Typically, the CPP platform remained based on nationalism and democratic principles while that of the opposition parties was based on regionalism and various forms of élitist traditionalism or neotraditionalism. The rest, however distasteful, was nothing but local and tactical deviations.

One more such argument is that the CPP leadership during the period of the Dyarchy got rid of several CPP left-wing backbenchers and took control of the Trade

Unions; it removed the former more independent leaders and replaced them by more disciplined CPP militants such as the new Secretary General, John Tettegah. By and large, this is true, but the "liquidation" of the left-wing of the CPP was limited to a few persons and on the issue of Tactical Action; it must be considered as part of the efforts of the leadership to maintain their control of the then new party. The problem of the Trade Unions is more important in the sense that the control of the Trade Unions from above by the party was to be paid in the form of the quasi-insurrectional strike of Sekondi-Takoradi in 1961. But it would be extremely naive to consider this as a specific Ghanaian problem. There is practically no ruling party in Africa, including the Algerian FLN, that proved capable of resisting the temptation of taking control of the Trade Unions. And it may not be without interest to recall that the Communist parties in the socialist countries have done just the same. What really matters here is not that the ruling parties take control of the Trade Unions but that they can do it so easily—which is another way of stating that the proletariat is a minor partner in the nationalist movement for independence.

In fact, neither the large proportion of nonvoters, nor the recruitment of the CPP, nor the party's political methods, nor its dealings with the Trade Unions and the expulsion of, *stricto sensu*, a handful of Communist fellow-travelers from the party can substantiate the identification of the CPP with a party of the Ghanaian petty bourgeoisie. This identification cannot be substantiated for the simple reason that the very notion of a Ghanaian petty bourgeoisie is not as clear as some seem to believe. In fact, although it is not easy to arrive at any definite conclusions in the under-studied field of Ghana's socio-economic structures, we have seen, in our second chapter, that however rudimentary the picture obtained, it is possible to put together some information in this respect.

And what then appears is not the image most observers present: neither simply the chiefs-intelligentsia-youngmen (commoners) grouping of earlier analyses, nor the bourgeoisie (agro-mercantile stratum) —petty bourgeoisie-working class (urban and rural proletarians) grouping suggested by Fitch and Oppenheimer. What did characterize the Gold Coast-Ghana in the early post-World War II period —was the existence, side by side, of an embryonic bourgeoisie, a marginal proletariat, and a large "middle class" of farmers, artisans and traders or petty traders, including an upper middle class of richer cocoa planters and cocoa brokers. And above all, these groups and classes represented a rather fluid combination and were confronted with a rapidly changing situation. These changes were more conjunctural than structural, but they were rapid and important. People tried to adapt themselves to such changing circumstances by even faster changes in their occupations and by betting on as many horses as they could. [27]

This phenomenon was not limited to the Gold Coast; it was fairly general in Africa; but the more-advanced development of the Gold Coast attracted a considerable influx of migrant labor from the North of the country and also from neighboring countries. Thus, a large proportion of the "rural proletariat" (the daily, monthly or yearly paid laborers) came from other countries and were not Ghanaians. To some extent, it is also true of the mines. This migrant labor cannot thus be assimilated to a rural working class or an industrial (mining) working class on which, as Fitch and Oppenheimer seemed to believe, a "truly revolutionary" CPP could and should have based its strategy. While part of the "proletariat" was migrant—thus, to say the least, unstable[28]—many in other groups also appeared to *migrate* constantly from one type of activity to another.

Thus, mobility was the spontaneous answer, the fundamental characteristic—not, of course, of a majority of the population, but of the majority already living in cities and towns and no longer satisfied with what the rural society and farming offered them. Mobility, however, was severely limited in one important respect. Many people had good reasons to move *out of* their jobs and out of the traditional rural society, but they very seldom had the possibility of moving *into* something better.

The development of primary education, the changes brought about by the war (many Ghanaians were sent to East Africa and Burma), the gradual erosion of the prestige of the chiefs and, by and large, rural traditional society values, combined with the examples set by the intelligentsia and the British of more attractive ways of life, constituted many motives for change. But at the other end of the process, promotional opportunities in the modern sector remained very scant; as already mentioned, changes were conjunctural (essentially, the rising prices of cocoa and relative rural prosperity) but the structures of the economy remained basically the same and thus also the structures and possibilities of employment. This explains why so many entered retail trade and other forms of tertiary activity. However, as most observers have already pointed out, such activities could not meet fully the rising expectations of most Ghanaians.

Hence, there was a general feeling of frustration on which nationalism fed; the British seemed to have represented the main obstacle to mobility toward better opportunities, particularly in the civil service. More deeply, the colonial system became increasingly perceived as the specific institutional obstacle to development, i.e., to the opening of new opportunities. This, as we shall see later on, remains to this day the fundamental historical "truth" of anticolonial nationalism—whatever the adjustments to be

made within the existing socio-economic system, an
essential improvement of the situation of *all groups* can
only come as the result of the building of a new system
and to begin with the building of a new, modern economy.

Apter puts it very well: "In some cases the gap
between aspiration and achievement was met with apathy;
in most parts of the Gold Coast, particularly in the South
and central areas, it was met with nationalism."[29] With
perhaps the exception of Northern rural communities, most
Ghanaians shared this general feeling of frustration, but
obviously in varying degrees and forms. Cocoa farmers
tried to oppose compulsory cutting of diseased cocoa trees
and objected to Cocoa Marketing Board margins. Urban
proletarians and, by and large, all those in the lower
income brackets in towns concentrated their grievances on
inflationary prices. Partially educated youngmen, and their
number increased rapidly, saw themselves as victims of
a kind of *numerus clausus* in the civil service and the
large foreign firms. Traders and businessmen equated the
colonial status with unfair competition from British and
"Syrian" firms. The chiefs and the intelligentsia naturally
shared such complaints but, at the same time, had to
maneuver to retain their positions of inheritors of British
power, for, in the words of Apter, "they considered
themselves logical trainees under indirect rule for positions
of authority."[30]

The leaders of the CPP in general were neither
"partially educated" nor especially young.[31] They were
not directly related either to chiefly families or to the few
fairly well-established Ghanaian business circles, and
thus, did not have the same reasons to be careful. Their
action, although it was much bolder, developed within the
same framework and sought to give expression and form to
the same frustrations.

The CPP in the 1950's was a mass party. As it was

struggling for power against the revived élitist groups
associated in the past with the chiefs and the intelligentsia,
the CPP was *popular* in its appeal and recruitment, and
populist in its methods and aims. Inasmuch as it was
opposed by the various regionalist movements and parties
of the Gold Coast and early Ghana, it was *nationalist* in
its objectives before and *after* independence. It was more
significantly nationalist inasmuch as it aimed at building
a modern nation, including a national economy, in Ghana,
which, *inter alia*, implied that it had to fight for the "total
liberation of Ghana." In its struggle, on all these fronts,
it tried to appeal to as many people as possible, and thus,
*was no more the party of the working class than the party
of the lower middle class, or any other group or class.*

These characteristics, and the fact that the CPP was
relatively well-organized, account for its electoral victories
of the 1950's and the general support it received in
practically all regions and from practically all sections of
the population, including the chiefs. The only group which
never accepted the CPP's leading role was the
intelligentsia, with the exception of some of the high-ranking
civil servants. Such "irredentism" among the intelligentsia
is to be explained mainly by the fact that the CPP frustrated
their ambitions. "To the main core of the opposition, the
CPP Government was anathema. Particularly for those
whose orientations were similar to those predominating
during indirect rule, the CPP Government represented a
violation by the British of their commitments to the chiefs
and to the intellectuals who, it was assumed, would take
over the reins of Government."[32] Indeed, while the CPP
managed, when it had definitely liquidated the opposition
as a political force, to become acceptable to almost all
sections of the population of Ghana, it was among the
intelligentsia that the opposition remained strong.

Somehow, the University, for instance, never accepted

the rule of the CPP. The rather clumsy efforts, in 1964 and 1965, to bring down this stronghold of resistance to the ideology of Nkrumaism and the control of the party and government provide a good illustration of the intelligentsia's contempt for the party and resistance to the changes which the Nkrumah-CPP Government sought to bring about in Ghana. The fact that this struggle between academic freedom and party indoctrination might have appeared rather grotesque at times should not obscure the more important fact that such a struggle could take place at such a late date. To the very end, the intelligentsia went on complaining about the government and party in the quiet of Legon's senior commonrooms and at private houses of those not living on Ghana's three campuses. Exceptions to this general attitude were very few. There was a handful of them at the University, including the most prestigious of them all, Willie Abraham, one-time pro-Vice-Chancellor and Head of the Department of Philosophy.

Outside the University, the civil service supplied the bulk of the few intellectuals supporting the government if not the party, including, up to a point, people like Omaboe, the Government Statistician, who, although he was responsible year after year for the publication of a rather critical Economic Survey of Ghana, is said to have belonged to Tawia Adamafio's ideological club,[33] and who, at any rate, like many of the other high-ranking civil servants, as already mentioned, served the government and country well. These apparently worried more about how the country was faring than about their personal fortunes.

To come back to the CPP and our earlier question concerning the failure of the Nkrumah-CPP Government to combine Tactical and Positive actions, it seems clear enough that this failure is not due to the fact that the CPP was the expression of the Ghanaian petty bourgeoisie with its fear of mobilizing the people, for, as a popular and

populist nationalist party, the CPP was not the party of
the petty bourgeoisie. Indeed, the party did not run away
from the people, it simply withered away. And, in fact, it
withered away in the later years of the regime, precisely
during those years when, according to Fitch and
Oppenheimer, the Nkrumah-CPP Government made an effort
to move away from the methods of the "Lewis era," during
the "pro-socialist" years of Nkrumah's Ghana.

The explanation of this phenomenon—the withering
away of the CPP—is not to be found in the class nature of
the CPP which was not only "ambiguous" (Austin), but
extremely vague, due to the fact that the party remained
open to the end, and that its leadership attempted to
appeal to almost everyone in Ghana. The explanation, we
believe, has to do with the strategic options made by the
Nkrumah-CPP Government. To implement their strategy, the
Nkrumah-CPP Government sought to mobilize all the
resources at their disposal, all sections of the population.
To do so, they tried to appeal to all and this eventually
resulted in a unique *policy of equilibrium* between all
groups. And, under such circumstances, the party is far
too fluid a type of organization to be an effective tool for
mass mobilization in "development battles," to implement
the government's development program. As an instrument
of this policy, the civil service on the contrary, is ideal. [34]
Now that the electoral battles are over, the party is
maintained but it has no specific role to play any more.

Apter saw it mostly as the decline of Nkrumah's
charisma. [35] More simply, Austin remarks that, in the later
years, Nkrumah relied less on the party to implement his
policies and more on the civil service:

> Indeed, it was to the leading figures of the civil
> service that Nkrumah was later to turn as the
> effective instruments of his own personal rule after
> the inner party quarrels, assassination plots, and

detentions of 1961. Flagstaff House (where the President established his offices) became a centre of budgetary and economic planning directed by Nkrumah and an able group of economists, statisticians, and administrators.[36]

We must now say a few words about this other phenomenon which developed parallel to the withering away of the CPP and which goes a long way to explain it.

NKRUMAH AND THE POLICY OF EQUILIBRIUM

Whether Nkrumah's charisma became ritualized[37] or whether this is a classic pattern,[38] what really matters is that, in the 1960's, we have in Ghana a type of evolution which is characterized by a formalization or a ritualization of CPP's activities and an emergence or re-emergence of the civil service. The state absorbed the party.

Whether the rise and fall of Tawia Adamafio in the beginning of this last period actually represented an abortive attempt to radicalize the policies of the government and give the party a more important and direct responsibility in the running of the affairs of the state, or whether this was nothing more than a problem of personal ambitions, or even part of a tribal (Ga) conspiracy, is not too clear nor too important. With or without Adamafio and his group in government, the involvement of the CPP in the policies of development remained and would probably have remained superficial. Mobilization of the people through the party for development actions was never given serious consideration. Apter puts it very clearly, when discussing the significance or not of the new institutions and organizations created by the ruling party, such as the Young Pioneers: "Once these changes had been introduced, however, the result was *revolution from above* [italics mine]. Government took it upon itself to transform society in its own image, even if political leaders were unclear about what that image ought to be."[39] With Tawia Adamafio and Coffie Crabbe or Kojo Botsio and Krobo Edusei at the helm, the CPP as a party was withering away.

From this point of view, one could argue that if 1960/61 is a dividing line in Ghana's contemporary history, it is the dividing line between a period during which Nkrumah ruled with and through the CPP (before 1960/61) and a period during which he gradually relied almost exclusively on the civil service (after 1960/61). During the Republic years, Nkrumah acted more as the Head of State than as the leader of the CPP. This, however, was perhaps obscured by the fact that, formally, party and ideology were given, after 1960/61, more emphasis than ever. These were the years of a vast verbal and formal attempt to identify the party and Ghana and to make Nkrumaism the official ideology of the country. The more formal Positive Action became, the louder the emphasis on ideology and party in the press, on the radio, and eventually on the television.

Such efforts remained, of course, largely unsuccessful and, in fact, the real situation was quite different and could perhaps be better characterized as a process of increasing fragmentation of power. In this connection, it may be useful to mention the debate that took place just before the launching of Nkrumah's *Consciencism* and which concerned the organization and even the conception of the party In these last years of the regime, the use of the press and other communication media as well as some speeches delivered by the President himself and the growing activities of the Kwame Nkrumah Ideological Institute at Winneba may have given the impression that essential ideological battles were being fought in Ghana and that the CPP was determined to defend, in Africa, the integrity of scientific socialism. (Nkrumaism was officially defined as the adaptation of scientific socialism to the concrete circumstances of Africa.) However, on a fundamental question of party organization, the debate between those advocating that the CPP remain a mass party and those supporting an avant-garde conception of the party ended in the victory of the former. Later on, this was to find an additional justification in *Consciencism*.

But it goes without saying that a mass party cannot as such be a revolutionary party; it is much too wide and much too fluid a type of political organization to bring about the revolutionary changes which the leadership may have in view, unless one "hides" an avant-garde party within the official, mass party (perhaps the mysterious "inner circle" so often and vaguely mentioned by most students of Ghana?). At the same time, an avant-garde party cannot be set up and organized without some measure of clarification (who should belong to the party?). An avant-garde party, traditionally, is a class party, if not *stricto sensu* in its recruitment, at least in its fundamental options and objectives. In contemporary Africa, after independence, considering the class structure of most countries, it may be possible, but it is extremely difficult, to conceive of setting up an avant-garde party which, at the same time, would be popular.

This choice in favor of the mass party even at the end also implies that if revolutionary changes are to be brought about, the agent of such changes will not be the party. As the only alternative is the state (in Apter's words "revolution from above"), we must now turn our attention to the state and government. And what we find at the level of government is a policy of equilibrium between conflicting forces, a policy of avoidance of major choices which not only prevailed to the end but indeed was almost institutionalized as a method of government. This policy is well illustrated by the composition of the Presidential

Commission. This three-member commission, officially meant to replace the President in his absence, was reappointed each year and each year it was composed in the same pattern: one traditional chief, one high-ranking civil servant, and one representative of the radical "left" (the "ideological wing"). The composition of the Commission, thus, formally reflects the balance of forces in the country and perfectly illustrates the Nkrumah-CPP Government's policy of equilibrium.

The chiefs have lost their power and much of their prestige but they still sit on their stools. For all practical purposes, as we have seen, the University is controlled by the intelligentsia which is opposed to the regime. The civil service, although it is constantly under attack and told to "change its mentality," is maintained in its prerogatives. This had already been clearly seen by Austin who remarked that

> in May, 1960, the Government issued a New Charter for the civil service which declared: 'With the achievement of independence the position of the Civil Service in Ghana was drastically altered but these revolutionary changes did not become immediately apparent partly because of the continuity of personnel.' But in fact very little was changed. The service remained under the control of a Civil Service Commission, and the New Charter itself recognized that 'the principle of loyalty to the State and to the Government... does not imply participation in party politics. Perhaps the most important feature of the civil service is its non-political character.' ... In general, the civil service, the police, the university at Accra, and the Kumasi College of Technology weathered a great deal of abuse without being greatly affected by it. Similarly, the courts remained free under magistrates and judges who were appointed by a Judicial Service Commission. [40]

The Trade Unions themselves were at the same time

strengthened and emasculated; their Secretary General became ex officio member of the Cabinet, but they lost their autonomy; they became, like the Young Pioneers or the National Council of Ghana Women, an integral wing of the party.

Within the party leadership itself the same fragmentation of power can be seen. Up to a point, with the exception of the Adamafio's period, the "ideological wing," the socialist "Young Turks," had to be content with the party and government press, but they were kept out of ministerial posts as this remained the restricted province of the "Old Guard" (Botsio, Kweku Boateng, Krobo Edusei, etc.) despite growing criticism. One had to wait to the very end, late in 1965, to see a change in this pattern, with the appointment of K. Amoako-Atta to the Ministry of Finance, of Chinebuah to the Ministry of Information, and then, to the Ministry of Education, and of J.E. Jantuah to the Ministry of Agriculture. And, even so, there were indications that these new and more radical ministers were still far from having gained the upper-hand in the government.

Indeed, it may well be that it was because they were kept out of power that the radical "Young Turks" gave to the Ghanaian press its amazingly violent and critical style. In the 1960's, the press of the party and the government read more like the press of a party in opposition than that of a ruling party, and, a fortiori, like the press of the government. Those familiar with The Ghanaian Times or The Evening News will remember the violent attacks on corruption and bribery, the criticisms of the police or the even more extraordinary and recurrent denunciations of Cabinet ministers. They will also remember that all this was to no avail, that nothing ever happened, that Botsio and Boateng and Krobo Edusei remained Cabinet ministers, not to speak of the continuation of bribery and corruption.

In other words, all forces were kept in a state of unstable equilibrium. And, according to the formula commonly used in Ghana at the time, "the party [was] supreme!" But, of course, this was fiction. For instance, within the party itself, the Ideological Institute at Winneba was pitched against the Central Committee on problems of doctrine; the party remained open to all, and, therefore, the same groups which made up the Ghanaian society were to be found in the CPP. Each element of the power structure was held in check by another element; the characteristic, therefore, was fragmentation, atomization of power. And there remained, in the last analysis, only one source of power which could resist this process of atomization, this deliberate policy of equilibrium, and this was the Leader, Kwame Nkrumah.

However, if this situation as well as the declining prestige of most other leaders known to be corrupt, resulted, by comparison, in enormously increasing Nkrumah's personal power, there remained the fact that his own power was itself undermined by the impossibility of basing such power on any particular social or organized force. This was not too important in the early 1950's when people came flocking to the party, when "within eighteen months of taking office, membership was up to 700,000,"[41] when in addition to "an appeal to the heart," the party also represented

> the promise of immediate, material benefits as soon as self-government was attained, when the common man would be able to enjoy all the blessings which it was supposed existed in a country able to control its own affairs. With the removal of the imperialists, there would be an end to the enforced destruction of the cocoa farmers' trees, and a return to a market price for kerosene, cloth, matches, rice, yam, plantain, and tinned fish, as to enable the ordinary

man to live within his income while he enjoyed the amenities of pipe-borne water, free schooling, cheap houses, smooth road, more hospitals, industrialization and a 'mechanized agriculture.' [42]

By the beginning of the 1960's, after ten years of Nkrumah-CPP power, all this had changed as people in Ghana had had to adjust their former "rising expectations" to whatever could actually be provided. Besides, "limited access to top positions had reduced the prospects for social mobility [and had tended] to reduce the effective base for further recruitment among the youth in the CPP." [43] This, among other things, implies that in the 1960's, outside the "Court" and a small group of ministers and dignitaries, people did not feel they had vested interests in the regime. Not that the government was not doing anything for anybody; on the contrary, but precisely because what was being done—and which was important—was done in a diffuse way, for everybody, through the administrative machinery of government and without involving the people through mass mobilization.

The building of a modern infrastructure, on which the government concentrated its efforts and investments, was by definition in the service of the whole community, of all. As a result, no social group could feel that the continuing existence of the Nkrumah-CPP Government was serving its own particular group interests, whether this was the proletariat, the lower middle-class or any other group. From a political point of view, the building of Tema harbor or of the Akosombo Dam on the Volta river was an abstraction.

Under such circumstances, the Leader, because he maintains the complex of all these conflicting forces in balance, is all-powerful. However, this is true only until such time as a serious attempt to overthrow him is made. Much like the king in the tale of Hans Christian Andersen, everybody may marvel for a long time over his beautiful garments, but it takes only a little boy to make everyone realize that he is stark naked. As soon as this happens, there is nothing or almost nothing to support him—hence, the absence of any resistance to the Coup in Ghana. And then, the political scene remains desperately empty; there is nothing to replace the Leader.

In the case of Ghana, this situation is rather well illustrated by the behavior of the press, the radio, and the television which, several months after the Coup, continued to attack with extreme violence the former President. One may wonder why this happened, why, after being the main vehicle of the personality cult, the Ghanaian press continued to be so completely obsessed with the person and actions of the former leader. The explanation is quite simple: It did not change; before or after the Coup, Nkrumah remained its main topic; before the Coup, the press was Nkrumaist, and then it was not different; it simply became anti-Nkrumaist. It used to carry the Word, and after there was no word to carry.

In this respect, a comparison between the issues of February 23 and 24, 1966, in *The Ghanaian Times*, constitutes a most extraordinary experience. There was no solution of continuity; the government paper came out on the twenty-fourth of February, with only a few hours delay. One might think that this was part of the plot, but it was not. Very simply, Osagyefo had become *Anti*-Osagyefo, the Font of Honor now a Font of *Shame*. Founder's Day, *Usurper's* Day, etc. And, basically, this has still not changed. The lack of any positive content, politically speaking, so many months after the overthrow of Kwame Nkrumah, cannot be dismissed as a mere accident.

In addition to this anti-Nkrumaist onslaught of the press, the new government organized, as soon as possible, a countrywide campaign to destroy the myth of Nkrumah, and this again appears as a negative counterpart to the former Nkrumaist campaigns. Revealing also the state of political instability and the political vacuum that followed Nkrumah's overthrow and the peculiar nature of his power (balance of forces), the Junta not only banned the CPP *and* all other political parties, which had already been banned by the CPP in the 1960's, but did not hesitate to take the unpopular decision of banning the association of former detainees (of the former regime's goals) a few days after it had been constituted. The political vacuum and instability after the Coup correspond to the atomization of power before; they represent, as it were, its most striking a posteriori evidence. Or else some organized form of opposition would have occupied the political scene and manifested itself in a positive way, including filling the press with the tale of its ambitions, hopes, and programs —or, alternately, the socio-political forces backing the former regime would have opposed some resistance to the Coup.

Before going any further, let us now summarize. *The Evening News*, the daily newspaper of the CPP, supplies a good starting point: It was published everyday with the motto "One Party, One Leader" next to its title—thus, identifying in one short formula, the political life of Ghana at that time. Indeed, the whole political life then seemed to be reduced to a dialogue between Leader and Nation, on the one hand, and the activities of the ruling CPP and its "integral wings," on the other. However, as the main mass organizations were integrated to the party—the "integral wings"—, neither these organizations, nor the groups which they were supposed to represent (workers, women, youth, etc.), nor anything else could, under such a system, express or manifest itself autonomously, Thus, there only remained the party. But, as we have seen, the CPP was a mass party, i.e., ideologically confused, and some of its leaders were corrupt and discredited, [44] thus, the party could only manifest and express itself with some authority through the Leader. There was, therefore, no real party; the whole political life in the 1960's in Ghana was eventually reduced solely to a dialogue between the Leader and the Nation. But with the Leader addressing himself to the whole nation—rather infrequently, for that matter, in the later years—the dialogue tended to become diluted in generalities to the point where communication almost ceased to exist. The Word was carried out by the press, by the party, by the government, by all those who wished to use it, and for a thousand contradictory purposes, so that the policy of balancing forces practiced by Nkrumah did not incline him to clarify. The Leader's Word became an umbrella which everyone used to suit his own purpose. An impasse was reached.

The next question then is obvious: Was this impasse due to tactical mistakes? It does not seem so, or at least not entirely. In view of the class structure of Ghana, it is quite clear that the policy of equilibrium which manifested itself at the level of the party by an option in favor of a mass party and the Leader personality cult did correspond to a socio-political reality, that of a *postcolonial society in transition.* In such a society, the new (modern) forces —proletariat and bourgeoisie—more or less balance each other; none is strong enough to determine clearly the course of events in its own interest; none is capable of proposing a truly national future to the country. Besides, in such a society the conflict between past and future, between the modern world and the ancient traditional world, is partly blurred by the lack of a clear-cut separation between the modern and traditional sector in the economy (and therefore, in society). This is due to the fact that economic growth and development during the colonial era was largely the result of a Ghanaian response to colonial incentives, particularly in agriculture with the emergence of a large and fairly prosperous cocoa farming community.

In former African colonies, characterized as they are by an unstable balance of forces and a relative fluidity of the social structure, it would seem logical that the most dynamic and the best prepared social group, or its political expression, should take the helm, establish itself in the leadership of the nationalist movement, and identify its own class or group or political interests with those of the whole country within the framework of nationalist opposition before independence and within the framework of national reconstruction and development after independence. In Ghana, in the late 1940's, the embryonic bourgeoisie and the intelligentsia seemed to constitute such a potentially leading group, and the then newly formed UGCC appeared both as the political expression of this group and the logical leadership of Gold Coast nationalism. [45]

It was among the Cape Coast intelligentsia and the Sekondi-Takoradi business circles that the first proto-nationalist movements were initiated, and this could only appear as one more argument in favor of this group's bid for the leadership of the nationalist movement. At the end of the 1940's, the "model colony" had its "model party" and the UGCC felt so close to the goal that it had even brought Kwame Nkrumah back from the U.K. to become its Secretary General, i.e., to organize the party in such a way as to popularize the UGCC's general option for independence, to bring into the party's fold the more popular strata of Gold Coast society. The aim was to make sure that, from the upper circles of the intelligentsia, the nationalist ideas would reach the entire population of the Gold Coast.

It is not necessary to discuss again the reasons and the circumstances which led Nkrumah to leave the UGCC, to create his own party, the CPP, and his own following. It is enough to recall here that, in the ultimate phase of

the nationalist struggle for self-government, Nkrumah's
dynamism and that of the CPP (largely made up in the
beginning of the former youth groups following the UGCC
leadership until then) and a more radical appeal to the
people's nationalist feelings ("Self-Government Now")
made it possible for the "left" (Nkrumah-CPP) to outrun
the intelligentsia at the end of the race and, in 1951,
assume power in its stead. No doubt, this might have been
more difficult without the "troubles" of 1948 and 1950
which involved a majority of the urban population of Ghana.
But, whatever the circumstances, the fact remains that, by
1951, the "logical trainees" had been clearly outrun by a
more radical and less élitist political party. At the same
time, it is also true that the situation had not fundamentally
changed and, as we have already seen in Chapter 3, it is
on a more radical version of a basically similar platform
that the CPP defeated the UGCC. This set a number of
limitations on the CPP's margin of movement. *Inter alia,*
it had to retain as broad a popular support as possible, it
had to remain the party of the people, of the whole people.

After 1951, and for almost a decade, a generally
favorable economic conjuncture facilitated considerably the
task of the Nkrumah-CPP Government in its struggle with
the opposition. The government and the CPP leadership
appeared all the wiser when they could fulfill their electoral
promises by implementing their huge "reconstruction"
program (Tema, Akosombo, roads, schools, health services,
etc.) without such investments preventing private income
from rising. Under such—atypical—circumstances, the
opposition to the CPP was reduced to regionalism (Ashanti,
Northern, Ewe) and to trivialities on democracy and liberty
(UGCC, Ghana Congress Party, UP in succession). In sum,
this first decade was, despite the fierce electoral battles,
a period of respite for the CPP. It had to fight on one
front only, i.e., the internal political front, while it was

able, as a government, to carry out a vast development program without having to restrict private consumption.

It is in this period and under these circumstances that the "style" of the Nkrumah-CPP Government gradually emerged from daily practice—a nationalist and populist Government building a welfare state and a modern economy. Against such a platform the opposition was powerless and, indeed, it was possible to turn the Republic of Ghana in the 1960's into a one-party system, first *de facto*, then *de jure*. But the effectiveness of such a style of government depended in a large measure on the possibility of investing large sums in development programs without having to reduce private consumption.

After 1961, this possibility no longer existed. And the opposition, which had been practically eliminated in the late 1950's, reappeared with the first economic difficulties. As it had been banned, it manifested itself in the form of bomb attempts (starting with the Kulungugu incident of 1962) and pamphlets of exiled leaders, such as Busia of the former GCP and UP or Gbedemah, a former cabinet minister expelled from the CPP. The opposition also expressed itself in private conversation as already mentioned. To fight this opposition, as the party was allowed to wither away, Nkrumah hoped he could also use his policy of machinery (e.g., ban the UP) and his personal guard. It seems that Nkrumah hoped he could also use his policy of equilibrium, and the fragmentation of power would prevent any group from being able to take the initiative of striking blows against the only element that kept the whole system in balance, Nkrumah himself.

Thus, in Ghana, the withering away of the party and the progressive fragmentation of power are two elements of the same process which results from the leadership's policy of equilibrium. This can partly be explained by the limitations set upon the nationalist leaders by the origin of their power—the broad anticolonial movement and its high expectations. To retain their power the leaders, after independence, have to maintain as broad a popular support as they can. To do so in Ghana, under the circumstances of the 1950's, the Nkrumah-CPP Government used what was readily available: It invested both in the economic and social infrastructure at the same time as private income rose;[46] it kept the doors of the party wide open, thus illustrating, at the expense of the opposition, the party's slogan that "the CPP is Ghana" in two ways. First, in offering membership to all in Ghana, and second, in undertaking the process of building the new (welfare) state and the new economy (infrastructure).

However circumstantial this policy—to back the CPP's struggle against the opposition—may appear it has a deeper justification, and, fundamentally, this remains the justification of the whole anticolonial nationalist movement until the foundations of a modern national economy have been laid. It is again in discussing one of Fitch and Oppenheimer's theses that this comes out most clearly—and this points to the great usefulness of their essay, which, like Fanon's *Les damnés de la terre*, poses essential questions. When Fitch and Oppenheimer say that the acceptance of Arden-Clarke's offer by the CPP (to enter the election and to form the first government, i.e., to move from "Positive" to "Tactical" action) was their first and last mistake, they are right. They are right in the sense that unless one waits until there is a complete historical coincidence between a class movement and the nationalist movement, the party which forms the first government can only hope to accomplish a "partial revolution" as opposed to a "total revolution," i.e., socialist proletarian. But what does this mean? Simply what has been common knowledge for quite a time, i.e., that colonial countries are not industrial countries and that, as they are not industrial countries, the industrial proletariat cannot be a dominant force.[47]

At the same time, although the colonial system has not permitted the colonial countries to develop, it has introduced enough contradictions in these countries to trigger off strong anticolonial movements. Thus, under the circumstances of post-World War II Africa, the major contradiction was not within the colonial countries but between the nationalist movements and the colonial powers. And, therefore, the intimation that, outside the action of a truly proletarian party, there can be only "petty bourgeois mystifications," under the guise of nationalism, is not founded. It does not fully recognize the particularities of colonial history and colonial economics in Africa. Independence does not solve, but poses, the problems in Africa. And the central problem is that of the liberation of the country's economy and the building of a national economy. The question was not, and could not be, that of building socialism (despite government and party literature). The question was, and still is, that of the party and government's determination to give concrete and positive content to nationalism after independence, for nothing can be done before.

In such an undertaking much more is needed than the support of the "real oppressed class," "the landless agricultural laborers and sharecroppers,"[48] i.e., in Ghana a relatively small minority of the population even if one adds the urban proletariat. The idea—the Fanonist idea —that, because they are more oppressed, the poor peasants or the landless peasants of Africa alone can accomplish a "total revolution," i.e., perform the same role in Africa "as the industrial workers in Europe," is in part an extrapolation of the Algerian situation which was that of a settlers' colony with a dense European agricultural settlement (i.e., up to a point, an exception) and in part a superficial Marxist analogy in the sense that, in the Marxist analysis, the industrial workers are not only expected to "expropriate the expropriators" because they are oppressed, but because in the process of socialization of modern production they are both the "masters of technology" and the only indispensable "factor of production." In Fanon's analogy, the modern and technological elements of the Marxist analysis are both absent. [49] On the contrary, these elements are very much on the mind of the nationalist leaders.

FROM NATIONALISM TO SOCIALISM?

Their problem is that when the main objective of the nationalist movement—independence—has clearly been reached, when the most obvious external signs of the colonial period have been removed, and when the nationalist party is solidly established in government, the pre-independence platform no longer suffices. The time has come for the addition of a more concrete dimension to nationalism, if nationalism is to mean something after independence. In point of fact, it is then and only then that it is possible to give a positive content to the nationalist program. The country is now independent and its political independence must be consolidated by the development of a national economy. The struggle for independence is to be continued by the building of the nation. In other words, a program of industrialization and modernization of agriculture must be initiated. In Ghana, as more or less everywhere else in independent Africa, the accession to independence was followed by the adoption of a series of programs of industrialization to be embodied eventually in the comprehensive Seven-Year Development Plan. We have already discussed the merits of this strategic option and

seen its main results. What we now have to examine is why
this program of industrialization and modernization, which
is fully justified within the strategy of postindependence
nationalism, was in Ghana, as in most independent
countries in Africa, equated by the nationalist leaders to
a socialist policy of development.

Beyond the technical and financial difficulties it
raises in any former colony, industrialization poses a
fundamental political problem to the nationalist party.
Unlike its main pre-independence objective—independence,
which tended to unite all forces in the country in the
anticolonial struggle—industrialization, inasmuch as it
represents the main postindependence objective of the
nationalist movement, may either accelerate the process of
class stratification or, if it is carried out almost exclusively
within the public sector, will represent a considerable
burden for the entire taxable population. In contemporary
Africa, due to the importance of both the foreign firms and
the national public sector, what matters most is the cost of
industrialization and the emergence of a bureaucracy whose
development is parallel to the growth of the public
industrial sector.

In the former colonies of Africa, if one excludes
foreign firms, the industrial sector is public. This is also
true of Ghana despite the development of a number of
small and medium Ghanaian enterprises. All the important
plants set up since independence are state corporations or
foreign firms or a combination of the two, but typically
they are state corporations. This is known by everyone
and due to the fact that practically no African entrepreneur
can mobilize the financial and technical resources needed
in modern industry. This also implies that the development
of an industrial sector in Africa will increasingly result
—unlike what happened in Latin America—in the
development and the consolidation of a technocracy and a

bureaucracy, and not in that of a national bourgeoisie. This is the fundamental fact as far as industrialization is concerned in Africa.

Under certain circumstances, on the fringes of this industrial public sector, a number of small national businessmen and industrial entrepreneurs may also prosper. This depends on the political orientation of the countries concerned as well as on the previous, i.e., pre-independence, development of a business class. But this remains a marginal phenomenon, the essential is the development of the national economy by a national bureaucracy.

Thus, what may be expected in Africa, if a serious process of industrialization is actually to take place in the near future, is not so much an acceleration of class stratification but a polarization between a bureaucracy of higher civil servants and directors-managers of state corporations as well as technicians, on the one hand, and a growing industrial and semi-industrial proletariat, on the other hand. At the same time, the huge farming communities will become increasingly directed in their activities by a network of state-run marketing boards, agricultural extension services or "co-operatives" and other forms of rural "encadrement."

The general tendency in all countries to modernize and rationalize the economy is likely to be opposed by the various groups whose interests are threatened by such a rationalization-modernization process, in particular, the large section of the population engaged in retail trade. In this connection, it is interesting to note that in Ghana the "mammies" (market women), who had been in the forefront of the nationalist struggle in the late 1940's and in the 1950's, who had given their financial and vocal support to Nkrumah and the CPP, strongly and rather effectively opposed all attempts made in the 1960's at controlling retail prices. In 1964 and 1965, the economic

difficulties were increased in Accra and in other cities in
Ghana by the hoarding of goods and black marketing by the
"mammies." With or without Nkrumah and the CPP, the
government will have, sooner or later, to come to grips
with the problem posed by the distribution system
prevailing in Ghana, and this will no doubt be opposed
strongly by the powerful corporation of market women and
their petty trader clientele throughout the country.

More generally, the cost of industrialization will
represent a heavy burden on most groups upon whom
unpopular austerity policies will be imposed. As we have
seen in Chapter 4, the psycho-political difficulties inherent
in any policy of austerity are compounded by the persistence
of much higher standards of living among the expatriate and
national higher employees of the foreign firms established
in the country.

In Ghana, as up to a point elsewhere in independent
Africa, industrialization has been and still is presented as
a gigantic national effort of modernization. The difference
between Nkrumah's Ghana and neighboring countries or the
present regime is only a matter of emphasis. Because the
state will play the essential entrepreneurial role, one
seems to imagine that, just as the Ghanaian peasants had
managed to develop the agricultural sector of the colonial
economy in Ghana (by modernizing themselves enough to
become cocoa farmers but, at the same time, integrating this
modern economic activity in the traditional framework of
Fanti and Ashanti society),[50] Ghana would be able to
industrialize without giving up the permanent and essential
values embodied in the Ghanaian social structures and
way of life, the much talked about "African personality."
And the main argument given in support of this prognosis
is precisely that industrialization will not follow a
"European" pattern, will not result in an acceleration of
class stratification, will not result in the constitution of a

dominant national bourgeoisie. As we have seen, this is
quite possible, even likely. Due to the role of the state as
entrepreneur, it is probable that the industrialization of a
country like Ghana, among others in Africa, could be
achieved and controlled by a bureaucracy which would
eventually emerge as the truly leading group in the country.
It is likely, but what has this to do with socialism?

There is no good reason to identify socialism with a
policy characterized by the leading role of the state in the
industrialization of the country and the substitution of a
bureaucracy (which may not remain open for very long) to a
national bourgeoisie as the country's leading group. To be
sure, this is not capitalism either. It is, in fact, a new
model which contains elements inherited from the colonial
type of capitalist enterprises set up before independence
and elements of Soviet socialism, but above all, it contains
new and specific elements. These correspond to the
problems posed by the passage of a traditional economy and
society, which have been modified and altered by the
colonial impact, to a more-advanced stage of economic and
and technical development. This "African way to socialism"
is not entirely different from the way followed by some of
the least-advanced countries of Eastern Europe (e.g.,
Bulgaria or Romania), but it nonetheless presents some
specific characteristics.

Taking into consideration all this confusion (partly
innocent, partly not) on the very meaning of socialism, one
may now wonder why Ghana under Nkrumah, among many
other independent African countries, did not seem to be
able to consider the possibility of its development outside
the framework of socialism. Many answers can be found in
the Ghanaian press and other documents of the time.

The following are typical: Capitalism is too complicated
for Africa; traditional African society is fundamentally
communalistic, thus socialist; Africa must develop rapidly

and socialism only can ensure a high enough rate of
growth; the state must be active in all sectors of the
economy in the absence of a real bourgeoisie; because
there is a lack of private capital; because capitalism in
Africa is colonialism, and so on. Such answers and many
similar ones can be found daily in the African press
particularly in Ghana until the Coup. Although a good
many of them are not too convincing, they are given as
peremptory arguments. But they have in common one
essential underlying historical truth: Capitalism has
already had its turn in Africa, for 50 years, 100 years or
more, and Africa is underdeveloped. In other words,
*capitalism, as far as development is concerned, is seen as
having already failed.* Moreover, capitalism is foreign
inasmuch as first, precolonial Africa was also precapitalist
(especially if one excludes North Africa); and second, during
the colonial period, capitalist enterprise was the province of
foreigners. This argument seems finally to be the decisive
one because it is not simply a technical or an economic
argument but truly a deep political reason and one which
fits perfectly in the general framework of the nationalist
strategy. This comes out quite clearly in the last books by
Kwame Nkrumah *(Consciencism* and *Neo-colonialism: The
Last Stage of Imperialism)*—in particular, in *Consciencism.*

"CONSCIENCISM": AN IDEOLOGICAL PARRY
OR THE ESSENCE OF NKRUMAISM?

It is hard to say whether *Consciencism*[51] is mainly an
ideological parry, an attempt at justifying theoretically and,
a posteriori, the policies followed by the Nkrumah-CPP
Government for fifteen years, or whether it truly represents
the essence of Nkrumaism. It may be that *Consciencism*
only reflects problems and questions of a transitional

period, and thus, only represents the theoretical justification of the policy of equilibrium. If it is so, the book was only written for the benefit of the Young Turks of *The Spark* and the expatriate socialist friends of Nkrumah's Ghana. However, it was not well received by these people because of its lack of Marxian orthodoxy.

If, on the contrary, *Consciencism* does represent the essence of Nkrumaism, the intimate political thinking of Nkrumah, then it is quite clear that, *volens nolens*, Nkrumah gives a most unexpected support to what he and his ideological *epigoni* had until then so sternly fought, viz., "African Socialism" and its "specificities." Quite obviously, the historical evolution of Africa has followed, and is still following, a pattern different from that of the industrial countries of Europe and America. But, with all the changes introduced in African societies by the intrusion of European capitalism, it is hardly possible to describe the African society as essentially homogeneous, "communalistic," free from antagonistic contradictions, threatened only by external forces, and, at the same time, present such conclusions as the result of a Marxist analysis.

Consciencism is mentioned because it is the only book by Nkrumah which deals with these problems at the ideological level.[52] To be sure, the book only briefly touches on the problems of building socialism in Africa and appears mainly as a re-examination of the history of philosophy (in fact, mostly Western philosophy), but the thesis on the transition of African societies from communalism to socialism is clearly linked up with the book's central thesis on the relations between the "outside" and the "inside." Besides, this thesis was later further developed in several theoretical articles, in particular in a long series of articles in *The Spark* by Habib Niang.

Its political implications may be summarized as follows: Colonialism (intrusion of the "outside" on the "inside")

has modified the internal situation in colonial countries
(e.g., Ghana) both negatively and positively. The
development of the nationalist movement, because of the
nature of its fundamental objective (independence), is a
conflict of the "inside" against the "outside." It
re-establishes a positive equilibrium in the colonial
countries (the "inside"): first, by uniting in one movement
the whole people, and second, by bringing back the powers
or centers of decision to the country. It also integrates the
positive elements of the external influence (technology,
modern culture, etc.). The nationalist movement only
rejects those nationals who maintain links with the
"outside," who are the links of the "outside" with the
"inside," with the country—the "traitors," as it were.

After independence, only those who persist in their
role of agents of the "outside" (now neocolonialism) are
rejected, once again, because they are the agents of
external interests and forces. In sum, "inside" (i.e., in
the colonial country, in Ghana, before and after
independence) there are no antagonistic contradictions.
There are only the Ghanaians, the people, all, together,
and a few "traitors," local agents of the "outside," i.e.,
neocolonialism. Thus, one way or the other, we are led
back to the thesis of communualism so dear to the
theoreticians of African socialism. Although not completely
homogeneous, the contemporary African society does not
harbor antagonistic class or other interests. There may be
some internal conflicts, but they are not antagonistic
contradictions. This contemporary African society thus
remains fundamentally communalistic and, therefore, the
transition to socialism is only a matter of acquiring modern
technology.

What lies between contemporary African societies and
socialism is modern technology and industrialization. Thus,
socialism will not be achieved as the result of a class

struggle and the "expropriation of the expropriators" but by the modernization of the whole people who will acquire modern technology and embark on a program of industrialization of the country. This has been well defined by Colin Legum when he says that (according to Nkrumah's *Conciencism*) "in relation to African traditional society, socialism is historically revolutionary but genetically evolutionary."[53]

Whether *Consciencism* was only an ideological parry or the essence of Nkrumaism, it seems to indicate that Kwame Nkrumah had no intention in the mid-1960's of altering significantly his strategy and tactics, that the policy of equilibrium would not only be maintained as a provisional expedient but would be justified theoretically; it would be the "Ghanaian Way."

One more question must be raised. Why should Ghana's claim, that its nationalist policy was socialist, be taken more seriously than similar claims in other countries? The answer is not simple. It has to do with a combination of elements; the first one is the very real existence of Ghana. As compared to many African countries, Ghana had more reality, more density as a country. It was richer, it had more schools, more qualified civil servants; it existed more conspicuously. This is partly due to pre-Nkrumah, pre-CPP facts, such as the development of the main export crop by Ghanaian farmers and, through cocoa farming, the spread of a relative but obvious prosperity. Through this prosperity came the possibility of investing in infrastructure and education, with an ultimate result of a comparatively large national élite of administrators and intellectuals in Ghana. Besides, the country's values were not completely destroyed by the period of colonization; Ghana or rather the then Gold Coast had not been a settlers' colony. This persistence of various "national" cultures in Ghana perhaps performed a role similar to that of Islam and the

Arabic language in the North African countries; it held the community together in its confrontation with the world around it. The Ghanaians knew they existed and the world was soon made to know it too, as it became accustomed to the strong voice of the kente-clad Ghanaian delegates attending the various conferences and assemblies of the world.

The other elements which made Ghana's claim more credible than that of other African countries are essentially to be found in what was called in Ghana, before 1966, the "vision," Nkrumah's vision. This vision embraced both Ghana and the whole of Africa. In Ghana, it was being gradually materialized in the form of the huge infrastructure and in as many different and successfully realized projects as the building of a new port town (Tema), the setting up at Legon of a remarkable Institute of African Studies, or the existence of a nuclear research center near Accra. On the African scene, it was expressed by pan-Africanism, and later, by Nkrumah's advocacy for African Unity. On the world scene, it was expressed by the conspicuous participation of Ghana in the activities of the neutralist group of states. Ironically, it is when absent on a peace mission to Hanoi —a mission unthinkable only a few years earlier when Africa was still a mere object in world politics—that Nkrumah was overthrown.

Thus, the "vision" meant that in Ghana a nation was in the making and that Africa could not only complete its liberation struggle, but could also have a major role to play in the world—if only it could unite. The novelty as well as the audacity of this vision coupled with the relatively advanced economic position of Ghana could not be missed: Something was happening, this was the African revolution. From a distance and given the insistence of the Ghanaians that theirs was not merely African socialism but scientific socialism applied to Africa, it could be taken for socialism—at least, it seems established that many people did think so.

NOTES

1. The Tunisian example again is relevant here. According to the official propaganda of the Neo-Destour and the Tunisian Government, between 1957 and 1961, Tunisia was engaged in a series of "battles": the "battle of the Dinar," the "battle of foreign trade," etc.; 1961 was simply and globally the year of the "economic battle," while 1962 was the "year of the Plan."

2. *See,* Dennis Austin, *Politics in Ghana: 1946-1960.* (London: Oxford University Press, 1964), p. 31. Austin states that

> in June, 1959, Nkrumah revived a claim which had been allowed—perforce—to lapse. On the occasion of the tenth anniversary of the CPP, a large party rally in Accra was told: 'Comrades, it is no idle boast when I say that... the Convention People's Party is Ghana. Our party not only provides the government but is the custodian which stands guard over the welfare of the people.' The corollary to this claim was drawn a year later by John Tettegah, General Secretary of the Ghana TUC, who was reported as telling a local party rally that 'those who sit outside the ranks of the CPP forfeit their right to citizenship in the country. For it is only within the CPP that any constructive thing can be done for Ghana.'

3. Formally, this was illustrated by the fact that the Nkrumah-CPP Government even gave the country its name. They may not have invented the name, but they meant to "invent" the country, modern Ghana.

4. Provisional Government of the Algerian Republic or *gouvernement provisoire de la republique algérienne (GPRA).*

5. Frantz Fanon, *Les damnés de la terre* (Paris: Maspéro, 1961) (our translation).

6. *Ibid.,* pp. 127-38.

7. Austin, *Politics in Ghana*, pp. 12-13.

8. David Apter, *Ghana in Transition* (Rev.ed., New York: Atheneum, 1963), p. 304.

9. *Ibid.*, p. 165.

10. *Ibid.* Cf., I. Wallerstein, *The Road to Independence, Ghana and the Ivory Coast* (Paris-La Haye: Mouton, 1964) p. 138. This problem is by no means limited to Ghana, and Wallerstein is quite right in saying that "the immediate consequences for social change [of education] were very great, particularly in the colonial period, when acute status inconsistency, brought about by not finding appropriate employment for the educated, was a primary motorforce of nationalism." What was true of all educated men in the Gold Coast (including the so-called intelligentsia) was, of course, even truer of the thousands of partially educated, the "Standard VII boys," who had even more trouble and difficulty in finding an outlet for their ambitions. It may also be said that such a phenomenon is not restricted to the colonial period and, after independence, the problem posed to African governments by their numerous *chômeurs de luxe* (educated youngmen who are loath to take menial jobs) is only too well known.

11. Apter, *Ghana in Transition*, p. 166.

12. Austin, *Politics in Ghana*, p. 77.

13. Another name given to the militant CPP members, who were supposed to be too poor to have houses of their own to sleep in and had to use rich people's verandahs.

14. Austin, p. 77

15. Robert Fitch and Mary Oppenheimer, "Ghana: End of an Illusion," *Monthly Review* (Special Issue; July-August, 1966), Vol. 18, No. 3, p. 53.

16. *Ibid.*

17. *Ibid.*, p. 24.

18. According to figures given by Austin and quoted by Fitch and Oppenheimer, the CPP only won 55 per cent of the votes cast in 1956, and this only represented 32 per cent of the registered electorate, or 16.5 per cent of the eligible electorate. Fitch and Oppenheimer's comment is that on the eve of

independence "only one out of six Ghanaians eligible to vote supported the CPP." *Ibid.*, p. 75.

19. Cf., *supra*, our Chapter 2.

20. Austin, pp. 287-88.

21. An exception should perhaps be made for the very last years. But even then, this was done in very general terms—the "workers" being substituted in the propaganda for the *people*—and not even consistently.

22. In particular, Roger Murray's "Second Thoughts on Ghana," *New Left Review*, (London), 42, (March-April, 1967), pp. 25-39.

23. Fitch and Oppenheimer, p. 73.

24. *Ibid.*, p. 76.

25. Cf., Austin, pp. 360-61, and then, Fitch and Oppenheimer, pp. 76-77.

26. Austin, pp. 314-15.

27. Wallerstein and Austin give some details on the changes of occupation of MPs before their election (Austin) and on the number of associations to which people belonged (Wallerstein).

28. Many were unconcerned with Ghanaian politics, particularly if they were staying in Ghana alone, expecting to return after a given period of time to their villages in the North, or in Togoland, the Ivory Coast, or the Upper Volta, not to speak of more distant places, where they had their families and more often than not some farming activities.

29. Apter, p. 158.

30. *Ibid.*, p. 149.

31. Most of them were in their mid- or late thirties.

32. Apter, p. 227.

33. Austin, n. 77, p. 407.

34. It may be interesting to note that the same comment has been made recently about Bourguiba and the *parti socialiste destourien* in Tunisia:

> *la seule issue pour le pouvoir est d'osciller dans une*

politique de concessions à toutes les classes, et
d'arbitrer les conflits de la société. Parce que tous
ces conflits se répercutent en son propre sein, elle
a besoin d'un arbitre suprême; Bourquiba, qui jouit
d'un grand prestige auprès des masses, joue ce rôle
à merveille.

Groupe d'études et d'action socialiste tunisien, Les
caractéristiques de la période actuelle du développement de la
Révolution arabe [Paris?, 1967?] p. 16.

35. Apter, p. 329.

36. Austin, p. 367.

37. Apter, p. 337.

38. Wallerstein, pp. 156-62.

39. Apter, p. 336.

40. Austin, pp. 336-67.

41. *Ibid.*, p. 171.

42. *Ibid.*, p. 131.

43. Apter, p. 311.

44. Cf., Wallerstein (p. 161) who sees, in this tendency to
discredit the lieutenants of the charismatic leader, a fairly
general pattern and a way of prolonging and preserving the
leader's charisma.

45. This is almost what Apter and Austin say when they refer
to the intelligentsia as the "logical trainees," the "heir apparent"
of British succession. But such expressions may partly obscure
the fact that the party which assumes the leadership of the
nationalist movement is not in a logical relationship with the
colonial authorities, but in a dialectical one, whatever
compromises made on both sides.

46. The extent of the resources at its disposal, as well as the
struggle with the opposition, probably partly account for the
considerable emphasis placed on social amenities during the
first and second five-year development plans.

47. We have already mentioned that the cases of the U.S.S.R.
and China are different in that, although the industrial proletariat

only represented a relatively small fraction of the total population, *in absolute terms*, it was already, in 1917 and 1949, a very large group.

48. Fitch and Oppenheimer, p. 22.

49. This criticism has already been leveled against Fanon's "poor peasants theory." Cf., the article on Fanon by Nguyen Nghe, in *La Pensée* (Paris), February, 1963.

50. As illustrated, *inter alia*, by the use of the traditional systems of *abusa* and *nkotokuano* for the mobilization of the necessary additional labor force.

51. Kwame Nkrumah, *Consciencism* (London: Heinemann, 1964).

52. His other books, including *Neo-colonialism: The Last Stage of Imperialism* (London: Nelson, 1965), and *Africa Must Unite* (London: Heinemann, 1963), discuss the same problem at a much more practical level.

53. Colin Legum, "Socialism in Ghana: A Political Interpretation," *African Socialism*, ed. by W. H. Friedland and C. G. Rossberg, Jr. (Stanford, Calif.: Stanford University Press, 1967, 1964^c), p. 156.

CHAPTER 6 CONCLUSION

LA TRAGEDIE DU ROI CHRISTOPHE

In the *economic field* what was undertaken, and partly achieved, by the Nkrumah-CPP Government is immense. It is the "Tower" of King Christophe,[1] or at least, its foundations.

Gigantic sums were invested—and whatever was diverted by a few individual ministers or wasted for uneconomic prestige projects represents very little when compared to the infrastructure built in the course of these years. This must be said once and for all to clarify the nature and scope of the problem. The result of this policy (including Africanization, which was one of its modalities) is not only that the basis for the modernization and industrialization of Ghana has been laid but also—as we have just seen and this is even more important—that Ghana exists, is a country, *is*. It takes only a tour in the interior of Ghana to realize it. And this is not only a matter of roads, schools, electricity, and hospitals, but, much more deeply, a matter of men.

In Ghana, for a few years, expatriates had been confined to expert and technical jobs. With very few exceptions, key positions, executive posts had been Africanized and not only formally, but really, at the level of decisions. One might say that what made Ghana stand out among other tropical African countries was not so much

215

that Ghana was doing better (this was not always true) but that Ghana, for better or for worse, was really in charge of her own affairs; if she were to commit mistakes, they were committed by herself, under her own responsibility! This was in striking contrast with the situation of most neighboring countries and this is the only true school of development. And to whoever stayed for some time in Ghana, it was quite obvious that Ghanaians were aware of the particularity of their situation in this respect. It is not without interest that this has also been clearly emphasized by Nkrumah:

> The road of reconstruction on which Ghana has embarked is a new road...A certain amount of trial and error in following the road is inevitable. Mistakes we are bound to make, and some undoubtedly we have already made. They are our own and we learn from them. That is the value of being free and independent, of acquiring our experience out of the consequence of our own decisions, out of the achievements of our own efforts.[2]

This is an important achievement, but this is about all that was achieved. Beyond this, the economic results remain modest and, as we have seen, it would be too much to say that Ghana had already succeeded in freeing her economy; she had not even managed to find a serious alternative to the quasi-monopoly of her traditional Western trading partners. A good deal of the industrial production was in private and sometimes foreign hands and several large foreign trading companies were still active in the country. In sum, the essential in this field was, once more, the successful building of a huge modern infrastructure which contained the promise of an accelerated process of industrialization at a later stage. In fact, this was the main assumption of the Seven-Year Development Plan, which had been initiated two years before the fall of Nkrumah, and which, for the first time, had put the emphasis on productive investments as opposed to infra-structural ones.

In this policy of modernization, the two key elements were Kwame Nkrumah's "vision" of a modern Ghana, and the civil service as the specific instrument of implementa-tion. It is a venture in which the state played the main role—and this can easily be explained as, at this stage, it was essentially a matter of building the infrastructure. A few foreign firms associated themselves with this venture, among them, Kaiser (U.S.) and Parkinson-Howard (U.K.). Such a profitable cooperation was to constitute the first step, at the level of the infrastructure, of a wider cooperation which was to include the productive sector, especially in industry. Kaiser, again, as well as the Italian ENI, Unilever, and other firms, had already by their investments in the industrial sector clearly indicated that the type of mixed economy on which the Government of Ghana seemed to rely for the transitional period of rapid industrialization could find partners among the large expatriate firms.

It goes without saying that the description of this policy in terms of a socialist experience is misleading. To be sure, the state is becoming the main industrial and commercial entrepreneur; to be sure, in addition to one million individual farmers and their families, the state has set up a few large state farms, but these are rather symbolic; they are part of the many "signals"—"Here: Socialism!" Neither the 5,000 hectares or so put under cultivation by the Workers Brigades nor the few state farms, nor the thirty state corporations (some of which were very modest in size), nor the existence of a large state-run department store (GNTC), nor that of a large state building corporation (GNCC) can alter the fact that production remains essentially a private affair. Nor does this represent an earnest democratization of the production process.

The objectives appear clearly. They are the modernization and the development of the economy and these are implemented by the state, *from above*. The increasingly important role of the state corresponds to a double necessity: to make up for the inadequacy of Ghanaian private entrepreneurship in the modern industrial sector, and to protect and develop the national economy. That is all.

Politically, it is obvious that, despite the official doctrine, the experience of Nkrumah's Ghana is not a socialist experience—and we should not be surprised that it is not. Strategically, the country's modernization is identified with socialism, i.e., a reduction of socialism to one of its modalities, viz., the dominant role of the state in the building of a modern economy. At the level of implementation, the situation is somewhat more subtle. On the one hand, there is the whole panoply of socialist "signals" (the CPP, the Young Pioneers, the Young Farmers, the Co-operatives, the Ideological Institute at Winneba, the teaching of Nkrumaism, etc.) and, on the other hand, there is the daily practical evidence of the futility of these signs. Despite all the noise made by the CPP, its mass organizations, its press, and the Winneba ideology propagandists, the country's modernization (i.e., the party and government's strategic objective) is being organized *from above*, is the affair of the government, not of the party, and the specific instrument of this policy is the civil service. And, as we know, the civil service, although it is nationalist-minded and earnestly bent on modernizing the country despite its sometimes old-fashioned habits and methods inherited from the colonial period, is not imbued with socialist ideas. And neither the press nor the party, which denounce the civil service day in and day out and want the civil service to "change its mentality," can help it. Day after day and year after year, what is anticolonial nationalism is being renamed socialism.

Apter saw this and thought that what was happening was a form of neotraditionalism. "What is emerging in Ghana in the name of socialism is a national form of traditionalism. This is the reality which lies behind the term 'African personality.' The nation has replaced the ethnic community. The Presidential-monarch has replaced the chief."[3]

> Supporting him as a Presidential-monarch is a political religion. In it, the term 'African personality' disguises neo-traditionalism and emphasizes the unique qualities of Ghana life. If African socialism supports state enterprise, but compromises on the issues of property and classes, remaining thoroughly ambiguous on both these matters so fundamental to classical socialists, it also does not contradict traditional views of property and land tenure.[4]

However perceptive such a judgment—which includes the possibility of the ultimate destoolment,[5] and thus, may seem all the more correct as it appears to have been confirmed by the most recent history—it does not account for the most important dimension of anticolonial nationalism, its modern dimension, the thrust forward, the "vision." The nationalist movement or the nationalist leader is not in search of a static equilibrium; what they are after— almost desperately—is the breakthrough, the solution ahead, the way out. Nkrumah's policy of equilibrium can only be fully understood by recognizing that the frantic building of the infrastructure was conceived as the only way out. The main contradiction is seen as being between the underdeveloped countries (such as Ghana) and the advanced industrial countries. As long as this industrial gap exists, the relations between the two can only be defined within the general framework of neocolonialism. The contradictions within Ghana are only minor. The

strategy of the nationalist movement, therefore, is simple
enough: First, achieve independence, for nothing can be
done before; second, consolidate the power of the
"country's leaders," i.e., consolidate, against all forces
of division, the power of the party which has received the
people's mandate to free the country; third, "build a
socialist society."[6]

The first stage was completed by 1957. Due to the
instability inherent in any period of Dyarchy (1951-57),
the problems of the second stage—consolidation of
power—posed themselves before the first stage was
completed, in particular ever since the 1954 election. By
1960, the second stage, formally at least, was completed,[7]
and the Nkrumah-CPP Government was confronted with the
third stage, i.e., that of the "struggle for the total
reconstruction of society."[8]

Once the power of the country's leaders is consolidated, when all power is concentrated in their hands, the
policy of equilibrium is expected to serve to mobilize all
the resources of the country for the "total reconstruction
of society," and, first of all, for the accelerated process
of industrialization. Thus, equilibrium is not to be a
permanent feature, but only a way for achieving the main
objective of the transitional period—industrialization:
When this process is advanced enough, the potential
conflicts of the early period of the nationalist movement
will have been surpassed, the economic structures will
have been completely altered, and the social structures
also.

This is the vision, the dream. It is the dream of a
patriot, the vision of a nationalist leader, but not
specifically that of a socialist militant and leader. African
hero, dedicated and dedicating his country to the total
liberation of Africa, Kwame Nkrumah eventually appears as
a new Henri Christophe, who had also set for himself and

his people "some impossible task" to achieve.[9]

In reading *La tragédie du roi Christophe*, one wonders whether Césaire had not Nkrumah in mind rather than Henri Christophe or some other African or black leader, so precisely the description of Christophe seems to fit Nkrumah's own situation. One thinks of the lack of a sense of measure of which Nkrumah was accused and of the answer lent by Césaire to Christophe who was also accused of lacking this sense of measure and "of taking all in his own hands, of settling everything by himself, [of being] the huge figtree that eats up all vegetation around him." And here is Christophe's answer, which could also, *mutatis mutandis*, be Nkrumah's:

> I say that this people must seek, must want, must achieve some impossible task. Against Fate, against History, against Nature. Ah, ah. The uncommon attempt of our bare hands. Made by our wounded hands, the furious challenge! On this mountain, the rare cornerstone, the solid foundation, the tested block. ... Look. Imagine, this extraordinary platform turned toward the magnetic North, the walls are 130 feet high, 20 feet wide ... Not a palace. Not a castle to protect my acquired possessions. I say the Citadel, the freedom of a whole people. Built by the whole people ... Built for the whole people! ... It is a city, a fortress, a heavy battleship made of stone... inexpugnable, inexpugnable! Yes, to each people its monuments! To this people that was forced on its knees, there was needed a monument to put it on its feet again. Here it is. Surging! Watching! Look...do look! It lives. It hoots in the mist. It lights up in the night. Negation of the slave trader! The formidable ride. ... Let my people, my black people hail the Future's tidal smell.[10]

The analogy with Akosombo, with Tema, and also, unfortunately, with the OAU palace, the famous "Job 600," is striking.

Thus, the fall of Nkrumah does not appear as the end

and failure of a socialist experience in Africa, but rather as bringing to a formal close a transitional period and its illusions. By and large, the period stretches to 1965 and the illusions focused on the central idea that nationalism (the struggle for independence) would be more or less naturally followed by socialism (i.e., the "African way to socialism" as a specific method of development). Although the CPP and Nkrumah tried hard to identify Nkrumaism with the application of "scientific socialism" to Africa, a systematic and unprejudiced examination of their policies in the economic and political fields as well as an analysis of the ideology—"consciencism"—clearly show that Ghana was no exception to the general rule. Its socialism was, in the final analysis, but another brand of African socialism. In other words, the essence of this experience does not lie in the fact that it contained elements of socialism, but that it was a form of postindependence nationalism centered on an all-out effort to build a modern economy and a modern society.

In economic terms, these fifteen years (1951-66) can be described as a transitional phase of mixed economy, and in political terms, this period was characterized by an attempt at establishing and then maintaining a dynamic balance of forces both inside and outside Ghana. This resulted in a systematic policy of equilibrium, whose most conspicuous external characteristic was the personality cult of Kwame Nkrumah.

Nkrumah and the CPP ideologues attempted to justify this policy both to a majority of Ghanaians at home and to as many people as possible abroad, in Africa and outside the continent, both to socialists and, on different grounds, to nonsocialists. To this end, they used many arguments, at all possible levels, from the crudest to rather sophisticated ones, as in *Consciencism*, from the Bible to "Materialism and empirio-criticism," from the rhythms and popular poetry of the high-life to a new interpretation of Western philosophy, but the best justification can be easily summarized.

Historically, the "Ghanaian Way," inasmuch as it is a coherent and consistent nationalist policy after independence, is justified by the building of a modern nation. *Politically*, it is justified to the extent that it concentrates on the essential problem, viz., the establishment of a new relationship between the former colony, which is underdeveloped, and the advanced industrial countries, including the former *métropole*. The assumption is—and we believe it is fundamentally a correct one—that the main contradiction in a former colony is not between the various economic and social components of the society but between the former colony and the advanced industrial countries, including the former *métropole*.

Ideologically, the "Ghanaian Way" is justified by the "specificity" of the African situation, i.e., according to *Consciencism*, the persistence of a basically communalistic society in Ghana, or the absence of antagonistic classes. We do not believe that this is a correct analysis, for classes exist in Ghana and they are, as everywhere else, potentially antagonistic, but these classes are embryonic as far as the modern ones are concerned (bourgeoisie and proletariat) and they balance one another. Furthermore, and this is the most important point, none of them have proven capable of organizing the development of the country on its own terms. The only fully developed modern instrument of development is the state and its public servants—in other words, what was originally set up by the colonial power to organize the modern sector of the economy, and, by and large, to run the affairs of the colony according to the criteria of the British Civil Service, i.e., relatively speaking, according to modern criteria, along relatively modern lines. Thus, for all practical purposes, the ideological justification given in *Consciencism* can be accepted, although, *stricto sensu*, it is not correct. Indeed, the specificity of the African situation, i.e., the specificity of the socio-economic and political problems of former colonies in Africa has to be recognized—although it is not characterized by the absence of antagonistic classes.

The specificity of this situation is that colonization is not the industrial revolution; in other words, it is only marginally that the colonial countries have been brought into the modern capitalist system. Thus, the modern socio-economic classes—bourgeoisie and proletariat—are still either embryonic or marginal, but, because the whole country was put under colonial control, the state machinery and its bureaucracy are relatively well developed, and, with the attainment of independence, are growing more rapidly than ever. Colonization has not resulted in bringing about the development of the colonies, but it has introduced enough tensions and contradictions to trigger off a nationalist movement, as a more or less spontaneous indigenous political response to this situation. The real products of colonization are, therefore, the state machinery and the bureaucracy (directly) and the nationalist movement (dialectically).

Independence means that, one way or another, the nationalists take over the state machinery. And for some time, this is all they have at their disposal. They soon find out that this is not very much, for this administrative machinery was no more than the local wheel of a larger establishment. It is not in Accra, in Tunis, or in Dakar that the prices of cocoa, of olive oil, or of ground nuts are fixed. It is not in these capitals that loans are floated. Expatriate firms in these countries are only branches or subsidiaries of larger firms. The powers of decision have been brought back from London to Accra, but the decisions which can be taken in Accra are limited. Just as before independence, the main contradiction still lies, as far as the former colonies are concerned, between these former colonies and the industrial countries. This is, politically speaking, the essence of underdevelopment in former colonies. Any policy of decolonization, or of development, must be based on the full recognition of this fact.

Ghana's strategy of decolonization and development was based on the recognition of this.[11] And this explains most of the apparent contradictions of the Nkrumah regime. Similarly, the intuition first and then the clear awareness (as expressed in the Seven-Year Development Plan, for instance) that Ghana, and for that matter most if not all African countries, could not fully develop within their colonial limits alone, gave additional force to Nkrumah's pan-Africanist stand.

In sum, this is the essence of the Nkrumah-CPP's experience. If one does not see it, if one insists on discussing these fifteen years outside the framework of postindependence nationalism, the whole period, the whole experience remains a closed book—whatever the Marxist, Fanonist or other subtleties of the analysis.

But Nkrumah failed. In other words, despite what appears as a generally correct strategy and a reasonably effective implementation of this strategy, after fifteen years, Nkrumah's regime had only partially achieved its economic objectives and, politically, had ended up in a global failure—Nkrumah's ouster and the absence of Nkrumaist resistance to the Coup.

A likely explanation—and a tentative lesson to be drawn from Nkrumah's ultimate overthrow—is that the major contradictions in Africa's former colonies can only be solved by the development of these countries; but, at the same time, the means to achieve development are sadly limited in relation to the nature and scope of the job. This is particularly true of small countries, such as most former

African colonies. In the absence of larger regional
regroupings, external assistance on a fairly large scale is
necessary, but assistance is not a one-way street and it
implies risks (fast-increasing external debt, external
pressures, internal dichotomy between the expatriate
sector and the rest of the economy and society, etc). But,
if such risks are not taken, very little can be undertaken,
or very slowly, in the modern sector at least, in countries
which, more often than not, have neither the capital nor the
technological know-how to modernize their agriculture and
initiate a process of industrialization.

Thus, the duty of the nationalist leaders after
independence is clearly to switch to nation-building (with
all its implications, including a thorough process of
Africanization) and to concentrate on development,
whatever the risks such a policy represents or whatever
the internal tensions this is bound to create (austerity,
constraints of all kinds). But, despite efforts and successful
achievements (when the former are made and the latter
come by), the ultimate result of the "battle for development"
is not guaranteed—particularly if the African countries
persist in fighting this battle in isolation from one another.

To go through the long and frustrating transitional
period of industrialization and nation-building, the political
leaders do not have much at their disposal. They may
either attempt to raise the level of political consciousness
of the people (popular participation, mass mobilization,
"Positive Action," etc.), or they may consolidate their
power by strengthening their military and police establishments (but, as the most recent history tends to indicate,
this may prove very dangerous indeed). One original
aspect of Ghana's experience is that Nkrumah and the CPP
followed neither course, but, taking advantage of favorable
circumstances (the rising price of cocoa in the 1950's and
Ghana's sterling reserves), they tried to avoid the problem

and the tensions of development by investing enormous sums in an accelerated program of development without restricting individual consumption.

Considering the circumstances of Ghana in the 1950's, when this policy was initiated, Nkrumah's tactical choice (accelerated building of a modern economy) seems well justified and consistent with the strategic objective (modernization and industrialization). The decision of maintaining and even accelerating the pace of industrialization in spite of a completely altered conjuncture (falling price of cocoa, dwindling reserves) appears to be more open to debate, but, by then Nkrumah's margin of movement had been considerably reduced. The job had to be completed and it was probably already too late to bring back to life the CPP and attempt to resort to a new type of "Positive Action." It may, however, be partly a feeling of growing isolation in the wake of increasing tensions and frustrations in the country due to the high cost of this development policy in the 1960's, which prompted Nkrumah to press, in 1964 and 1965, for the total—but terribly formal—"Nkrumaization" of Ghana.

Whether this interpretation is correct or not, this was one of the most obvious tactical mistakes Nkrumah committed, for there is no possible justification for an ideological campaign to be launched at the same time as the party had been allowed to wither away and as the economic tensions have reached a peak. Whatever the importance of this tactical blunder, the game is over and Nkrumah has been thrown out. At his personal level, as a political leader, this constitutes the ultimate failure, the Guinean exile; and, if no drastic change is soon to take place in Ghana, this will also imply Nkrumah's final political exit as a major African leader. From a more general point of view, however, one may feel that the fall of Christophe-Nkrumah does not represent the definitive failure of a policy, of Nkrumaism, but that it merely emphasizes the perils and the limits of this policy. Like the hero of the Greek tragedy, "his struggle, including his meaningful death, contains a promise, the promise that the hero's deeds have contributed to freeing us from Fate."[12] Indeed, despite the fall and emphatic rejection of Nkrumah in Ghana, a complete abandon of his policies seems hardly conceivable. *Volens nolens,* the new regime will have to resume from what has been left by fifteen years of Nkrumaism. And this is not limited to a material legacy (a physical infrastructure and the first elements of a modern industry). It also includes the enormous Ghanaian and African ambitions of the Nkrumah-CPP years.

For the time being it would seem that Ghana is in a process of digesting these fifteen years—at the economic level, this takes the form of a most desirable streamlining and sorting out operation. But, it goes without saying that this economic consolidation cannot constitute a program of government nor can a negative and unattractive policy of simple anti-Nkrumaism. Sooner or later, the nationalist program of development will have to be resumed in Ghana on a large scale, for the simple reason that the program is fundamentally the only one and it was not completed by the former regime. Not to speak of the future problems which will be posed by the many youngmen of the Nkrumah primary schools, secondary schools, and three universities!

In Africa, the fall of Nkrumah has also raised questions. Mali, for example, almost immediately set up a "Council for the Defense of the Revolution." But essentially the fall of Nkrumah has added a sobering postscript to his fifteen years in power; it has added the sobering notion that an accelerated program of development creates almost as much tension as the absence of such a program, at least in the short period. The fall of Nkrumah, the abrupt end of the "Ghanaian miracle" (more advanced, more developed, and officially, more revolutionary) has contributed to a better appreciation of the total process of development in contemporary Africa.

If "neo-Nkrumaism" is ever to mean anything, it should probably not be expected from an hypothetical "return from Elba," for a hundred or more days, but from a clearer consciousness of the total process of development. Nkrumah's Ghana, for fifteen years, showed the way by its very success in building a modern economy at the same time as it fostered some illusions concerning the actual cost of development due to the particularity of the situation of Ghana during the 1950's. Nkrumah's fall emphasizes the risks and dangers of any serious policy of development. The civil servants in Accra, who may have thought at the time of the Coup that the hero had somewhat outlived his usefulness and that the job could be better done from then on under their sole and competent responsibility, may now be pondering over the lesson of the rise and fall of Kwame Nkrumah—just as much as the few other heroes still at the helm here and there in Africa.

NOTES

1. Aimé Césaire, *La tragédie du roi Christophe* (Paris: Presence africaine, 1963). Cf., *infra*.

2. Kwame Nkrumah, *Africa Must Unite* (London: Heinemann, 1963), p. 120.

3. David Apter, *Ghana in Transition* (Rev. ed.; New York: Atheneum, 1963), p. 361.

4. *Ibid.*, pp. 369-70.

5. "One cannot help wondering whether or not this neo-traditionalism will eventually include destoolment of the Presidential-monarch." (Apter, p. 370).

It may also be worth mentioning that General Ankrah also used this comparison (Cf., *West Africa* (London), 2545, March 12, 1966) in a broadcast on February 28, 1966, stating that the army and police had acted in accord with "the oldest and most treasured tradition of the people of Ghana, the tradition that a leader who loses the confidence and support of his people and resorts to the arbitrary use of power should be deposed."

6. For an exposé of these three stages in CPP political terminology, see, *Some Essential Features of Nkrumaism*, by the Editors of *The Spark* (New York: International Publishers, 1964) especially, pp. 28-29.

7. Marked formally by the election of Nkrumah as the first President of the Republic of Ghana.

8. *Some Essential Feature of Nkrumaism*, p. 29.

9. Symbolically, Christophe had decided to erect an impregnable Tower, for the building of which all the resources of the country were mobilized.

10. Aimé Césaire, *La tragédie du roi Christophe*, pp. 65-66 (our translation).

11. Although, paradoxically, I believe the word "under-developed" was never applied to the situation of Ghana in either party or government literature.

12. André Bonnard, *Civilisation grecque* (our translation). *"La lutte du héros contient jusque dans sa mort-témoignage une promesse, la promesse que l'action du héros contribue à nous affranchir du Destin."*

BIBLIOGRAPHY

BIBLIOGRAPHY

Several books and many articles have already been devoted to interpreting the fifteen *Nkrumah years* of the contemporary history of Ghana.

Some of these are almost classics and indispensable: David Apter's *Ghana in Transition* and Dennis Austin's *Politics in Ghana*. Robert Fitch and Mary Oppenheimer's "Ghana: End of an Illusion" represents essential reading for the questions it raises, if for no other reason.

Ghanaian sources and interpretations are not lacking either. First in importance are Kwame Nkrumah's several books, and in particular: *Ghana: The Autobiography of Kwame Nkrumah* (1957); *Africa Must Unite* (1963); *Consciencism* (1964); and *Neo-colonialism: The Last Stage of Imperialism* (1965). Other Ghanaian sources for presenting the CPP viewpoint include two daily newspapers, *The Ghanaian Times* (Government) and *The Evening News* (Party), as well as the weekly ideological paper, *The Spark*, and many less important publications. During the period of the "Dyarchy" (1951 57) and the first postindependent years, the press and other publications of the opposition, (UGCC, GCP, NLM, etc.) were also quite important.

Throughout these years, the London-based weekly, *West Africa*, has supplied a wealth of information and comments on Ghana's political and economic evolution.

In addition to numerous articles published in Ghana (particularly in the *Economic Bulletin of Ghana)* and outside Ghana, the first volume of *A Study of Contemporary Ghana* now provides the student of Ghana with a comprehensive economic study of Ghana and an excellent specialized bibliography.

For a general bibliography, one can refer to A.F. Johnson, *A Bibliography of Ghana, 1930-1961* (London:

Longmans, 1964), as well as to the bibliographies given by Apter and Austin.

The bibliography given hereafter only mentions the books, documents, and articles which have been specifically quoted in this book.

BIBLIOGRAPHY

BOOKS

Amin, Samir. *Trois experiences africaines de développement: le Mali, la Guinée et le Ghana.* Université de Paris. "Institut d'étude du développement economique et social (IEDES). Tiers-Monde." Paris: Presses universitaires de France, 1965.

Apter, David. *Ghana in Transition.* Rev. ed. New York: Atheneum, 1963.

Austin, Dennis. *Politics in Ghana: 1946-1960.* London: Oxford University Press, 1964.

Birmingham, Walter B., Neustadt, I., and Omaboe, E.N., eds. *A Study of Contemporary Ghana.* Vol. I: *The Economy of Ghana.* London: Allen and Unwin, 1966.

Césaire, Aimé. *La tragédie du roi Christophe.* Paris: Presence africaine, 1963.

Fanon, Frantz. *Les damnés de la terre.* Paris: Maspéro, 1961.

Fitch, Robert, and Oppenheimer, Mary. "Ghana: End of an Illusion." Special Issue. *Monthly Review* (New York), Vol. 18, No. 3, July-August, 1966.

Groupe d'études et d'action socialistes tunisien. Les caractéristiques de la période actuelle de développement de la Tunisie et les instruments de la Révolution Arabe. [Paris?, 1967?]

Guelfat, Isaac. *Doctrines économiques et pays en voie de développement.* "IEDES. Tiers-Monde." Paris: Presses universitaires de France, 1961.

Hill, Polly. *The Gold Coast Cocoa Farmer—A Preliminary Survey.* London: Oxford University Press, 1956.

Hodgkin, Thomas. *African Political Parties.* London: Penguin Books, 1961.

Nkrumah, Kwame. *Africa Must Unite.* London: Heinemann, 1963.

———————. *Consciencism.* London: Heinemann, 1964.

——————— · *Neo-colonialsim: The Last Stage of Imperialism.* London: Nelson, 1965.

Some Essential Features of Nkrumaism. Editors of *The Spark.* New York: International Publishers, 1964.

Wallerstein, Immanuel. *The Road to Independence, Ghana and the Ivory Coast.* Paris-La Haye: Mouton, 1964.

Wills, J. B. *Agriculture and Land Use in Ghana.* London: Oxford University Press, 1962.

ARTICLES

Bourguiba, Habib. Speech. November 18, 1961.

Decraene, Philippe. *"Les régimes militaires de l'ouest africain."* Part III: "Ghana: *Des officiers qui ont la faveur du peuple."* Le Monde* (Paris), July 2, 1966.

Killick, Tony. "Making Ghana Grow Again." *West Africa* (London), 2568, August 20, 1966.

Legum, Colin. "Socialism in Ghana: A Political Interpretation." *African Socialism.* Ed. by W.H. Friedland and C.G. Rossberg, Jr. Stanford, Calif.: Stanford University Press, 1967 (1964^c).

Mohan, Jitendra. "Varieties of African Socialism." *Socialist Register.* Ed. by Ralph Milibrand and John Saville. London: Merlin Press, 1966.

Roger, Murray. "Second Thoughts on Ghana." *New Left Review* (London), 42, March-April, 1967.

Nghe, Nguyen. "Fanon." *La Pensée* (Paris), February, 1963.

Riad, Hassan. *"Les trois âges de la société égyptienne."* *Partisans* (Paris), No. 7, 1962.

Seers, Dudley. "The Stages of Economic Development of a Primary Producer in the Middle of the Twentieth Century." *Economic Bulletin of Ghana* (University of Ghana, Legon, Accra), Vol. VII, No. 4, 1963.

Wallerstein, Immanuel. "Ghana as a Model." *Africa Report* (Washington), May, 1967.

GOVERNMENT REPORTS AND DOCUMENTS

Ghana. Census Office. *1960 Population Census of Ghana.* Advanced Report of Volumes III and IV. Accra: Government Printer, 1962.

_____. Central Bureau of Statistics. *Economic Survey 1964.* Accra: Government Printer, 1965.

_____. Office of the Planning Commission. *Seven-Year Plan for National Reconstruction and*

Development. Financial Years 1963/64–1969/ 70. Accra: Government Printer, 1964.

Program of the Convention People's Party for Work and Happiness. Accra: Government Printer, 1962.

Seers, Dudley and Ross, C. *Report on Financial and Physical Problems of Development in the Gold Coast.* Accra: Government Printer, 1952.

United Nations. Economic Commission for Africa. *Investment Laws and Regulations in Africa.* (E/CN.14/INR/28/REV.2), 1965.

INDEX

INDEX

-A-

Abraham, Willie E. 183
abusa workers 27, 33-34, 57n.19, 172,
   214n.50
acts
   Avoidance of Discrimination 92
   Capital Investment 71, 129, 154n.8
   Deportation 92
   Emergency Powers 92
   Local Government Ordinance 44
   Preventive Detention 92
Adamafio, Tawia 7, 183, 185-86, 189
Africanization 45, 57n.21, 73, 81, 149,
   215, 226
"African personality" 100, 203, 219
Akosombo 67, 139, 148, 191, 196, 221
Algeria 52, 80, 105-6, 116n.75, 137,
   152, 162, 178, 199, 210
Amin, Samir 4, 13n.4, 143
Amoako-Atta, K. 189
Anlo Youth Association 92
Apter, David 14n.13, 35, 44, 48,
   114n.46, 166-67, 175, 177, 181,
   184-87, 219
Arden-Clarke, Sir Charles 82-83,
   113n.40, 198
Armah, Kwesi 155n.9
asantehene 39, 43
Ashanti Goldfields 25
austerity policy 7, 100, 144-46, 150,
   160, 203, 226
Austin, Dennis 8, 14nn.9 and 11, 35,
   38, 48, 84, 93-96, 165-66, 168, 170,
   172-73, 176, 184, 188

-B-

Balandier, George 35, 48
banks 79, 101, 128-29
   Bank of West Africa 129
   Barclays Bank 129
   Central Bank 128
   Ghana Commercial Bank 128-29
Bettelheim, Charles 153
Birmingham, Walter B. 14n.12, 55n.3
Boateng, Kweku 189
Botsio, Kojo 186, 189
bourgeoisie 24, 52, 70, 74, 183, 194,
   205, 223-24
   agro-mercantile stratum 51, 170, 179
   embryonic bourgeoisie 25, 34-36, 50,
      52-53, 169-70, 179, 195, 223
   embryonic urban bourgeoisie 25, 52
   rural middle bourgeoisie 24, 34,
      50-51, 56n.16
Bourguiba, Habib 93-94, 105-7, 212n.34
Burns Constitution (1946) 44, 50
Busia, K.A. 45, 96, 197

-C-

Césaire, Aimé (*La tragédie du roi*
   Christophe) 215, 221
charisma 54, 166, 184-86, 213n.44
chiefs 37-54, 44n.36, 58nn.32 and 33,
   81, 90, 111n.11, 165, 167, 169,
   179-82, 188, 219

China 2, 151, 213n.47
Chinebuah, K. 189
Christianity, Christians 42, 47, 58n.39
Cie française de l'afrique occidentale
   (CFAO) 25, 129
civil service 36, 46-47, 53, 65, 75, 81,
   99, 108, 117n.76, 131, 135, 149,
   164, 180-86, 188, 202, 208, 217-18,
   223, 229
cocoa 51, 90, 95-99, 102, 133-35, 146,
   149, 208, 226
   annual laborers 30 Table 2, 33, 36
   "cocoa boom" 6, 17, 155n.17
   export 22-26, 66, 97, 127n.4, 170
   fall in cocoa prices 7, 105-6, 141,
      143, 227
   farmers 17-18, 22-25, 29-36,
      30 Table 2, 50, 53, 68, 81, 90,
      94, 171, 179, 181, 190, 203, 208
   farming 18, 21, 26, 30 Table 2, 31,
      180, 195
   prices 6-7, 23, 90-91, 96, 98, 180,
      224
Cocoa Duty and Development Funds
   (Amendment) Bill 90
Cocoa Marketing Board (CMB) 181
Cocoa Purchasing Company (CPC)
   114n.48, 177
Code of Foreign Capital Investment
   137
colonialism 21, 35, 62n.4, 113n.40,
   153, 207
   colonial system 22-23, 40-43,
      48n.41, 50-55, 57n.21, 59, 63,
      65, 70, 72, 79-82, 86-87, 100,
      103, 107, 128, 136-38, 148, 165-66,
      169-70, 180, 194, 199-200, 204-5,
      211n.10, 218, 223-25.
   colonization 22, 39, 42-47, 50-51,
      169, 208, 224
   (*see also* neocolonialism)
commoners (see youngmen)
Communism 6, 81, 162, 170, 174, 178
consciencism 186-87, 205-8, 222-24
Convention People's Party (CPP)
   13nn.3 and 5, 59-60, 81-86, 92,
   114n.46, 162-96, 210n.2, 218
   aims and methods 60-63, 83-87,
      94-96, 99, 116n.72, 117n.76, 121,
      150, 165-85, 230n.6
   ambiguity of its class nature 35-36,
      41, 83, 166-68, 173-75, 184
   and the press 47, 189, 192-94, 218
   as a mass party 13n.8, 54, 81, 150,
      160-61, 165, 173-75, 181, 187,
      193-94
   as a revolutionary party 13n.8, 80-
      83, 187
   constitution (1949-51) 94, 111n.11,
      114n.51, 121
   leaders of 6, 35, 59, 70, 75, 80-83,
      87, 89, 91, 110, 122, 149-50, 164,
      166, 177, 189

Convention People's Party (cont'd.)
  left-wing 6, 130, 170, 177-78
  "Old Guard" 189
  opposition to 6, 45, 53, 76, 84,
    87-97, 102, 115n.58, 122,
    156n.25, 163, 170, 182, 196-98
  party organization 5, 13n.7, 46, 49,
    54-55, 88-89, 187, 195
  Tarkwa Conference (1952) 60
  withering away of 184-86, 197, 227
  (see also "integral wings")
coups 1, 9, 76, 112n.27, 140, 147, 165,
  192, 205
Coussey Report 59, 110n.1
Crabbe, Coffie 186

—D—

Danquah, J.B. 5, 45-46, 92-93
decolonization 3, 5, 8-12, 60-61, 85,
  108, 225
development strategy 4-5, 8-12, 60-64,
  74, 78, 84-85, 97, 110, 123-27, 137,
  141, 144, 149-53, 159, 225
  options 24, 79, 83, 108, 110,
    115n.62, 184
DuBois, W.E.B. 153
Dyarchy 59-60, 83-89, 92-93, 110, 122,
  148, 156n.25, 160, 177, 220

—E—

Edusei, Krobo 90, 114n.48, 186, 189
Egypt (see United Arab Republic)
elections 84-97, 115n.58, 121, 170-73,
  176-77, 182-84, 196, 198, 211n.18
  by-elections 89, 92, 161, 176
  1951, first election 5, 13n.8, 54-55,
    59-60, 82-83, 87-90, 95, 167-68,
    170-72
  1954, independents' election 5, 60,
    87-88, 114n.46, 90-91, 95-96,
    161, 172, 220
  1956, third election 6, 60, 86-91,
    96-97, 161, 172
  1960, Presidential election 7, 93,
    100, 161
  1964 referendum 7
élite groups (see intelligentsia, chiefs,
  and youngmen)
expatriate firms (see investment)
expatriates 25, 38, 40, 46, 140, 150,
  159, 215, 226

—F—

Fanon, Frantz 35, 79, 116n.75, 162-63,
  198-200
  Fanonist 166, 199, 225
  "the party and the state" 162
  (see also Marxist-Fanonist)
Fitch, Robert 9, 14n.14, 35, 78-84, 86,
  97, 100, 111n.19, 113nn.35 and 40,
  114n.43, 122, 128, 166-67, 170-71,
  175-76, 179, 184, 198
foreign trade 19, 22-23, 56n.7, 102-4,
  128-35, 141, 163, 216-18
  with socialist countries 133 Table
    4, 134-35, 139-40

foreign trade (cont'd.)
  (see also investment)

—G—

Ga Adangme Shifimo Kpee 6, 91-92
Gbedemah, K.A. 48, 90, 156n.25, 197
"Ghanaian Way" 123, 125, 140, 148-
  54, 223
Ghana National Construction
  Corporation (GNCC) 217
Ghana National Trading Corporation
  (GNTC) 129
government 98-105, 108-110
  Nkrumah-CPP 3, 5, 8-12, 22-26, 35,
    47, 54-55, 59-63, 69-74, 80,
    83-84, 97, 117n.76, 121, 123-26,
    128, 130-32, 136, 141, 144, 145,
    148, 149, 153, 160-64, 182-84,
    186, 188, 190-91, 196-98, 202-5,
    210n.3, 215, 220, 225, 228
  Planning Commission
  (see also self-government)
Great Britain (see United Kingdom)
gross domestic product (GDP) 127n.4,
  142 Tables 6 and 7, 141-47
gross national product (GNP) 10, 128

—H—

Hill, Polly 29-31, 33
Hodgkin, Thomas 35, 48

—I—

independents' election (see elections)
indirect rule 40-44, 54, 81, 181-82
  "Iugardian" concept 41
  native authority 41
industrialization 4, 13n.5, 27, 50, 62,
  62n.4, 64-67, 70-74, 100, 104, 109,
  116n.72, 136-39, 146-47, 149, 153,
  191, 200-204, 207, 215-17, 220,
  226-27
inflation 17, 127, 181
"integral wings" of the CPP 189, 193
intelligentsia 22, 37, 40, 44-54, 89-93,
  96, 165, 167-71, 179-83, 188, 195-
  96, 211n.10, 213n.45
investment 6, 34, 69, 75-78, 99-104,
  109, 125, 141, 216-17
  expatriate firms 2, 25, 27, 42, 50,
    52, 53, 70, 217, 224
  foreign 25, 68, 69, 72, 74, 79, 81,
    83, 129, 135-40, 153, 154n.8,
    159, 163-64, 181, 201
  infrastructural 12, 76, 77 Table 3,
    99, 109, 136, 148-49, 191, 196-
    98, 207, 215-16, 219, 227

—J—

Jantuah, J.E. 189

—K—

Kaiser Aluminum 67, 99, 217
Killick, Tony 14n.9, 55n.3, 56n.8, 72,
  126-27
Kingsway 129
Kulungugu incident (1962) 197

–L–

labor 21, 30 Table 2, 172, 179
  mining 27, 116n.70, 172
  mobility of 33, 35, 179
  (see also cocoa)
Legon (the University) 46, 182-83,
  188, 209
Legum, Colin 58n.29, 208
Leventis *(see* Ghana National Trading
  Corporation)
Lewis, W. Arthur 78, 112n.25
  "Lewis era" 79, 103, 113n.35,
  122, 184
  "Lewis model" 80, 83, 85
  Report on Industrialization and the
  Gold Coast 103

–M–

Marxism, Marxist 79-80, 86, 153, 200,
  206, 225
Marxist-Fanonist 9, 167
mass media 4, 47, 148, 186, 189, 192-
  94, 205
middle class 24-26, 29, 34, 36, 81,
  166, 168-69, 191
  rural middle class 26, 34, 51, 53
  semimodern rural middle class
  21, 50
  urban middle class 26
  (see also traders)
"misfits" *(see* youngmen)
mixed economy 69, 75, 77, 111n.17,
  125, 150, 154, 217
mobilization 74, 78, 164, 180, 185,
  191, 220, 226
  by the CPP 35-36, 161-63, 183
"model colony" 17, 50-51, 195
modern, modernization 44, 109, 164,
  200-202, 215, 217-18, 226-27
Moslem Association Party (MAP) 92

–N–

National Council of Ghana Women 189
National Liberation Movement (NLM)
  6, 53, 86-92, 94, 96-97, 102,
  115n.57, 172, 174-75, 177
nationalism, nationalist 2, 4, 17, 22,
  35, 38-39, 46-52, 64, 70, 74, 78, 80,
  90, 108, 122, 159, 166, 169-70, 177,
  180-82, 195, 199-205, 211n.10, 219-
  20, 222, 224, 226
  anticolonial nationalism 85, 121,
  180, 198-99, 201, 219
  proto-nationalist movements 54,
  168, 195
  (see also colonialism)
native authority *(see* indirect rule)
  (see also chiefs and traditional)
neocolonialism 63-65, 69, 79, 80, 83,
  102-3, 113n.35, 135-38, 148-49,
  156n.25, 207, 219
neo-Weberian 9, 37, 167
Neustadt, I. 14n.12, 55n.3
Niang, Habib 157n.30, 206

nkotokuano 33, 57n.24, 172, 214n.50
Nkrumah, Kwame 1, 11, 22, 24, 46-49,
  54, 59-60, 70, 76, 80-83, 91, 93, 96,
  113n.40, 116n.72, 121, 130, 132,
  141, 149, 150-53, 161-68, 184-86,
  190-93, 195-97, 202, 204-5, 208,
  216, 218, 221-22, 227, 229
  and the press 4, 35, 47, 130, 148
  as *le roi* Christophe 220-21, 227,
  230n.9
  Ideological Institute *(see* Winneba)
  "Nkrumaist vision" 78, 110, 209,
  217, 219-20
  Osagyefo 192
Nkrumaism 9, 35, 81, 183, 192-93,
  205-8, 218, 222, 227-29
  anti-Nkrumaism 192, 228
  definition of 63, 186-87
  official ideology 7, 183, 186
nkwankwaahene 38
Northern People's Party (NPP) 6, 87-
  88, 92, 96, 176-77

–O–

Omaboe, E.N. 14n.12, 55n.3, 61,
  117n.76, 131-32, 183
Oppenheimer, Mary *(see* Fitch, Robert)
Organization of African Unity (OAU)
  60, 151-52, 221
  "African Unity Now" 60, 72, 151
  (see also pan-Africanism)
Osagyefo (see Nkrumah, Kwame)

–P–

Padmore, George 153
pan-Africanism 151-53, 209, 225
  Sixth Pan-African Congress 81
Parkinson-Howard 217
parti socialiste destourien (see
  Tunisia)
petty traders *(see* traders)
Plan for the Nation 95
plans 77 Table 3, 117n.76, 131n.11,
  213n.46
  first Development Plan (1951-56) 8,
  95
  Second Development Plan (1959-64)
  8, 61, 79, 110n.2
  Seven-Year Development Plan (i.e.,
  the Plan) 3, 8, 13n.5, 61-62, 72,
  75-78, 83-86, 93, 109-110,
  111n.17, 112nn.25 and 27,
  117n.76, 130-32, 137, 140, 143,
  200, 216-19, 225
Population Census, 1960 26, 36, 46,
  55n.2, 56n.15
Positive Action 5, 13n.8, 59, 82,
  113n.40, 160-61, 164, 183, 186, 198,
  226-27
Presidential Commission 188-89
Presidential election 1960 *(see
  elections)
Program for Work and Happiness (i.e.,
  the Program) 3, 60-75, 83-86, 110,
  111nn.11 and 17, 162

proletariat 24, 26-27, 34-36, 50, 52,
    138, 223-24, 169-72, 174, 178-79,
    181, 191, 194, 199, 201
                    –R–
referendum (1964) (see elections)
regional, regionalism 87-88, 95-96,
    182, 196
    macro-regionalism 177
        Ashanti 89-91, 177, 196
        Ewe (separatist tendencies) 90-
        91, 96, 196
        Northern 88, 90-93, 95-96, 177,
        196
    micro-regionalism 175, 177
        Brong 177
revolutionary African countries 137,
    152
Riad, Hassan 86
riots of 1948 5, 17, 167-68, 196
Ross, C. 23
    (see also Seers, Dudley)
                    –S–
Sagoe, Julius 130, 155n.9
Seers, Dudley 100-105, 108-9, 112n.25,
    122, 148
    "Dudley Seers's model" 97-98, 100-
    105, 108-9, 115n.63
    Seers-Ross 23, 56n.14, 126-27
self-government 2, 3, 5, 17, 23, 53, 89,
    196
"Self-Government Now" 13n.8, 54, 59,
    89, 111n.11, 167, 172, 196
Seven-Year Development Plan (see
    plans)
socialism 1, 4-5, 61-65, 69-70, 74-80,
    83-85, 94-95, 100, 110, 111n.11,
    121-23, 125-29, 139, 146, 151, 153,
    163-64, 199-210, 217-20, 222
    African 150, 157n.28, 204, 206, 209,
    219, 222
    problem of dimension 150-53
    "scientific socialism" 63, 150,
    157n.28, 186-87, 209, 222
    the "Iron Curtain" model 150-51
    (see also Union of Soviet Socialist
    Republics)
Soviet Union (see Union of Soviet
    Socialist Republics)
"Standard VII boys" 167-68, 211n.10
    (see also youngmen)
strike, i.e., Sekondi-Takoradi quasi-
    insurrectional (September, 1961) 5,
    7, 27, 73, 100, 102, 104, 178
Szereszewski, Robert 14n.12, 19-20,
    56n.9, 143, 145, 155n.16

                    –T–
Tactical Action 13n.8, 59-60, 89, 103,
    160, 164, 178, 183, 198
Taylor, Kurankyi 176
Tema 67, 70-71, 139, 149, 155n.15,

    196, 209, 221
    artificial harbor 99, 109, 191
Tettegah, John 178, 210n.2
Togoland Congress (TC) 87, 92, 96
Tokyo Joes 91
    "Verandah Boys" 91
    (see also youngmen)
traders 26, 179, 181
    "mammies" 202-3
    petty traders 19-20, 36, 56n.5, 81,
    179, 203
    (see also middle class)
Trade Union Congress (TUC) 27,
    64n.11, 65, 72-74, 210n.2
Trade Unions 178, 188
traditional, traditionalism 22, 39-40,
    169, 177
    power 38, 42, 44n.36
    neotraditionalism 46, 66, 166, 177,
    219, 229n.5
    rule 39
    societies 35, 39, 42, 45, 48, 50, 78,
    169, 180, 204, 208
    values 39, 41-42, 180
Tunisia 80, 93-94, 105-6, 210n.1,
    212n.34
                    –U–
Unilever 25, 70, 71, 217
Union of Soviet Socialist Republics
    (U.S.S.R.) 2, 79, 83, 134 Table 5,
    135, 150-51, 162, 213n.47
Union Trading Company (UTC) 25, 129
United Arab Republic (U.A.R.) 86, 152,
    155n.13
United Gold Coast Convention (UGCC)
    5, 13n.7, 45-49, 48n.41, 54, 80-81,
    90, 95, 167-68, 171, 174, 195-96
United Kingdom (U.K.) 36, 132, 143,
    153-54, 195
    (see also civil service)
United Party (UP) 6, 45, 92-93, 102,
    174-75, 177, 196-97
United States (U.S.) 132, 143, 153-54
urbanization 44, 50
Volta River project 64, 95, 99, 109,
    148, 191
                    –W–
Wallerstein, Immanuel 9, 13nn.2, 5 and
    6, 14n.13, 35, 48, 58n.27, 59, 166-
    67
welfare state 61, 95, 197
Winneba, Kwame Nkrumah Ideological
    Institute 7, 73, 156n.25, 156n.25,
    186, 190, 218
Wright, Richard 46
                    –Y–
youngmen 35-40, 45, 48-54, 81-83, 86,
    167-71, 179, 181, 211n.10
    "petty bourgeois stratum" 69, 81,
    83, 166, 169-70, 178-79, 183
Young Pioneers 185, 189

ABOUT THE AUTHOR

Roger Genoud, a staff member of the Training and Research Division of the United Nations Development Programme, has had extensive firsthand experience in African affairs. He lived in Africa from 1959 to 1966, both north and south of the Sahara, in French-and English-speaking countries. He taught economics at Tunis' Teacher Training College, worked on the staff of the Institute of Public Education of the University of Ghana, and served as Director of Ghana's Institute of Languages under the Office of the President.

Dr. Genoud has published articles in leading journals of African studies, assessing the relationship between anti-colonial nationalism and economic development. In 1966, he joined the staff of the Centre for Developing-Area Studies at McGill University in Montreal.

A Swiss citizen, Dr. Genoud studied economics and humanities at the College de Calvin and the University of Geneva and received his doctorate from the University of Geneva.